Gender in the
Rhetoric of Jesus

Gender in the Rhetoric of Jesus

Women in Q

Sara Parks

LEXINGTON BOOKS/FORTRESS ACADEMIC
Lanham • Boulder • New York • London

Published by Lexington Books/Fortress Academic
Lexington Books is an imprint of The Rowman & Littlefield Publishing Group, Inc.
4501 Forbes Boulevard, Suite 200, Lanham, Maryland 20706
www.rowman.com

6 Tinworth Street, London SE11 5AL, United Kingdom

Copyright © 2019 The Rowman & Littlefield Publishing Group, Inc.

All rights reserved. No part of this book may be reproduced in any form or by any electronic or mechanical means, including information storage and retrieval systems, without written permission from the publisher, except by a reviewer who may quote passages in a review.

British Library Cataloguing in Publication Information Available

Library of Congress Cataloging-in-Publication Data Available

Library of Congress Control Number: 2019949507

ISBN 978-1-9787-0200-4 (cloth)
ISBN 978-1-9787-0199-1 (electronic)

To Meredith Warren and Shayna Sheinfeld, the best academic co-conspirators a woman could ever ask for.

Contents

Acknowledgments ix

1 Methods and Mapping 1
2 Q and the Q People 27
3 What are They Saying about the Gendered Pairs in Q? 51
4 Gendered Pairs in Q: Taxonomy and Analysis 77
5 Were There Gendered Parable Pairs before Jesus? 111
6 Gender Pairs in Contemporaneous and Later Texts 127
7 Conclusions and Next Directions 151

Appendix: The Q Gender Pairs in English 161
Bibliography 165
Index of Ancient Sources 185
Index of Modern Authors 187
Subject Index 189
About the Author 191

Acknowledgments

From the earliest inklings of my idea that perhaps the question of women in Q might be different from the question of women in the Gospels, Prof. Gerbern Oegema provided non-stop encouragement, and Dr. Aaron Ricker was my most patient sounding board. At the University of Nottingham, Prof. Frances Knight and Dr. Jon Hoover ingeniously bought out a few weeks of my Greek teaching so I could focus on revising the manuscript; thanks also to Jonny Rowlands' willingness to teach for me on short notice. As I crossed the finish line of the last proofs, Dr. Matthew Anderson provided everything from meals to footnotes to celebrations (and read every word with a sharp eye). My parents, Rev. Dr. Winston and Shirley Parks are, and have always been, unconditionally loving and supportive, even when they had no idea what I was doing or why on earth it was taking so long. Through it all, Drs. Meredith Warren and Shayna Sheinfeld, who are so much more than my Writing Group, were there with "track changes" and good humor. The Society of Biblical Literature Q Section often sharpened my thinking with helpful input. Neil Elliott of Fortress/Lexington was a delight to work with and made everything fun. The reviewer Neil selected, whose identity I may never know, suggested erudite and profound improvements, all of which I have gratefully incorporated. Over the years, my undergraduate students at McGill, Concordia, and Nottingham have been wellsprings of inspiration and assurance that there is always more to learn. Thanks are also due to Hilary Floyd for swiftly creating the indices. I offer my deep gratitude and affection to everyone mentioned here and many not mentioned who know full well they, too, are entitled to enormous credit for anything that shines herein. I alone take credit for the bits that still need work.

Chapter 1

Methods and Mapping

> Consider the ravens; they neither sow nor reap nor store up, and yet God feeds them. Are you not of more value than the birds?
> Consider the lilies; they neither card, nor toil, nor spin. Yet I tell you, even Solomon in all his glory was not arrayed like one of these.
> (Q 12:24)

The sayings of Jesus of Nazareth have been captivating audiences since they were first uttered in Galilee. Yet, only recently has anyone formally investigated how Jesus' words, in form and content, relate to women. At first, this question of what Jesus had to say to, and about, women struggled at the academic margins, but this is not the case today. The woman-centered and gender-aware approaches to the study of Jesus that have emerged in the last half-century continue to expand in depth and appeal,[1] and the relationship of women to the early Jesus movement is a flourishing area of research.[2]

It is somewhat surprising, then, that despite an unfailing interest in Jesus and a newly flourishing interest in his relationship to women, few have systematically directed such questions toward what is probably the earliest evidence for Jesus' treatment of women—his teachings in Q. Not all the sayings of Jesus recorded in the New Testament are thought to have been handed down intact and much of the speech placed in the mouth of Jesus over half-a-century later (such as the lengthy orations in John's gospel) is highly unlikely to have originated with the Galilean teacher in its current form. However, historical Jesus researchers look to the short sayings and parables[3] that are repeated in both Matthew and Luke as a likely place for original material. It is to this collection—known as the *Quelle* (source)—that this book turns for its examination of gender in the teachings of Jesus.

Whether or not one agrees with the *boundaries* of the reconstructed Q (as the sayings list is nicknamed), the words of Jesus shared across Matthew and Luke are, as James Robinson states, "generally agreed to provide the oldest surviving layer of material brought together by Jesus' disciples."[4] Gerd Theissen and Annette Merz describe the Q material as "certainly the most important source for reconstructing the teaching of Jesus."[5] N. Siffer and D. Fricker also argue that Q is our most ancient piece of evidence for Christian origins and our best chance of accessing any of the words of Jesus.[6]

It seems almost stunning that so little investigation has been done into the treatment of women in such a collection. This is despite the fact that Q is not only rich with references to women but it also boasts a unique literary device that seems to place women on par with men in an unmistakably deliberate way. Scholars have referred to this device as the "gender doublets."[7] I have labeled this rhetorical device, which I argue was coined by Jesus of Nazareth, the "parallel gender pairs."[8] These gendered pairs are at the heart of this book.

Jesus' parallel gender pairs work as follows: he presents two matching didactic pieces (twin parables or twin similes about the *basileia* of God),[9] such as the parable of the Lost Sheep (Q 15:4–5a, 7) and the parable of the Lost Coin (Q 15:8–10). The two lessons or sayings are verbally parallel—sometimes nearly identical—except that one lesson features a male character or characters and the other features a female character or characters. Alternatively, rather than referring to a man and a woman, first-century indicators of masculinity and femininity may be inferred more subtly, such as by mentioning two tasks, one of which is normally done by the men of the day and the other normally performed by the women. For instance, the twin parables of the Ravens and the Lilies do not mention any people, but the ravens' connection to farming recalls the work of men, whereas the lilies' connection to spinning brings to mind the work of women. Additionally, smaller scale binary gendered pairing also occurs throughout Q, such as in passing phrases like "sons and daughters" (Q 12:53) or "father and mother" (Q 14:26). A complete list of the gendered pairs of Jesus in English translation is included in the appendix.

According to my findings, until Jesus spoke, using stories, to the everyday situations of both women and men in this carefully paralleled way, such a device is unattested[10] in Hellenistic and early Jewish[11] literature. This is a unique rhetorical strategy that appeared for the first time in Jesus' sayings material, and—as we shall see—it intentionally treats male and female listeners with a certain equality.[12] Yet, although these pairs in Q and their uniqueness in Greco-Roman literature seem like such a promising resource for the history of wo/men[13] in early Jewish and early Christian[14] antiquity, to date there are only a handful of feminist scholars who discuss this literary device in Q. In chapter 3, I engage with these authors. My synthesis and clarification of their sometimes disparate approaches and findings should prove useful to future scholars and others interested not only in women in Q but in Jesus and women more generally.

The pairs do not have any Greek or Hebrew literary precedent; nowhere in the literature of Jesus' past is this paralleled gender pairing performed. We will look at some contenders in chapter 5. However, there are plenty of echoes of this innovation in literature that immediately *followed* Q. As Margaret Beirne has shown, there is certainly gendered pairing at a broader narrative level in the Gospel of John, as in Luke.[15] There also seems to be a unique gender-paired saying in Mark's gospel[16] and at least one extensively gender-paired passage in the letters of Paul.[17] This means that a classic criterion in Historical Jesus Research for a greater likelihood of authenticity—namely, that of multiple attestations in independent sources—can be brought to bear on gendered pairing and Jesus. The fact that gendered pairing is echoed in a number of disparate and separate sources around Jesus serves to strengthen the notion that the rhetorical gender equality preserved in Q sayings can be traced back to him more solidly.[18]

Of course, any study of Q is a study of the historical Jesus.[19] As Burton Mack writes, "Q puts us as close to the historical Jesus as we will ever be."[20] Not only is there an interesting array of gendered pairs in the literature that is close in temporal proximity to Jesus, but the fact that it appears in independent streams of tradition means that what Historical Jesus Researchers call the criterion of multiple attestation comes into play. This historian's criterion "focuses on sayings or deeds of Jesus witnessed (i) in more than one independent literary source (e.g., Mark, Q, Paul, or John) and/or (ii) in more than one literary form or genre."[21] Highlighting possible vestiges of this rhetorically innovative binary gender pairing in both Mark's and John's gospels and in Paul's letters alerts us to the probability that the idea was "in the air" prior to its appearance in the New Testament sources; that is, it can be traced back to earlier (indeed, to the earliest) stages of the Jesus movement. Given the lack of tenable examples of gender pairs in Jewish or Hellenistic works prior to Q, the link between gendered pairing and Jesus of Nazareth himself is further strengthened.[22]

There are, however, caveats. This project shows that the Q pairs and their traces in later early Christian texts do indicate a relationship between Jesus' *logia* and an interest in pairing binary gender in a way that sometimes implies spiritual—although not full social—equality, but a conclusion that Jesus programmatically advocated "egalitarian" values or had as a project the dismantling of patriarchal[23] norms does not automatically follow. Although almost everyone can agree that Jesus spoke in these gender-paired ways, there is little agreement on what that meant (or means) for women. Some feminist readings use these sayings to argue that there was full gender equality in the Jesus movement; others see no such thing there. Perhaps the disagreement between optimistic and pessimistic readings of the pairs stems from overlooking the nuance that my research has uncovered—namely, that while there is indeed equality implied in the Q pairs in terms of delivering the same message to both men and women, it is not, generally speaking, disruptive of gendered social expectations. Q remains ambiguous in this regard.

Jesus' didactic method may have been innovative in its effective strategy for the inclusion of wo/men listeners, but it did not seek to overturn the gendered expectations that were in keeping with the androcentrism[24] and kyriocentrism[25] of the day. In his stories, men still sow the crops, and women still spin the wool. At the same time, though, this teaching method certainly indicates that women were among the expected recipients of Jesus' teachings and expected to be able to process the same intellectual and religious content as men.

The distinction between these two things implied by Jesus' teaching: accepting typical gendered roles, on the one hand, yet at the same time abandoning gender as a criterion for membership in the movement, on the other, may resolve a scholarly division between those who argue for a gender-leveling message in Jesus' sayings material and those who argue that Q simply reinforces and participates in patriarchy. By unpacking the specific ways in which the gender parable pairs do, and do not, level the genders, I shift the conversation in such a way as to validate arguments on both sides of the debate. Additionally, through comparison with other instances of equally ambiguous gender inclusion from the time (i.e., from Stoicism, Philo, and the Pseudepigrapha), I demonstrate that it is possible to avoid careless supersessionism in feminist New Testament analysis by highlighting the elements in the Q sayings that are woman-positive without resorting to denigrating the Jewish *milieu* in which Jesus lived. As Schüssler-Fiorenza points out, "scholarly as well as popular studies continue to stress the positive attitude of Jesus toward women and to draw 'Jesus the feminist' against the patriarchal background of Judaism, which generated the 'depraved status' of Jewish women in the first century."[26] The present study confirms that Jesus is situated firmly within, rather than over and against, a Jewish milieu in which women were active participants in diverse circles in myriad ways. In this way, I hope this work avoids "reproducing Christian anti-Judaism" and unwittingly perpetuating "anti-Jewish tendencies in discourses about Jesus."[27]

It is with great hesitation that I have sometimes used qualifiers such as "intellectual," "spiritual," and "religious" (juxtaposed against "social") to describe the ways in which women and men are (and are not) construed as equal or similar in the gender pairs. Intellectual/spiritual/religious is a cluster of etic (outsider) concepts that can be useful in limiting and contextualizing Q's brand of gender equality, as opposed to a more absolute (and more contemporary) gender equality. A juxtaposition between "spiritual" and "social" is employed by other scholars of women in Early Judaism and Christianity in a similar fashion.[28] These terms, however descriptive they may be of what is happening with gender in Q, are not without their problems; to dichotomize between the social and the religious does not fit the ancient Mediterranean any better than it fits today. And yet, the gendered pairs themselves do indicate gender equality in some ways and not in others.

To be very careful and clear about what is meant when less-than-ideal shortcut terms such as intellectual/spiritual/religious are used, I will elaborate. I needed to find some way to show that the gendered parable pairs assume that their women hearers *are not in any way different intellectually* (meaning: in their ability to comprehend and apply the lesson) and/or *religiously* (meaning: in their inclusion in the *basileia* movement and thus in their implied value to God) from male hearers of the pairs. At the same time, it is important to note that the pairs do not assume that there is anything problematic about men and women's existing socially expected tasks and livelihoods. Although these are observations arising from the texts themselves, it is important not to retrojectively map contemporary notions of gender equality onto them. So, when the words "intellectual," "spiritual," and "religious" are used in this book as adjectives describing how the pairs denote a gender equivalency, I ask my readers to read them as qualifiers in a limited sense, as also meaning essentially "not acting to dismantle socially gendered roles." In other words, women and men may be *equal* in the world of the *basileia*, but this does not extrapolate to women and men being *identical* in that world. Gender is an irrelevant criterion when it comes to inclusion or exclusion from the message of the pairs, but it is not erased entirely.

When compared to previous texts from Hellenistic and early-Jewish antiquity, the gender pairs stand out as innovative for their overt and repeated use of matching masculine and feminine examples to teach an identical lesson—not separate lessons for men and women, but the same lesson for both. Yet, in this same context, the Q sayings maintain unremarkable, status quo expectations for externally visible gender roles such as male and female occupational tasks and social relationships. This tension can be resolved by discerning that Q can accept typically gendered social tasks, while at the same time deliberately transcending gender when it comes to intellectual capabilities and religious expectations.

WORDS ABOUT METHOD: ENGAGED HISTORICAL CRITICISM, LITERARY EVIDENCE, AND GENDER

Engaged Historical Criticism

My primary interest in the text of Q is as an historian, so my methods are historical-critical to the extent that I am interested in reading the sayings in relation to their contemporaneous surroundings. Despite a postmodern shift away from confidence in historical-critical scholarship, I believe that the goal of working toward elucidating antiquity through a variety of methodological lenses remains relatively possible and useful, although an interpreter is never devoid of her own subjectivity. For example, in addition to my historical interest in Q is my feminist interest in Q; I describe myself, like Elisabeth Schüssler Fiorenza, as "a 'connected critic' who speaks from a marginal location and that of an engaged position."[29] I am interested in reading the Q gender pairs, vis-à-vis their first speakers, hearers, and compilers, but it is also specifically my interest as a woman and as a feminist[30] to uncover stories and experiences of ancient women for their own sake, and, by uncovering their stories, to affirm and value modern women and Wo/man. "Connected critics" may employ historical criticism, but with a self-reflexive and skeptical eye. They make inquiries that are not necessarily standard; instead they ask about those marginalized by, in, and around the artifacts in question.[31]

This recent honing of historical-critical methods reflects a move toward an awareness of those who are being marginalized by the texts and by our interpretations of them. Not all scholars have abandoned historical-criticism as being overly confident about the possibility of scholarly objectivity;[32] some continue to improve and develop the method to fit contemporary needs and incorporate the contemporary understanding that every scholar is inevitably "situated."[33] Those who continue to identify as historical-critical scholars in postmodernity must, of course, do so with the humility that comes with this erosion of the illusion of objective analysis of artifacts from the past. Dale Martin, in his recent monograph on gender and biblical interpretation, critiques those who hold on to a belief in the possibility of objectivity:

> We must admit that we are without secure foundations for knowledge. In the end there are no guarantees that we or anyone else will not use the text unethically. There are no reliable foundations. The answer to that problem is not just to keep insisting that there are, but to learn to live faithful and ethical lives without secure foundations.[34]

This book puts historical-critical methods to work, but with the humility that comes with these "unreliable foundations." I know that my own situatedness as a white ecumenical Christian Canadian, a critical biblical scholar, and a feminist, unquestionably leaves its mark on my findings, as does any researcher's context.[35] As an engaged historical critic, I do not approach the elucidation of ancient women's history with neutrality; rather, I consider elucidating women's history to be an ethical requirement—one which not only improves wo/men's present-day but also happens to produce better historical analysis.

Schüssler Fiorenza's "third thesis" on the "ethics of interpretation" suggests that to interpret ancient texts *without* an awareness of marginalization and of one's own participation in intersecting lines of oppression is essentially *unethical*. She mends the perceived wide gap between "objective" scholarship and engaged scholarship and attempts "to overcome the assumed dichotomy between engaged scholarship (such as feminist, postcolonial, African American, queer, and other subdisciplines) and scientific (malestream) interpretation."[36] She critiques the historical-critical approach for hiding behind "scientific" discourse in order to maintain comfortable hierarchies that benefit the privileged:

> Whereas the [engaged approach] is allegedly using ethical criteria, the [scientific, malestream approach] is said to live up to a scientific ethos that gives precedence to cognitive criteria. Instead, I would argue that a scientific ethos demands both ethical and cognitive criteria that must be reasoned out in terms of standard knowledge and at the same time intersubjectively understandable and communicable.[37]

In order to produce scholarship that is both rational *and* ethical, I assume that historical criticism and scientific rigor, such as they are, do not suffer from working in tandem with—and adapting to—an interest in the marginalized. The practice of acknowledging one's engagement *overtly* is a means of legitimizing and acknowledging as scholarly a concern for those marginalized by a text and its interpretations.

In the same work, Schüssler Fiorenza states, "if texts and discourses are studied without reference to human agency or socio-historical situation, then language and texts become a closed system that takes on the character of 'scientific law.'"[38] The claim that one can undertake historical work from a "neutral" or "unbiased" standpoint is problematic at best[39] and violent at worst. Claiming scientific neutrality, while ignoring minority voices, is not only impossible but also unethical. All scholarship *is* engaged and has political and sociohistorical consequences; only some scholarship admits it.

Yet, I maintain that this inevitable engagement, and even enthusiastic engagement, can exist while retaining respect for ancient historical evidence and for the discipline of history. To approach the question of women in Q as an historian and as a feminist means, for me, to attempt to recover as much as possible about ancient women, whether what we uncover reveals kyriarchal oppression, or moments of emancipation from forcibly gendered modes of being, or—more likely—a complex combination of both.

Feminist scholarship has sometimes been criticized for analyses that use evidence selectively in an attempt to salvage patriarchal ancient literature for theological purposes.[40] Comparing the secondary scholarship on women in Q becomes complicated because some feminist Q scholars identify primarily as theologians and others seem not to identify in this way, although they may be historians who work from feminist perspectives. Part of the tension arises because the performance of theology allows for texts to function differently than does the performance of history, although of course agreement of results from both methods is often possible. I have endeavored to acknowledge this tension among my sources and to allow the analysis of primary texts in this project to be guided more by curiosity about gender in Q than by any program to redeem or condemn the Jesus movement at the outset. The project is feminist, in that it seeks to understand the place of women in the Q sayings and to elucidate the historical situation of first-century female members of the Jesus movement, but it is not theological, in that it does not set out to look for certain outcomes, whether to expose patriarchy/kyriarchy in the text or to uncover points of emancipation there. For me, inquiring into the role of women in Q—or any ancient text—with greater nuance is service enough to feminism. I have made every effort to let Q and its surrounding literary context guide the discovery and description of what might be said of women and Q, rather than setting out to evaluate whether Q's view of women (and thus, for some, Jesus' view of women) has passed or failed some test of patriarchy, according to this or that modern feminist set of standards.

It is my hope that by the time the reader reaches the concluding chapter, it will become obvious that asking ancient texts to answer questions about ancient women is not simply a niche or fringe concern. Nor are the results of such a study only of interest to one particular marginalized group. Rather, it is only when asking questions from all possible angles and with diverse interests in mind that we do ancient texts—and the contemporary search for knowledge about them—any justice at all. As this research shows, examining the role of women in Q also provides answers to longstanding text-critical questions about Q's so-called literary strata, establishes that the historical Jesus or someone in his earliest movement was a rhetorical innovator, and helps better position the development of early Jesus movements within a broader literary and social context.

Sociohistorical Claims from Literary Evidence

For an historian of women in antiquity whose evidence is primarily literary, the question of how far the evidence may be allowed to reach must be addressed. Textual evidence can sometimes point to socio-historical realities for real women of the time, but often the nature (and the dearth) of our evidence restricts us to the history of *men's attitudes* toward women. Since almost all ancient literary sources are male-authored and directed to a male audience, even texts that do focus on historical women or on female characters may not offer useful data for ancient women's sociohistorical realities, instead only providing evidence for the expressions of ancient male authors.[41]

In this book, both of these aspects of women's history—experienced social reality and imputed historical attitudes—intersect. My examination of Q as an early stratum of the evidence for the Jesus movement uncovers not only some ancient attitudes toward women but also elucidates the sociohistorical reality of some actual wo/men in the first century. The way in which Q points to a leveling of gender roles at a literary/rhetorical level indicates a strong women's presence at a socio-historical level. What I mean is that paired sayings that take real-life examples in order to teach a lesson imply, by their systematic inclusion of women from the surrounding context, that *there are actual women in the audience*. Of course, this is an observation that is corroborated by the parade of named and unnamed women throughout the texts of the New Testament. This means that, unlike those ancient texts that may mention women, but are clearly by men for men, in the case of the gender-paired sayings of Jesus, we may move more confidently from the text to the fact that there were women in its orbit. With Q's gender pairs, we are able to modestly reconstruct something of the women mentioned in the pairs and rhetorically implied in their audience. These women are not mere symbols, tropes, or fantasies, but are reflections of the women hearers of the *logia*, women who surrounded Jesus as he taught, supported him financially as he traveled, and advanced his teachings after his death.

The process of moving from ancient literary data to ancient sociohistorical realities is one that typically requires humility and care, and it is rife with pitfalls. "One cannot," in Claudia Camp's words, "make the error of equating 'women's roles' with 'female images,' lest one equate historical or sociological data with literary creations."[42] Randall Chesnutt points out, "what is feasible for women in literary fiction is not necessarily feasible in social reality."[43] Nonetheless, the tentative reconstruction of sociological history using literary evidence is a step that is commonly and necessarily taken by scholars undertaking a quest for the historical Jesus and one that, with caution, must also be undertaken in any quest for the women who surrounded and followed him. This study uses Jesus' rhetoric of gender to move toward some cautious conclusions about women in the Jesus movement. Q is well situated to answer such questions, not only because questions about women should be asked of all ancient texts, and not only because Q is such an early piece of data for the Jesus movement, but most importantly because *Q itself invites such questions*. It does so by making women, in everyday situations pulled from the Galilean countryside, a deliberate focus, a rhetorical move that, as I hope this book demonstrates, implies their significant presence in first-century Judaism and at the foundations of nascent Christianity.

A Note on the Use of Gender as a Category

The choice to lift out binary gender as an interpretive lens, in an age when scholarship is making such important strides toward a less topically segregated and more intersectional approach, warrants further explanation. The use of a gender binary has been replaced by more nuanced approaches, developed in sociological discourses in the 1960s and 1970s and in biblical studies in the 1980s by Elisabeth Schüssler Fiorenza and others. Ever since Simone de Beauvoir first remarked that one is not born a woman, but rather *becomes* one,[44] modern scholarship has been shifting toward the understanding that gender is, to a great degree, constructed socially.[45] De Beauvoir did not imply that biology is irrelevant altogether, but that the "behavioural characteristics and expectations inscribed on female identity were culturally constructed to be the 'other' to . . . male identity."[46] Butler's recent definition of gender is in keeping with this:

> Gender is the apparatus by which the production and normalization of masculine and feminine take place along with the interstitial forms of hormonal, chromosomal, psychic, and performative that gender assumes. To assume that gender always and exclusively means the matrix of the "masculine" and "feminine" is precisely to miss the critical point that the production of that coherent binary is contingent, that it comes at a cost, and that those permutations of gender which do not fit the binary are as much a part of gender as its most normative instance. To conflate the definition of gender with its normative expression is inadvertently to reconsolidate the power of the norm to constrain the definition of gender.[47]

This shift away from an essentialist gender dichotomy is one I fully support; in many fields, a discourse that is more intersectional and gender-complex is blossoming.[48] However, as an historian of antiquity, I am careful to use not only these latest etic (outsider) categories of analysis but to also pay attention to the emic (insider) categories suggested by ancient texts themselves. Gender could be seen as complex in antiquity as well, but in the case of the Q gender pairs, a focus on gender as a binary is supported by the sayings. Q clearly participates actively in the bifurcation of gender, by highlighting binary gender as a focus both in its content and its rhetoric. Since Jesus' gender-paired parables repeatedly present their recipients with two lessons that are verbally parallel except for small variables, and those variables are consistently related to masculine and feminine examples, the category of binary gender is a highly appropriate key to the interpretation of these texts, which construct gender as a male/female dichotomy even while employing rhetoric that in some ways closes a gap between male and female audience members. A series of verbally parallel parable pairs where the only variable is a gendered masculine/feminine binary clearly flags to the reader that gender is not only present in the text, but is one of the key elements of its design. It is certainly best practice to be alert to the fact that we inevitably bring anachronistic questions and etic categories to antique evidence, and to be cognizant of our distance from the world of the text,[49] but in this case, binary gender is an unmistakable focus of the Q sayings themselves.

Q AND WOMEN'S HISTORY

Among the collected Q sayings exists a record of a rhetorical treatment of women that was unprecedented within early Jewish and Hellenistic antiquity. Through its unique gender-paired examples, Q presses against the boundaries of the patriarchal/kyriarchal framework of first-century women's roles, reflecting a very early[50] example of women's inclusion within the Jewish Jesus movement. Q's several clear instances where an identical lesson is taught twice in a row, once with a male example and once with a female example, are the first known examples of this particular sort of "equal-opportunity" rhetoric in Greco-Roman antiquity. Other instances in Q of shorter phrases that also use gender-pairing reinforce an observable tendency to address both genders simultaneously and equally and thereby to both confirm and affirm the presence of women in the movement.

This reading of Q is not without controversy. Those who analyze these sayings are not unanimous on the ramifications of the gender pairs, vis-à-vis women. On the one hand, this curious device that deliberately addresses male and female audience members[51] with the same content provides evidence for gender inclusivity in the earliest accessible stratum of Jesus movements. The gender pairs have been rightly flagged as being of great significance for the history of women, by scholars eager to affirm women's important standing in early Christianity. Alicia Batten points out that the Q pairs indicate "a deliberate challenge to societal norms"[52] and Jean-Francois Racine writes that the gendered pairing "is an indication that Q addresses equally men and women."[53]

On the other hand, others caution that any gender equality to which Q's gendered pairs point is circumscribed. Kathleen Corley warns that "such a reconstruction of Jesus' preaching and practice can function as a foundational myth for modern Christian feminism,"[54] a practice that Corley deems an inappropriate use of the evidence. Corley's premise is that pairs are not evidence for an egalitarian gender situation, but that any freedom that happened to have been afforded to women in the movement was instead a result of a generalized emancipation that had occurred across many Greco-Roman and/or Jewish religious and political communities during the late Republic;

her book argues that Jesus indeed conducted a program of social critique, but for class, not gender, and that feminist readings of Jesus as gender-egalitarian are idealistic and exaggerated.[55] William Arnal contends that "the Q couplets do not in and of themselves serve as any convincing indication of a tendency toward gender inclusiveness,"[56] by positing a different, non-gendered rationale for the pairings, which he thinks were rooted instead in repetitive scribal tendencies unrelated to actual women and men. Amy-Jill Levine finds that any efforts to derive a positive feminist reading from Q are "hampered by Q's androcentric language"[57] and argues that Q does not ultimately provide solid evidence for gender-leveling activity.[58]

How is it that experts come to opposite conclusions about Jesus' sayings and women? It might seem that the two ends of this spectrum are irreconcilable. I propose that this is not the case. These sayings of Jesus do indicate a teaching and a movement in which women were viewed equally alongside men in terms of being recipients and distributors of the message. The latter scholars, however, are also correct insofar as Q does not provide evidence for a teacher who transcended a patriarchal historical context or had as an overt goal the denial of gendered norms. The paired sayings contained in Q did challenge the status quo for women, but the particular challenge was in their seemingly deliberate equal valuing of wo/men as recipients of the *basileia* message. Being included on this level sometimes required wo/men to break out of social expectations (such as dividing household members from one another as in Q 12:53), but not always, not all expectations, and not programmatically.

In other words, the characters in the pairs—and thus the wo/men listening to the teachings—are not expected to become indistinguishable from men socially; women more or less remain spinners of cloth and housekeepers, for instance, and men more or less remain farmers and shepherds. The very rhetorical power of the sayings in fact depends on their duality and so on an ongoing recognition of such gendered divisions. This retention in the sayings of the occupational *status quo* is not because such gendered occupations are being depicted as divinely ordained or because they have any deep theological import in the text, but because overturning gendered occupations is simply not one of Q's concerns. The parables draw from the audience's surroundings in rural Galilee; the women who form a part of these immediate surroundings, become part of the warp and weave of the examples used in Jesus' short stories. Both women and men in the audience can see themselves in the lessons.

These women in Q's audience are expected to be: equally capable of understanding, internalizing, and implementing Jesus' teachings; equally worthy recipients of the teachings; and equally important promulgators of the teachings. Whatever their gendered social tasks may be, everyone in the audience of Q's parabolic messages is clearly understood as having an identical capacity for receiving and applying Jesus' lessons, as well as an identical potential value and responsibility as proponents of the lessons for others.

This view that the Q pairs offer an equality that is specifically circumscribed in the above way is compatible with scholarship on both sides of the debate on gender-valuation and the Q pairs. On the one hand, my view of circumscribed equality supports the concern that any equality within the gender pairs is tempered by factors such as Q's overall patriarchal language and context,[59] and the concern that using Q as evidence to argue that Jesus himself programmatically sought to destroy patriarchal gender limitations stretches the evidence too far.[60] I agree with Kathleen Corley's caution that "the notion that Jesus established an anti-patriarchal movement or a 'discipleship of equals' is a kind of feminist Christian myth."[61] Moreover, I commend her for disputing the notion that "patriarchal Judaism" is an apt foil against which to set up Christianity as the alleged emancipator of women.[62] As Corley goes on to say,

> The fact that women played a role in Jesus' movement [. . .] means that we can place Jesus' movement and the early Christianities solidly within Jewish Palestinian and larger Greco-Roman environments, both of which were far more open to women's involvement in religion, society, and politics than has previously been assumed.[63]

On the other hand, my view of circumscribed equality is also compatible with more positive views of Q's attitude to women. When one analyses the gender pairs in Q against their Hellenistic and early Jewish literary contexts, one cannot altogether reject the notion that the Jesus of Q, in his gender pairs, is working deliberately to level the gender playing field in one specific regard, although scholars such as Arnal, Corley, and Levine, may not see the evidence in this way.[64] As I will show in chapter 3, "What are they Saying about the Gendered Pairs in Q?," explaining away the presence of gender-balancing as scribal wordplay (Arnal)[65] or transferring all credit for gender equality in Q to the wider Hellenistic world while only crediting Jesus for an interest in class equality (Corley)[66] does not do justice to the evidence. Further, while Levine's negative evaluation of what the pairs mean for women[67] is part of her crucial project to highlight anti-Judaism[68] in the Christian Testament[69] and to redeem Second Temple Judaism from undue blame for patriarchy,[70] she may have thrown out what *is* unique about the gender pairs with the proverbial bathwater in service to that (albeit important) task.

I argue that Jesus in Q is indeed assuming an intellectual and religious equality for wo/men, which was both made possible by, and also unique within the diversity of, the broader Hellenistic-era women's movement mentioned by Corley and Batten. That said, his inclusion of wo/men cannot be exaggerated into an advocacy for gender equality in the modern sense. The stereotypical and bifurcated gender roles used and reinforced in the Q pairs indicate that the sayings do not advocate for identical or interchangeable social roles for men and women. The limited and nonsocial nature of the equality found in the pairs is, as we shall see, completely in keeping with other first-century instances of brief-and-complicated flashes of wo/men's equality such as Philo's description of the Therapeutrides or Musonius Rufus's treatises on women's philosophical education. This is not to say that Q is "against" more widespread gender equality. Indeed, sometimes Q's insistence on the inclusion of wo/men may mean the transgression and transcendence of patriarchal and familial obligations (e.g., Q 12:51–53). But these transgressions remain a side effect of the apocalyptic nature of the message, not its central project.

A Map of this Book

The next chapter begins with an overview of the Q hypothesis as I see it. Some readers may be asking at this point, "Are we ever going to get to the part that explains what Q is?" Chapter 2, "Q and the Q People," is where non-specialists can read a general introduction to key Q issues and a discussion of the contribution of Q to our knowledge of the early Galilean Jesus movement. The chapter goes on to amalgamate the diverse secondary literature on community in and around Q, to posit a social background of Q.

The puzzle pieces that come together in this next chapter begin to form a picture of a social context, perhaps a community, of Jews who are keenly interested in the sayings of Jesus but not necessarily in his biography and who collect and transmit Jesus' particular habit of referring to the *basileia* of God. Both sapiential (wisdom-oriented) and apocalyptic (judgment oriented), this posited Jewish group may make use of itinerant messengers, with a message that is deliberately subversive of the dominant urban cultures of Rome and Jerusalem.

Although, for centuries, scholars only discussed Q in order to solve text-critical problems about the relationship among Mark, Matthew, and Luke, they have recently begun to consider the people around Q. We have not reached (and may never reach) a point of sufficient consensus on "Q People" to speak of them with confidence as a single community around a single Q document. Therefore, chapter 2 explains that this book does not make claims based on a physical community around the written Greek translation of Jesus' sayings known as Q. I ask the reader to instead have in mind, as will I, the recipients of Jesus' oral sayings first and foremost as the implied audience of the text. Of course, it is sensible to assume some continuity and overlap with whoever collected and translated that oral material.

The second chapter concludes by narrowing our focus to the *women* addressed by the text, highlighting Q's special importance for understanding women's role in the earliest Jesus movements, most strikingly present in the rhetorical strategy of gendered pairings[71] which assume that both men and women are among those expected to engage with the spiritual content of the lessons. The reconstructed Q collection provides an excellent lens through which to focus on the treatment of women at a place and time much closer to Jesus' Galilean Judaism than to the increasingly non-Jewish and urban movement Christianity had become in less than a century, and to which the Gospels, the letters of Paul, and virtually all of the New Testament bear witness.

Chapter 3, "What are they Saying About the Gendered Pairs in Q?," begins by untangling scholarship on the gendered pairs in Q from scholarship on the pairs in the Lukan context in which they were first noticed. In general, study of the Lukan pairs has been impervious to considerations of the Q hypothesis, but examining the pairs in their Q context offers a unique perspective, providing a stark contrast to the highly embellished narratives of the Gospels. The chapter summarizes the secondary literature on the gendered pairs as they appear in Q; as the examination of these pairs in their Q context is a relatively recent and undeveloped field of research, the chapter is able to comprise most feminist discussion on the pairs to date.[72] Rather than reviewing the literature chronologically, I arrange the scholarship on the Q gender pairs into two main streams—those who find "equality" in the rhetoric of the pairs and those who do not. The themes around which I have grouped this scholarship are the widely differing analyses of the import of the pairs for women; the relative comfort or caution with which authors apply the concept of (gender-)egalitarianism to ancient literature; and the way in which feminist analyses of Jesus either show or do not show sensitivity to anti-Judaism and supersessionism. The chapter concludes with my own evaluation of this secondary literature: I share the caution of those who are wary of finding "equality" too easily in antiquity, and I prioritize the warnings against anti-Jewish readings. At the same time, I also align with those who insist that something of importance for women is indeed happening in Q's rhetoric. The gendered pairs do push against the boundaries of the status quo for women in unique and important ways while, in other ways, simultaneously reinforcing social gender roles. This chapter establishes the importance of Q as a significant locus of evidence for women in the early Jesus movement, in a way the Gospels alone cannot, and demonstrates through current debate that the interpretation of this important evidence is as yet unresolved. My method of analyzing the pairs may provide a useful way through the dilemma.

Chapter 4, "Gendered Pairs in Q: Taxonomy and Analysis," finally jumps into the texts. The chapter begins with my definitions of the "full pairs" and the "shorter pairs," which consist of an equal juxtaposition of masculine and feminine concepts or characters within short metaphorical narratives or sayings. A full taxonomy and description of each pair of primary texts is accompanied by analysis that shows how both "sides" of the women-in-Q debate can be reconciled, with greater precision around *what sort/s* of equality may (and may not) be inferred from the texts.

Rather than advocating an erasure of socially gendered roles (which is often part of our contemporary expectation of gender equality), the sayings imply an equality that has to do with an individual's response, regardless of gender, as a hearer and proponent of the *basileia* teachings. Specifically, the paired sayings are implying that men and women are equally expected to hear and spread Jesus' message and equally capable of contributing to the religious community. In other words, they are equally capable on an intellectual and spiritual level to understand and apply Jesus' lessons and equally called upon to contribute to the spread of his message.

For a text to imply that men and women are equal, or even identical, at the level of their intellectual and spiritual capacity, or even to imply that men and women are both called to the role of itinerant prophecy for the *basileia*, does not necessarily imply that men and women are being called to otherwise smash out of all gendered social roles—nor does it necessarily presume an "egalitarian" or "anti-patriarchal" social program. This is the observation that may resolve the tension among Q pairs scholars, some of whom insist that the pairs point to a more or less "feminist" Jesus, while others caution that any utopian "discipleship of equals"[73] in the earliest Jesus movement may be a lovely theological trope, but is simply too good to be true from a historian's standpoint. In effect, both so-called sides are responding to elements that are present within the sayings material. Being able to describe more precisely where the pairs imply, condone, or promote equality, as well as *what types of equality* are implied, lends clarity to a debated issue. The pairs indicate a real tendency in Q, not only toward gender inclusivity but also toward gender equality; however, that equality does not map neatly onto definitions of gender equality today.

How the Q pairs relate to other literature in the ancient Mediterranean world is addressed in chapters 5 and 6, "Were there Gendered Parable Pairs before Jesus?" and "Gender Pairs in Contemporaneous and Later Texts." Chapter 5 establishes a stark lack of literary precedent for the rhetorical device of gendered parable pairs in Hellenistic and Jewish antiquity. Chapter 6 goes on to report a number of places in later first-century literature from the Jesus movement and early Christianity—that is, in Paul, Mark, and John—where the rhetorical device of gendered pairing is employed and echoed. Some of these later cases show discomfort with the gender pairing tendency and work to mute its gender-leveling rhetoric (e.g., Luke/Acts). Together, these cases function as independent attestations to literary gender-pairing in early Jesus-movement literature. This works to reinforce chapter 5's argument that the gender pair technique is an innovation of the historical Jesus. At the same time, other contemporaneous texts outside the Jesus movement discussed in chapter 6, such as *De Vita Contemplativa,* Musonius Rufus' Stoic treatises on women's equal education, and *Joseph and Aseneth,* demonstrate that Jesus of Nazareth did not hold a monopoly on depictions of parity between women and men.

In the final chapter, I conclude that Q's encouragement of women's agency is indeed not from a vacuum, but is in keeping with some of the contemporaneous discourse on women in and around the first century. The active participation of Q's women recipients is in keeping with the greater freedoms for women that had arisen since the late Republic, and literary discourses of equality between women and men were arising in various other contexts. Yet, the gender pairs nonetheless represent a rhetorical innovation that merits attention for its creativity as well as its concern with women's agency and value.

Using the methods of historical-Jesus research to investigate other Hellenistic Jewish literature before and after the composition of Q shows that Q's innovative pairing device can be linked as closely as anything else can to the historical Jesus. This innovation of Jesus cannot be hailed as part of a programmatic gender-egalitarianism or an organized anti-patriarchy on the part of Jesus or his early followers; Q's comfortable and frequent use of androcentric language and its overall retention of stereotypical gender roles mitigate such a program. That said, the importance of the gender pairs in Q for Historical Jesus Research and for an understanding of Jewish women in the first century is worthy of notice, by Jesus scholars and Jesus followers alike.

NOTES

1. For a history of approaches to the question and a careful discussion of method in the earlier part of the last century, see A. Yarbro Collins, ed., *Feminist Perspectives on Biblical Scholarship*; (Chico: Scholars, 1985), for the end of the twentieth century, see E. Schüssler Fiorenza, ed., *Feminist Biblical Studies in the 20th Century* (Atlanta: Society of Biblical Literature, 2014), and for a reflection on changes in feminist biblical hermeneutics since the twenty-first century, see J. E. McKinlay, "Reading Biblical Women Matters," in *The Oxford Handbook of Biblical Narrative* (ed. D. N. Fewell; NY: Oxford University Press, 2016), 398–410.

2. According to Sidnie White, "interest in the role and status of women in Second Temple Judaism (and generally in Judaism and Christianity) has increased exponentially in the past twenty-five years." S. A. White, "Women: Second Temple Period," in *The Oxford Guide to People and Places of the Bible* (Oxford: Oxford University Press, 2001), 330. According to C. Murphy, in *The Word According to Eve*, "until recently,

[the Bible] was studied by female scholars hardly at all, let alone by female scholars who were interested specifically in what the Bible had to say about women. This has changed, to put it mildly." (Boston: Houghton Mifflin, 1998), x. Volumes dedicated to uncovering the historical realities of women in antiquity are beginning to appear as well, as, for example, Harvard University's five-volume history of women from ancient goddesses to the twentieth century, *A History of Women in the West* (series eds. G. Duby and M. Perrot; Cambridge: Harvard University Press, 1994–1996).

3. The definition of a parable is hard to pinpoint. See Dieter Roth's wonderful compilation of the various attempts in D. Roth, *The Parables in Q* (London: T&T Clark, 2018), 6–12. For our purposes, a parable is a short didactic narrative with a double meaning, one literal (if fictional) and one a metaphor or simile.

4. J. Robinson, "The Critical Edition of Q and the Study of Jesus," in *The Sayings Source Q and the Historical Jesus* (ed. A. Lindemann; Leuven: Leuven University Press, 2001), 27.

5. G. Theissen and A. Merz, *The Historical Jesus: A Comprehensive Guide* (Minneapolis: Fortress, 1998), 29.

6. N. Siffer and D. Fricker, *Q ou la source des paroles de Jésus* (Paris: Cerf, 2010).

7. People who discuss this literary device often use the terms "gender doublet" or "gender couplet" to refer to what is more precisely a type of parallelism. The choice of the term "doublet" is potentially confusing in this context, for the simple reason that "doublet" is a text-critical term used frequently in Synoptic studies to mean something else; there, a doublet is a repetition of the same verse in a different literary context. For this reason, I have chosen to discontinue the trend of referring to the parallel Q pairs as "doublets." Likewise, I avoid the term "couplet," simply because of its use to mean something else in poetry. To me, it only makes sense to guide any future discussion of the gender parallelism in Q toward precision by using the terms "gender parallels," "gender pairs," or "parallel parable pairs." These are the sorts of terms I use in this book.

8. See chapter 4 for a complete definition and description of the literary devices in question.

9. Due to the frequency of the use of "Kingdom of God" language in Q and elsewhere, I refer to the movement surrounding Jesus of Nazareth as a *basileia* movement. I prefer to leave *basileia* untranslated since, as Schüssler Fiorenza notes, "it is difficult to translate the term *basileia* adequately because it can either mean kingdom, kingly realm, domain or empire, or it can be rendered as monarchy, kingly rule, sovereignty, dominion and reign. In any case it[s English translation] has not only monarchic but also masculinist overtones" and this is all the more important since the *basileia* is a "central symbol" in Jesus' movement. E. Schüssler Fiorenza, "Jesus of Nazareth in Historical Research," pages 29–48 in *Thinking of Christ: Proclamation, Explanation, Meaning* (ed. T. Wiley; New York: Continuum, 2003), 45.

10. Chapter 5, "Were there Gendered Parable Pairs before Jesus?" is dedicated to demonstrating the innovative nature of the gendered parable pairs.

11. By "early Jewish" I mean the area of scholarly study that coincides roughly with the Second-Temple period, and I include both geographical (e.g., Judaean) and religious (e.g., Torah-abiding) designations. The terms "Judaism," "Jewish," or "early

Jewish" are never used over and against the terms "Hellenism" or "Hellenistic" but are rather a specific subcategory within Hellenism, which I trust would please the late Martin Hengel, whose thesis on Judaism and Hellenism has been one of the most game-changing works of the last century for biblical scholars: M. Hengel, *Judentum und Hellenismus: Studien zu ihrer Begegnung unter Berücksichtigung Palästinas bis zur Mitte des 2 Jh.s v.Chr.* (Tübingen: J.C.B. Mohr, 1973). As for the recent trend to refer to "Judaeans" rather than Jews, which took hold beginning with Steve Mason's article ("Jews, Judaeans, Judaizing, Judaism: Problems of Categorization in Ancient History" *JSJ* 38 [2007]: 457–512), I instead follow Adele Reinhartz and others who prefer to continue to refer to Jews, accompanied by the caveat that ancient divisions between categories such as ethnicity and religion are not identical to our own (A. Reinhartz, "The Vanishing Jews of Antiquity" in *Marginalia Review of Books*, 24 June 2014, n.p. [cited July 15, 2015]. http://marginalia.lareviewofbooks.org/vanishing-jews-antiquity-adele-reinhartz). C. Baker's thorough and sensitive discussion of the term "Jew" in the introduction to her book *Jew* (New Brunswick: Rutgers, 2016), 3–13 is a must read.

12. For the purposes of this project, I employ the terms "equality" and "egalitarian" in a limited sense—that is, as useful shortcuts for describing a process of "leveling" that brings members of separate social categories closer together in some way into a new, shared category that is less hierarchical. Wherever these words and their derivatives are used throughout, this will be the intended definition. Egalitarianism is a modern category of analysis, not an ancient one, and must be clearly defined in order to avoid anachronistic readings when attempting to describe social or literary phenomena in the ancient world that allow people to transgress expected boundaries of class, gender, or status. See J. H. Elliott, "Jesus was not an Egalitarian: A Critique of an Anachronistic and Idealist Theory" *BTB* 32 (2002): 75–91 for a critique of scholars who, in Elliott's view, paint too rosy a picture of early Christianity at the expense of historicity. Elliott calls, rightly, for a definition of "egalitarian" by any who choose to use the term (76). For Q, cf. the "limited 'egalitarian' ideology" in tension with "social reality" in the Matthean and/or Q communities, described by D. Duling in "'Egalitarian' Ideology, Leadership, and Factional Conflict within the Matthean Group," *BTB* 27 (1997): 124–137.

13. Throughout this work, the term "women" means human beings of the female gender. However, the term "wo/men" (with a slash) is to be understood as inclusive of all genders. This is one of the many useful neologisms of Elisabeth Schüssler Fiorenza. In her words, "In order to lift into consciousness the linguistic violence of so-called generic male-centered language, I use the term 'wo/men' and not 'men' in an inclusive way. I suggest that whenever you see 'wo/men' you understand it in a generic inclusive sense. Wo/men includes men, s/he includes he, and fe/male includes male. Feminist studies of language have shown that Western, kyriocentric—that is, master, lord, father, male-centered—language systems understand language as both generic and as gender-specific. Wo/men always must think at least twice, if not three times, and adjudicate whether we are meant or not by so-called generic terms such as men, humans, Americans, or citizens. The writing of wo/men with a slash re-defines wo/men not only in linguistic but also in socio-political terms," "Critical Feminist Studies in Religion," *CRR* 1/43 (2013): 48–49.

14. By "early Christian" I refer to offshoots of the Jesus movement after such time as they began to be referred to as *Christianoi*, never to the exclusion of the possibility of Jewish membership, co-identity, or leadership, as my view of the "parting of the ways" is akin to Daniel Boyarin's in terms of potentially late *terminus ad quem* and to Adele Reinhartz' in terms of complexity and fluidity. See D. Boyarin, *Dying for God: Martyrdom and the Making of Christianity and Judaism* (Stanford: Stanford University Press, 1999) and A. Reinhartz, "A Fork in the Road or a Multi-Lane Highway? New Perspectives on 'The Parting of the Ways' Between Judaism and Christianity" in *The Changing Face of Judaism, Christianity and Other Greco-Roman Religions in Antiquity* (ed. G. Oegema and I. Henderson with S. Parks; Gütersloh: Gütersloher Verlagshaus, 2005), 278–293. It is, of course, important to recognize the difficulty in designations for "Jewish" and "Christian" in the era before the "parting of the ways" coalesced. See the important essay by J. Lieu: "'Impregnable Ramparts and Walls of Iron': Boundary and Identity in Early 'Judaism' and 'Christianity'" *NTS* 48 (2002): 297–313 as well as J. J. Pilch's "Are there Jews and Christians in the Bible?" *HTS* 53/1 (1997): 119–125.

15. M. M. Beirne, *Women and Men in the Fourth Gospel: A Genuine Discipleship of Equals* (London: Sheffield Academic, 2003).

16. Mark 2:21–22 is discussed below.

17. Various pairs in 1 Corinthians 7 will be discussed, along with the wee pair in Galatians 3:28.

18. I am well aware that the criteria of authenticity (and the heavily form-criticism based notion of "in/authentic" itself) have been challenged in recent years, with some scholars calling for their abandonment or at least their revision. See C. Keith and A. Le Donne, eds., *Jesus, Criteria, and the Demise of Authenticity* (New York: T&T Clark, 2012). For a critique of the criterion of multiple attestation, see M. Goodacre, "Criticising the Criterion of Multiple Attestation: The Historical Jesus and the Question of Sources," 152–72 in that same volume. In my view, criteria (such as that of multiple attestation in independent sources) remain extremely useful, if not, as orality and memory studies may indicate, for examining *precise* textual transmission, then certainly still for elucidating the historical development of ideas behind texts, especially when used alongside the findings from other recent approaches.

19. For a recent argument that this is a link that should be more consistently acknowledged by Synoptics scholars and taken more frequently into account by historical Jesus researchers, see W. Arnal, "The Synoptic Problem and the Historical Jesus," in *New Studies in the Synoptic Problem* (ed. P. Foster et al.; Leuven: Peeters, 2011), 371–432.

20. B. Mack, *Who Wrote the New Testament: The Making of the Christian Myth* (New York: HarperCollins, 1995), 47.

21. J. P. Meier, *A Marginal Jew, Volume 4* (New Haven: Yale University Press, 1991–2015), 15.

22. Some scholars have suggested that "material which can be shown to be dissimilar to characteristic emphases both of ancient Judaism and of the early Church" is potentially more likely to be authentic: N. Perrin, *Rediscovering the Teaching of Jesus* (London: SCM, 1967), 39. Meier, who uses the term "discontinuity" to describe this criterion, says it "focuses on words or deeds of Jesus that cannot be derived either

from the Judaism(s) of Jesus' time or from the early church." Meier, *A Marginal Jew, Volume 4*, 15. In other words, if something placed in the mouth of Jesus cannot be traced to previous expressions of Judaism and Hellenism, as I demonstrate that the Q pairs cannot nor to agendas of the later Christian Church, then the possibility that they are indeed authentic individual teachings of the teacher himself is heightened. This criterion has rightly been criticized (see G. S. Oegema, *Apocalyptic Interpretation of the Bible* [New York: T&T Clark, 2012], esp. pp. 78–9) because its unbalanced use could lead to a reconstruction of the historical Jesus that is *unrealistically dissimilar* to the varieties of Judaism in and around the first century, but I do advocate its use in conjunction with various other criteria (such as the criterion of multiple attestation) and methods, which work together to avoid the construction of an overly anomalous Jesus, especially in conjunction with other approaches, including those that incorporate recent paradigms of memory and orality.

23. By "patriarchy" I mean a paradigm of "father-rule," that is, "the perspective of some powerful males over other males, and over most women and children." A. Loades, "Feminist Interpretation," *The Cambridge Companion to Biblical Interpretation* (ed. J. Barton; Cambridge: Cambridge University Press, 1998), 82. Schüssler Fiorenza's brief definition is also applicable: "a male pyramid of graded subordinations." *Bread Not Stone* (Boston: Beacon, 1995), xiv.

24. It is a given that the time period in question was male-dominated: "The major groups of texts of the Second Temple period are androcentric in focus, written by male authors for a male audience, and they mention women only rarely and usually in peripheral contexts." White, "Women: Second Temple Period," 331.

25. Schüssler Fiorenza used the term "kyriarchy" in order, in her words, "to connote a complex systemic interstructuring of sexism, racism, classism, and cultural-religious imperialism." "Feminist/Women Priests – An Oxymoron?" *New Women/ New Church* (Fall 1995): 18. This usage first appeared in her *But She Said: Feminist Practices of Biblical Interpretation* (Boston: Beacon, 1992). According to Schüssler Fiorenza, the term "kyriocentric" describes "ideological articulations that validate and are sustained by kyriarchal relations of domination. Since kyriocentrism replaces the category of androcentrism, it is best understood as an intellectual framework and cultural ideology that legitimates and is legitimated by kyriarchal social structures and systems of domination." *Jesus, Miriam's Child, Sophia's Prophet: Critical Issues in Feminist Christology* (NY: Continuum, 1995), 14. See also E. Schüssler Fiorenza, *Wisdom Ways: Introducing Feminist Biblical Interpretation* (Maryknoll: Orbis, 2001).

26. Schüssler Fiorenza, *Jesus, Miriam's Child, Sophia's Prophet*, 70.

27. Schüssler Fiorenza, *Jesus, Miriam's Child, Sophia's Prophet*, 71.

28. See, for example, C. Conway, "Gender Matters in John." Pages 79–103 in *A Feminist Companion to John: Volume II* (ed. A.-J. Levine; Cleveland: Pilgrim, 2003), 102.

29. E. Schüssler Fiorenza, *Rhetoric and Ethic: The Politics of Biblical Studies* (Minneapolis: Fortress, 1999), 19.

30. Elisabeth Schüssler Fiorenza often jokes at speaking engagements that she gets her definition of feminism from a bumper sticker she once saw, which reads: "Feminism is the radical notion that women are people." I agree with the simplicity

and broadness of this definition, but I also more formally employ the definition set out by A. Ogden Bellis in *Helpmates, Harlots, and Heroes: Women's Stories in the Hebrew Bible* (Louisville: Westminster John Knox, 2007), 6. Bellis defines feminism, broadly, as "a point of view in which women are understood to be fully human and thus entitled to equal rights and privileges."

31. See, for instance, Luise Schottroff's statement on the use of historical-critical methods by feminist theology: "I will inquire about the genres of texts and about their contexts in the history of thought and religion as does historical criticism, but always from the critical angle I have indicated. I ask about the *Sitz im Leben* (setting in life), but within the broad social sense of a social history critical of patriarchy. I inquire about the contents of the message of Jesus and his disciples, female and male, but always in the context of the question about their liberating or oppressive function and the praxis associated with them. I take a skeptical view of the methods of literary criticism and tradition criticism associated with the so-called historical-critical method." L. Schottroff, "The Sayings Source Q," in *Searching the Scriptures 2: A Feminist Commentary* (ed. E. Schüssler Fiorenza; New York: Crossroad, 1994), 510.

32. R. N. Soulen and R. K. Soulen, "Historical Critical Method," in *Handbook of Biblical Criticism, Fourth Edition* (Louisville: Westminster John Knox, 2011), 88.

33. On the complementarity of historical-critical and postmodern approaches, see J. J. Collins, *The Bible After Babel: Historical Criticism in a Postmodern Age* (Grand Rapids: Eerdmans, 2005).

34. D. B. Martin, *Sex and the Single Savior: Gender and Sexuality in Biblical Interpretation* (Louisville: Westminster John Knox, 2006), 16.

35. I acknowledge the long history of and the diversity within feminisms and agree with Ogden Bellis: "No one definition would satisfy all feminists." Bellis, *Helpmates, Harlots, and Heroes*, 6. My personal definition of feminism is the belief that all human beings have the right to be valued equally and to have a voice, regardless of their gender, and that a significant degree of one's gender has traditionally been and continues to be socially constructed in a way that reinforces an oppressive system whereby those considered "women" are given less agency, less value, and less voice. My feminism is intersectional in that I do not believe that any emancipation based on gender will be long-lasting, meaningful, or ethical unless co-emancipation occurs across all categories, such as class, race, culture, ability.

36. Schüssler Fiorenza, *Rhetoric and Ethic*, 195–6.

37. Schüssler Fiorenza, *Rhetoric and Ethic*, 195–6.

38. Schüssler Fiorenza, *Rhetoric and Ethic*, 97. See also Schottroff, "The Sayings Source Q," 511: "In traditional Western theology it is considered 'scientific' to adopt a (supposed) posture of neutrality toward the object of research and to take no account of one's own context. This 'neutrality' conceals the patriarchal biases expressed by a theological discipline that imagines itself to be independent of its social context."

39. As Achtemeier puts it, "there is no such thing as a neutral, historical-critical, scientific, objective interpretation of the Scriptures." E. Achtemeier, "The Impossible Possibility: Evaluating the Feminist Approach to Bible and Theology," *Interpretation* 42 (1988): 50.

40. For a scathing response to overly optimistic feminist readings of the Jesus movements and early Christianity that take place at the expense of historical accuracy

and with little to no sensitivity to the issue of anti-Judaism, see A.-J. Levine, "Second-Temple Judaism, Jesus, and Women: Yeast of Eden" in *A Feminist Companion to the Hebrew Bible in the New Testament* (ed. A. Brenner; Sheffield: Sheffield Academic, 1996), 302–331. From the same volume, see also both L. Siegele-Wenschkewitz, "In the Dangerous Currents of Old Prejudices: How Predominant Thoughts have Disastrous Effects and What Could be Done to Counter Them," 342–48 and E. Brocke, "Do the Origins Already Contain the Malady?," 349–54.

41. See Brooten on this distinction: "Recognizing that, for women, the state of the sources is similar to that for men and women for the periods usually deemed prehistorical should elicit in us the shock necessary for rethinking the way we use the sources. *Sources by men are also primarily about men*; they may have little or nothing to do with women's activities or perceptions of themselves" (emphasis mine). B. Brooten, "Early Christian Women and their Cultural Context: Issues of Method in Historical Reconstruction," in *Feminist Perspectives on Biblical Scholarship* (ed. A. Yarbro Collins; Chico: Scholars, 1985), 67. Cf. Schüssler Fiorenza: "Ideas of men *about* women ... do not reflect women's historical reality since it can be shown that ideological polemics about women's place, role, or nature increase whenever women's actual emancipation and active participations in history become stronger." E. Schüssler Fiorenza, "Remembering the Past in Creating the Future: Historical-Critical Scholarship and Feminist Biblical Interpretation," in *Feminist Perspectives on Biblical Scholarship* (ed. A. Yarbro Collins; Chico: Scholars, 1985), 57.

42. C. Camp, *Wisdom and the Feminine in the Book of Proverbs* (Decatur: Almond, 1985), 75.

43. R. Chesnutt, "Revelatory Experiences Attributed to Biblical Women," in *Women Like This: New Perspectives on Jewish Women in the Greco-Roman World* (ed. A.-J. Levine; Atlanta: Scholars, 1991), 123.

44. S. de Beauvoir, *The Second Sex* (New York: Vintage, 1973), 301.

45. A good example of the current conversation around gender as socially constructed is J. Butler's *Undoing Gender* (London: Routledge, 2014).

46. J. M. O'Brien, ed. *The Oxford Encyclopedia of the Bible and Gender, Volume 1 ASI-MUJ* (s.v. "gender"; New York: Oxford University Press, 2014), 264.

47. Butler, *Undoing Gender*, 42.

48. Cross-disciplinary scholarship is moving steadily toward postgendered, intersectional models. See G. Dvorsky and J. Hughes, "Postgenderism: Beyond the Gender Binary," *IEET White Papers* (March 2008): 1–18. "Postgenderists contend that dyadic gender roles and sexual dimorphisms are generally to the detriment of individuals and society" (2). "Postgenderism is a radical interpretation of the feminist critique of patriarchy and gender, and the genderqueer critique of the way that binary gender constrains individual potential and our capacity to communicate with and understand other people. Postgenderism transcends essentialism and social constructionism ..." (13). Intersectional feminism was first discussed by K. Crenshaw in "Demarginalizing the Intersection of Race and Sex: A Black Feminist Critique of Anti-Discrimination Doctrine, Feminist Theory, and Anti-Racist Politics," *UCLF* 140 (1989): 139–167. See also A. Carastathis, "The Concept of Intersectionality in Feminist Theory," *Philos. Compass* 9/5 (2014): 304–314.

49. For the "problem of social distance" from the world of the text in question, see further R. Rohrbaugh, "Introduction," *The Social Sciences and New Testament Interpretation* (R. Rohrbaugh ed.; Peabody: Hendrickson, 1996), 3. Rohrbaugh's example of the prevalence of belief in the "evil eye" serves as a reminder of differences in worldview between ancient text and modern Western reader.

50. Q scholars are not in an agreement about a date for the translation and compilation of sayings known as Q, but they are unanimous in Q's relative relationship to other early Christian evidence, in that it is among the earliest, if not *the* earliest Jesus-movement data, along with the early letters of Paul and perhaps the *Didache*. Mack calls Q "the earliest written record we have from the Jesus movement" in *Who Wrote the New Testament*, 47.

51. I am aware of the complexity of what it means to "read" in antiquity. By "audience" I mean "recipients," without speculating on the specific means of delivery. For information on ways in which a first-century audience may have received such sayings, see A. Millard, "Literacy in the Time of Jesus," *BAR* 29 (2003): 36–45 and *Reading and Writing in the Time of Jesus* (Sheffield: Sheffield Academic, 2000). In this project, I avoid commenting on differing literacy levels, whether auraliterate, oraliterate, oculiterate, scribaliterate, illiterate, etc. For a taxonomy of these and other types of literacy in the ancient world, see L. B. Yaghjian, "Ancient Reading," *The Social Sciences and New Testament Interpretation* (ed. R. Rohrbaugh; Peabody: Hendrickson, 1996), 208–209. There is also the question of whether one is speaking of the audience as a literary construct implied by a text or as a socio-historical group that formed a text's actual recipients. Because Q is a collection of sayings material, we must also distinguish between the hearers of Jesus' of Nazareth's sayings and the consumers of the written sayings in Q. For this project, I will specify whether the "audience" in question is that of Jesus of Nazareth's early sayings or that of the specific Greek written collection called Q. While some scholars seem to blend both, broadly speaking, under the umbrella "earliest layer of the Jesus movement," with the understanding that the members of pre-Gospel Jesus movements who may have heard the parable gender pairs do not span more than one generation, from original hearers to those who joined the movement at the time of Q, not enough can be known about Q's provenance to blend the two. For this reason, my focus here is on the audience of the original sayings (i.e., the audience of Jesus of Nazareth), to the extent that we have access to them through Q, and on the rhetorical work of the sayings, that is, the text's implied recipients. That said, the very presence of the gender pairs does say one thing about that audience: it contained women.

52. A. Batten, "More Queries for Q: Women and Christian Origins," *BTB* 24/2 (1994): 47.

53. J.-F. Racine and M. Beaumont, "Three Approaches to the Position of Women in the Q Document: Hal Taussig, Luise Schottroff, and Amy-Jill Levine," in *Women also Journeyed with Him* (Collegeville: Liturgical Press, 2000), 114.

54. K. Corley, *Women and the Historical Jesus: Feminist Myths of Christian Origins* (Santa Rosa: Polebridge, 2002), 1.

55. Corley, *Women and the Historical Jesus*. See also A. Bielman, "Female Patronage in the Greek Hellenistic and Roman Republican Periods," in *A Companion*

to *Women in the Ancient World* (ed. S. L. James and S. Dillon; Chichester: Wiley Blackwell, 2012), 238–248.

56. W. E. Arnal, "Gendered Couplets in Q and Legal Formulations: From Rhetoric to Social History," *JBL* 116/1 (1997): 92.

57. A.-J. Levine, "Women in the Q Communit(ies) and Traditions," *Women and Christian Origins* (ed. R. S. Kraemer and M. R. D'Angelo; New York: Oxford University Press, 1999), 150.

58. Levine, "Yeast of Eden," throughout.

59. As Schottroff states, "the Christian Testament as a whole, and the Sayings Source in particular, speak in androcentric language and presuppose a patriarchal system of relationships": "The Sayings Source Q," 510.

60. See Levine ("Yeast of Eden"), Elliott ("Jesus was not an Egalitarian"), and others who heavily critique the readiness to reconstruct an early "discipleship of equals" that has been embraced by some feminist Christian scholarship. I address this in detail in chapter 3.

61. Corley, *Women and the Historical Jesus*, 1. The term "discipleship of equals" was coined by E. Schüssler Fiorenza to describe the ideal community of the historical Jesus. The first mentions of it known to me are in 1993, in her monograph, *In Memory of Her* (New York: Crossroad, 1983) and in *Discipleship of Equals: A Critical Feminist Ekklesialogy of Liberation*. New York: Crossroad, 1993), and she refers to it frequently throughout her written and performed work, for example, in: "The Praxis of Coequal Discipleship," in *Paul and Empire: Religion and Power in Roman Imperial Society* (R. A. Horsley, ed.; Harrisburg: Trinity, 1997), 224–241. A thorough analysis of the ways in which the phrase is used by Schüssler Fiorenza has been published by Beirne, in *Women and Men in the Fourth Gospel*, 28–32.

62. Corley, *Women and the Historical Jesus*, 6.

63. Corley, *Women and the Historical Jesus*, 6.

64. See Arnal, "Gendered Couplets in Q"; Batten, "More Queries for Q"; K. E. Corley, *"Private Women, Public Meals: Social Conflict in the Synoptic Tradition* (Peabody: Hendrickson, 1993); Levine, "Yeast of Eden"; and "Who's Catering the Q Affair? Feminist Observations on Q Paraenesis," *Semeia* 50 (1990): 145–161.

65. Arnal, "Gendered Couplets in Q."

66. "An analysis of Jesus' teaching suggests that while Jesus censured the class and status distinctions of his culture, that critique did not extend to unequal gender distinctions." Corley, *Women and the Historical Jesus*, 1.

67. Levine, "Yeast of Eden," 302–331, esp. 320–323.

68. See A. Brenner, "Introduction," *Feminist Companion to the Hebrew Bible in the New Testament* (ed. A. Brenner; Sheffield: Sheffield Academic, 1996), 15.

69. I follow E. Schüssler Fiorenza and others who refer to the New Testament collection as the "Christian Testament" in an attempt at less value-laden terminology. (See Schüssler Fiorenza, *Rhetoric and Ethic*, ix.)

70. For an excellent treatment of women in Judaism during the Second Temple period that displays evidence for women in a wide spectrum of roles and social practices, thus counteracting any plausibility of a suddenly woman-friendly Christianity arising from a monolithically patriarchal Judaism, see L. S. Lieber, "Jewish Women:

Texts and Contexts," in *A Companion to Women in the Ancient World* (ed. S. L. James and S. Dillon; Chichester: Wiley Blackwell, 2012), 329–342.

71. It should be mentioned that there are other elements of Q besides the gender pairs that are also highly pertinent to the study of gender, including its use of Sophia language, which are not explored in this book. Melanie Johnson-Debaufre has written on the feminist ramifications of Q's eschatology and its use of Sophia imagery. See M. Johnson-Debaufre, *Jesus Among her Children: Q, Eschatology, and the Construction of Christian Origins* (Cambridge: Harvard University Press, 2005).

72. Scholars working specifically on this issue include, among others: Arnal, "Gendered Couplets in Q"; Batten, "More Queries for Q"; Corley, *"Private Women, Public Meals*; and Levine, "Yeast of Eden" and "Who's Catering the Q Affair."

73. Something that has been argued for cogently from the biblical text by Elisabeth Schüssler Fiorenza throughout her career, including in *Discipleship of Equals* and "The Praxis of Coequal Discipleship."

Chapter 2

Q and the Q People

At the core of this project are the uniquely gendered words of Jesus, not quite as they have come to us ensconced in the Gospels, but as we are able to discover them in the hypothetical Greek sayings list known as Q. Q reflects a situation much closer in time and demographic to Jesus of Nazareth himself than do our other extant sources for him. Being geographically and temporally closer to the earliest Jesus movement doesn't *automatically* make for "better" evidence for Jesus; the compiler/s of the sayings of Jesus would have had their own theology and their own tendencies just as any other author/s. However, with no writings left to us by Jesus himself, and little to no evidence for "ground zero" of the Jesus movement, Q, as an early Galilean sayings collection, is certainly something for historians to take seriously and for practitioners of Christianity to treasure. This book attempts to treasure and take seriously the attitude toward gender in these sayings, through a close look at the gender-paired parables, along with the ways that feminist scholarship has interacted with them.

Later on, I will provide a detailed analysis of these primary texts and of the conflicting interpretations of what they might mean for women; I will also work toward a proposed resolution to that debate. To begin, though, we will take some time for a more general introduction to key Q issues. This will be particularly useful for those not already familiar with the sayings gospel. This general introduction includes a sketch—necessarily speculative—of who the "Q People" may have been; a collection implies a collector, or perhaps even a blossoming community. The early translator/s, compiler/s, and consumers of the sayings of Jesus in Greek before they were folded into Gospels have been the object of much speculation. Many remain unconvinced that we can confidently make any sort of jump from a Q to a Q community, but others have not been able to resist guessing what such a community may have been like, based on the contents and arrangements of the sayings themselves. If nothing else, the sayings point to an implied or aspirational community.

This section serves to highlight the elements of Q's context that make a discussion of women and men around Q substantively different from typical discussions of "Jesus and women." While "Jesus and women" is usually short for "women in the Gospels," the exploration of "women in Q" is a distinct enterprise. These pursuits differ both from each other and from the pursuit of "women and the historical Jesus." In discussing the background to Q, I attempt to keep an eye on these sometimes subtle, but nonetheless conceptually substantial distinctions.

A BRIEF BACKGROUND TO Q

Q is the nickname for a lost[1] source of Jesus' sayings—lost, that is, if the Gospels of Luke and Matthew had not drawn upon it when they wanted to incorporate the way in which Jesus taught. No copy of Q has been unearthed, although it may have been referred to by patristic writers by other names, such as the Gospel according to the Hebrews[2] or the *logia*.[3] Its existence was first conceived of as the best solution to the problem faced by scholars wishing to explain the complex literary inter-relationship among Mark, Matthew, and Luke, including the many identical sayings of Jesus in the Gospels of Luke and Matthew. Since Luke and Matthew were not thought to have had access to each other, it was striking that their quotations of Jesus shared such strong verbal agreement, despite their different writing styles and aims; thus, these quotations, it was thought, had to have been taken from a shared, written Greek source.[4] Furthermore, the quotations largely appeared in the same order in both gospels,[5] although often inserted into different narrative surroundings and/or given different explanations. Although it had long been thought that Luke and Matthew had shared Mark as a source for Jesus' *actions* (the theory of "Markan Priority"), Jesus *teachings* are scarce in Mark, and so it was posited that there had been a collection of sayings used by Matthew and Luke in addition to Mark. With Markan priority established, the notion of Q was born quite naturally, as the simplest way of explaining the roughly 230 verses' worth of material—mostly sayings—shared nearly verbatim by Matthew and Luke, yet seemingly unknown to (or uninteresting to) Mark. These non-Markan sayings were attributed to a hypothetical[6] early sayings collection in Greek. It was surmised that "Matthew and Luke used the same two sources, Mark and a no-longer extant collection of sayings."[7] This two-source theory answered—and still answers—this puzzle of the literary relationships among the three Synoptic Gospels to the satisfaction of most scholars.

While the *setting of the sayings* is clearly Galilee, the *provenance of the Greek translation* Q is difficult to pinpoint. A majority of scholars nevertheless place Q in Galilee too.[8] As for a date, any time before the composition of Matthew and Luke is technically possible. Given the generally accepted earlier dating of Matthew, Q had to exist *before* Matthew's *terminus post quem*, which ranges anywhere from 80 to 100, but is most often placed in the 80s or 90s of the first century. Some imagine that the Greek sayings collection existed as early as the 30s or 40s, but those who specialize in Q tend to date it in the 50s or 60s, roughly contemporaneous with the undisputed letters of Paul.[9]

Significance of the Sayings List beyond the Synoptic Problem

For decades after the development of the Q hypothesis, Q's sole function remained steadfastly that of a variable in the Synoptic equation.[10] The puzzle of the literary relationships among Mark, Matthew, and Luke had been solved to the satisfaction of most, and it did not seem to dawn on them right away that Q, as a source for the canonical Gospels, was therefore evidence for a time considerably earlier than those Gospels, and consequently for a demographic closer to the first Jesus-followers. It took some time for Q to break free from the singular purpose of shedding light on the construction of Matthew and Luke and to be approached in its own right, for its own contents and context. Reconstructions of Q began to take shape,[11] and James Robinson writes: "Now Q need no longer remain purely hypothetical, a mere postulate lurking unattainably behind Matthew and Luke."[12] In other words, *Q became a text*.

It has taken more than a century since the rise of the theory of Markan priority and the two-source hypothesis for Q to reach its current status—namely, published in critical edition[13] and approached as a text.[14] Most scholars remain aware that we do not have enough evidence to confidently delineate the *boundaries* of Q, only its minimal core. While some have argued that the minimum (only sayings that overlap in Matthew and Luke) should be seen as Q's boundaries,[15] this is not commensurate with the way in which Matthew and Luke used Mark, so it does not make sense to assume they used Q markedly differently. Q was likely wider than Matthew–Luke overlap.

However tentative Q's boundaries, though, the study of the sayings on their own lends itself to questions about potential communities responsible for and interested in the material in Q, and also, significantly for this book, questions about the place of women in such communities. As John Kloppenborg observes, Q is now studied "because it is of intrinsic interest as one of the earliest expressions—perhaps the earliest expression—of Christianity in Palestine."[16] Scholars almost universally agree that we don't have enough data to confidently reconstruct such a community—some question whether a

"Q community" can even be said to have existed. That said, a variety of efforts are being put forward toward imagining Q's social location.[17]

The following section sketches the types of social settings for Q that have been posited. It is useful to keep in mind that there is a conceptual difference between the people toward whom Jesus first directed the gender pairs, and the people by and for whom they were collected and translated, and again between those who incorporated them into the canonical gospels, and those who were consumers of gospels. Although Q's community is a fertile field of speculation and creativity, it is not something that is necessary in order to analyze the pairs from a literary or rhetorical perspective. Yet these four distinct stages in the reception of the gendered pairs are worth bearing in mind for anyone yearning to try and reconstruct the social realities of first-century Jewish women.

"Q People"

The Q hypothesis or two-source hypothesis may have more or less consolidated into consensus, but the ways that scholars picture those who first translated, compiled, and listened to these sayings of Jesus have not.[18] Because Q is among our earliest evidence for an interest in preserving Jesus' teachings, the prospect of reconstructing its possible producers and/or consumers remains very attractive. Burton Mack is an example of a scholar committed to this project. In his view, it is a task we cannot afford to neglect, because "Q is the best record we have for the first forty years of the Jesus movements."[19] In Mack's words:

> [Q] documents the history of a single group of Jesus people for a period of about fifty years, from the time of Jesus in the 20s until after the Roman–Jewish war in the 70s. [. . .] It has enabled us to reconsider and revise the traditional picture of early Christian history by filling in the time from Jesus until just after the destruction of Jerusalem when the first narrative gospel, the Gospel of Mark, was written.[20]

This claim that Q "documents the history of a single group," and that this group stretches over five decades in an unbroken early history, surely overvalues Q while undervaluing other historical evidence for early Jesus movements, such as Paul's undisputed letters. On the other hand, dismissing Q entirely is also neglectful. Richard Horsley notes:

> [S]ince Q, as the source of Jesus' sayings for Matthew and Luke, apparently originated before the great Jewish Revolt of 66–70 C.E., which supposedly precipitated the separation of Jesus' followers from nascent 'Judaism,' it brings

the modern historian and believer a giant step closer to the circumstances of Jesus' ministry and the early stages of the movement in which the Jesus traditions took form.[21]

Although Q is undoubtedly an important clue for understanding the very earliest Jesus movements, there is wide-ranging speculation, and little to no agreement, about what *kind* of community evidence, if any, can be salvaged from one text, itself a tentative reconstruction. Despite this, some scholars, such as Kloppenborg, go so far as to subdivide Q into three literary "strata" and posit different social situations behind each stratum of development.[22] It's been suggested that attempting to identify specific communities with different recensions of Q material when not even one recension is extant is difficult, even problematic.[23] This book, with its focus on an analysis of the Jesus' practice of speaking in gendered pairs, does not require a tracing of development over specific stages in the reconstructed history of a hypothetical community of Q People. At any rate, the gender pairs occur across both of Kloppenborg's main strata, known as "Q1" and "Q2." Analyzing what gendered parable pairs might mean for their women hearers does not require a detailed reconstruction of stages of community development.

That said, this chapter will provide the reader who is unfamiliar with Q an introduction to some broad commonalities that tend to emerge in scholarly hypotheses concerning the consumers and producers of this early sayings material in Greek. There are several basic assertions about Q's social context, which are good to keep in mind as part of the fabric of Q scholarship. They include the following elements:

(a) a Galilean provenance;
(b) a deep interest in Jesus' teachings coupled with a lack of evident interest in a biography of Jesus;
(c) use of the language of the *basileia* of God;
(d) an interest in both sapiential witticisms and apocalyptic warnings of judgment;
(e) references to itinerant prophecy among community members;
(f) a rural agrarian demographic that is Jewish, as opposed to the more urban and mixed demographics represented in the Christian Testament; and
(g) a subversive or countercultural tendency.

Galilean Provenance

In some Q scholarship there is a tendency to posit that it is not only Jesus and his earliest movement that derived from Galilee, but that the early translation of his teachings into Greek also took place there.[24] Galilee is the backdrop against which the parables found in Q make the most sense. Based on literary and archaeological evidence for Galilee in the first centuries before and after the Common Era, Q's own internal evidence proves, according to Reed, that Q's "place names, spatial imagery, and themes fit the social and cultural setting of Galilee quite well."[25] Dunn concludes that "as to Q's *Sitz im Leben*, the strongest case has undoubtedly been made for Galilee."[26] Galilee is the most common backdrop against which Q scholars picture the creators and users of the Q material.[27]

So what does a Galilean context entail? A Galilean *setting* would imply that the community that Jesus addresses is neither urban nor wealthy, but rather primarily in a tenant-agrarian and resource-based economy, and more likely than not to be economically and socially disadvantaged.[28] Hypotheses of a Galilean *provenance* tend to suggest something similar about those concerned with collecting the sayings for posterity. Outside the small cities, the Galilean populace in Jesus' day was largely tenant farmers indebted to a handful of absentee landlords in whose ownership the vast majority of the wealth and resources were concentrated.[29] The Q compilers would be a part of that socioeconomic landscape—the noteworthy addendum being that Q's compiler/s could *write*, implying a degree of education, such as scribal training.[30]

In other words, it was what some might call a peasant[31] community, familiar with systemic social inequity, where social mobility was fairly curtailed. Q's imagery fits with this setting—the sayings refer to fruit trees (Q 6:43–44), harvest (Q 10:2), sheep (Q 10:3), sowing and reaping (Q 12:24), seeds (Q 17:6), and so on. Further, the geographic locations that are specifically mentioned are Galilean; the "woes" against local towns include Chorazin, Bethsaida, and Capernaum (Q 10:13–15).

It is possible that the probably Aramaic-speaking[32] audience of Jesus of Nazareth's teaching career might be different from the audience those teachings were intended to reach in their later Greek translation. Alternative theories of provenance place Q in as disparate settings as Qumran[33] and Jerusalem,[34] but the assumption of a Galilean setting *and* provenance continues to capture the approval of a majority of Q scholars.

Interest in Sayings over Biography

Q's clear interest in Jesus is as teacher or sage—in what he *said*. To that end, Q is primarily a collection of *teachings*—not of biographical details, nor accounts of wonderworking and healing.[35] Perhaps most notable is Q's apparent lack of material concerning Jesus' suffering, death, and resurrection; it has often been noted how this stands in sharp contrast to the strong emphasis on Jesus' death and resurrection to which virtually all other texts of the Christian Testament and most apocrypha[36] bear witness. (Paul, for instance, shows virtually no interest in Jesus' life apart from crucifixion and resurrection, and Martin Kähler famously over-stated that Mark is nothing but "a Passion story with an extended introduction."[37]) For Koester, this difference in focus could indicate a *divide* between the Galilean Jesus movement and the other ancient Jesus movements:

> Very early, different developments are evident in the way in which various circles of Jesus' followers expressed their relationship to the memory of Jesus of Nazareth. The circles that apparently gathered in Galilee made no recourse to Jesus' suffering and death. The community that preserved the earliest collection of sayings of Jesus, which eventually resulted in the composition of the Synoptic Sayings Gospel [. . .] did not value the recollection of Jesus' suffering and death but [. . .] emphasized the presence of the saving message of Jesus in his words as they were remembered.[38]

This is not to say that we can assume with confidence that Q is not interested in any other aspect of Jesus, as R. A. Piper demonstrates in his work on two miracles in Q,[39] but simply to say that, in Piper's words, "Q represents the *Gattung* of sayings, more than deeds."[40] As Kloppenborg notes, of the two miracles that do appear in Q (Q 7:1–10 relates the healing of the centurion's servant and Q 11:14 relates an exorcism), "in neither case does Q's interest lie in the miraculous as a *demonstration* of Jesus' identity. Rather, Q is interested in the *speech* or *teaching* that Jesus' miracles occasion."[41] What this means for the present study is that the gender pairs—and their repercussions for women audience members—form part of what is most important to the compilers of Q; they are *teachings*, at the Q collection's heart, not its periphery.

Language of the Basileia of God

The *basileia* (often translated as the "Kingdom of God") is a construct mentioned repeatedly throughout Jesus' teachings in Q.[42] Sanders asserts that before the time of Jesus, this concept had two compatible meanings that "would have been more or less self-evident given standard [apocalyptic] Jewish views"[43]:

> One is that God reigns in heaven; the 'kingdom of God' or 'kingdom of heaven' exists eternally there. God occasionally acts in history, but [. . .] completely and consistently governs only heaven. The second is that in the future, God will rule the earth. [. . .] (S)omeday he will bring normal history to an end and govern the world perfectly. Briefly put: the kingdom of God always exists *there*; in the future it will exist *here*.[44]

However, according to Sanders, the teachings of Jesus build an additional twist onto these existing meanings. In the sayings material, the *basileia* can begin immediately, becoming, in addition to a heavenly realm and a future state, "a special realm on earth, one that consists of people who are dedicated to living according to God's will and that exists both in and side by side with normal human society. [. . .] 'the kingdom is like leaven, which cannot be seen but which leavens the whole loaf.'"[45] Sanders' observation of this tangibility of the kingdom of God in Jesus' sayings seems accurate; despite the typically future-oriented nature of apocalyptic thinking, Jesus' *basileia* has also already begun (perhaps showing that, for Jesus's community, the end was beginning).[46]

This *basileia* of God is unquestionably a central concept in Q, if the following incomplete list of occurrences is any indication.[47] Those who take part in the *basileia* are said to be "more" than John the Baptist: "There has not arisen among women's offspring anyone who surpasses John. Yet the least significant in God's *basileia* is more than he" (Q 7:28). John's life is seen as an eschatological pivot point in the *basileia*: "the law and the prophets were until John. From then on, the *basileia* of God is violated and the violent plunder it" (Q 16:16). The location of the *basileia* is mysterious and inward and its timing somehow nonlinear:[48] "on being asked when the *basileia* of God is coming, he answered them and said: the *basileia* of God is not coming visibly. Nor will one say, 'Look, here!' or 'There!' For, look, the *basileia* of God is within you" (Q 17:20–21). Whatever or whenever the *basileia* is, instructions to itinerant messengers certainly feature it as a prominent part of their message: "whatever town you enter and they take you in, eat what is set before you, and cure the sick there, and say to them, the *basileia* of God has reached unto you" (Q 10:8–9). Not everyone is amenable to this message, however: "Woe to you, exegetes of the Law, for you shut the *basileia* of God from people" (Q 11:52). This *basileia* is promoted as the listener's first priority, after which other things fall into place: "do not be anxious, saying, 'What are we to eat?' or 'What are we to drink?' or 'What are we to wear?' For all these the Gentiles seek; for your Father knows that you need them all. But seek his *basileia*, and all these shall be granted to you" (Q 12:29–31). Importantly, the *basileia* is also the subject of several of Q's parables, including some of the gendered parable pairs under investigation in this project: "What is the *basileia* of God like, and with what am I to compare it? It is like a seed of mustard, which a man took and threw into his garden, and it grew and developed into a tree, and the birds of the sky nested in its branches. And again, with what am I to compare the *basileia* of God? It is like yeast, which a woman took and hid in three measures of flour until it was fully fermented" (Q 13:18–21).

It is clear from this non-exhaustive selection of *basileia* sayings in Q that the concept is central to the collection. This is useful for contextualizing the role of women in Q. It will become clear in the coming chapters that *Q takes care to include both women and men equally* in its vision of *basileia* membership, and to *hold both women and men equally accountable* when they behave counter to *basileia* priorities.[49]

Sapiential, Apocalyptic, Prophetic

In terms of the genres of the Q sayings, Q contains both lighthearted wisdom sayings ("The way you want people to treat you, that is how you treat them" Q 6:31) and more dour sayings of apocalyptic and prophetic[50] judgment ("The axe already lies at the root of the trees. So every tree not bearing healthy fruit is to be chopped down and thrown on the fire" Q 3:9). There is widespread agreement that there are elements of both wisdom and apocalypticism in the sayings source.

For some—Kloppenborg in particular, and many who have followed him—a perceived contrast between these two modes of discourse has led to a hypothesis that the two elements give us a glimpse into at least two different *stages* of redaction, each literary genre arising from differing external circumstances.[51] Kloppenborg, Mack,[52] and others,[53] imagine three distinct phases of community development, positing that the sapiential material is from an earlier and less organized "honeymoon" phase, directed more toward the group's own members (Q1), whereas the apocalyptic material came on the scene later as the group experienced rejection and persecution and is directed more toward outsiders (Q2).[54] Brief narrative portions (mainly the baptism in Q 3:21–22, and the temptation scene in Q 4:1–13) form the final smallest stratum (Q3).[55] The first two progressively worse situations correspond to Kloppenborg's two major strata, "Q1" (sapiential and less organized) and "Q2" (apocalyptic and galvanized by opposition).

Building on the wisdom material in the sayings, scholars such as Mack imagine a movement of small house groups that shared sapiential instruction about the lifestyle embraced by the group.[56] These sayings are characteristically wittier and less heavy-handed.[57] Kloppenborg and those who follow his stratification of Q posit that a situation of persecution could have given rise to the second main group of sayings, which focus on impending judgment and punishment, and take the form of warnings about divine revenge on other groups.[58]

In my view, however, sayings of wisdom and sayings of judgment do not require sequential stratification. They are sayings that could have come from Jesus concurrently and been carried on by the early Jesus movement concurrently. If the wisdom is indeed directed to insiders and the judgment to outsiders, there is no reason why these audiences could not both be addressed by the same teacher and subsequently collected in the same text, without necessitating distinct developmental stages.

Jesus' own mentor was made a violent example in a brutal beheading (Mark 6:14-29); there is no need to look any further than this for an explanation as to why Jesus himself would see the world as a sometimes hostile place and reflect this in apocalyptic and vengeful teaching. As for why violent sayings would then be preserved and translated in Q, we need look no further than Jesus' own violent death. Schüssler-Fiorenza argues against the need for stratification to account for conflict: "such a reconstruction of the development of Q does not account for the crisis introduced by the suffering and execution of Jesus . . . as a criminal."[59] In short, a later stage of persecution of Jesus-followers is not required in order to explain the perception of opposition and the harsh themes of judgment in the sayings material.

So, although many now speak of Q's redactional layers as givens, I do not see a necessity for them, and I do not have confidence that any such discussion can ever move beyond conjecture.[60] Scholars of early Judaism have long understood apocalyptic and sapiential discourses as deeply intertwined,[61] and apocalypticism does not automatically indicate a context of immediate persecution.[62] There are also text-critical reasons to be cautious about redactional strata. Different scholars have found commonalities across all the posited layers (see, for example, R. A. Piper's study of remarkably consistent attitudes toward wealth and poverty in the suggested "sapiential" and "apocalyptic" layers).[63] In fact, my research on the gendered pairs supports these reservations concerning distinct temporal strata because *the pairs occur across both main layers* (the "formative" Q1 and the "redactional" Q2) as well.

In other words, the community situations (and the sapiential and apocalyptic cultural and literary streams) that some scholars posit behind each so-called stratum are useful to bear in mind as background for a study of the sayings, but we are not obligated to follow them to the conclusion that the situations occurred in distinct linear sequence. Communities around and after Jesus likely involved a combination of house groups and itinerants who held at least some interest in sapiential and apocalyptic themes and who probably also experienced varying degrees of rejection—or perceived rejection—as they shared their *basileia* message.[64] What *is* of note for this book is that the Q gender pairs are included in both the sapiential "layer" and the apocalyptic "layer" of Q. At every level of the sayings gospel, there is evidence for the inclusion of women as fully equal recipients and proponents of wisdom, but also as fully equal agents of their own religious and spiritual lives and thus equal subjects of judgment.

Itinerant

Many scholars, Gerd Theissen foremost among them,[65] have used the Greek sayings collection to propose a community that involves two main sorts of members: the itinerant purveyors of the message of God's *basileia* and the sedentary "hosts" (and recipients of the message) who sheltered and fed the wanderers along their way.⁶⁶ Sayings like the following give rise to this picture: "Whoever takes you in takes me in, and, whoever takes me in takes in the one who sent me" (Q 10:16) and

> into whatever house you enter, first say, Peace to this house! And if a son of peace be there, let your peace come upon him; but if not, let your peace return upon you. And at that house, remain, eating and drinking whatever they provide, for the worker is worthy of one's reward. Do not move around from house to house. And whatever town you enter and they take you in, eat what is set before you. And cure the sick there, and say to them, the kingdom of God has reached unto you. But into whatever town you enter and they do not take you in, on going out from that town, shake off the dust from your feet. I tell you: For Sodom it shall be more bearable on that day than for that town. (Q 10:5–12)

Some scholars think it probable that women were among the itinerant prophets traveling through early Jesus communities, which will be discussed in the next chapter.

The itinerancy/settled host model is not the only hypothesis for the backdrop of Q.⁶⁷ William Arnal has argued strongly against this dominant thesis, in favor of a scribal setting linked to economic upheavals.⁶⁸ According to Arnal, the collection, translation, and arrangement of Q stems from unrest among Herodian village scribes with a desire to maintain solidarity among Galilean villages in the wake of the creation of the city of Tiberias in 20 C.E., which brought about "significant social and economic changes" and disrupted scribal and village autonomy.⁶⁹

However, that there were at least *some* itinerant *basileia* prophets is clear from the sources that give instruction on the rules for itinerants. Whether women made up some significant part of this group sometimes enters the discussion around gender pairs; for instance, when Luise Schottroff⁷⁰ uses the Q gender pairs to argue for gender equality in this movement, the notion of female itinerant prophets figures prominently. My arguments for the presence of a (limited, specific) gender equality that levels the playing field (albeit not in every sense) for women do not hinge on the presence or absence of itinerancy, whether at the level of Q or at the level of earlier Jesus followers. Rather, my arguments for the equality of women in and around Q hinge on the rhetoric of the sayings themselves.

Jewish

Q is a Jewish text. This shouldn't need saying, but it seems that interpreters of the New Testament and its adjacent texts still need constant reminders that the primary context in which to place first-century Jesus-movement literature is that of Second-Temple Judaism. It is obvious throughout the Q sayings that the community in question is familiar with Jewish literature[71] and is wrestling with Jewish concerns; the sayings refer frequently to characters and traditions from Israel's past and to issues in first-century Judaism.[72] Q warns its detractors not to think that having Abraham as their forefather is enough to protect them from judgment (Q 3:8). When Q's Satan quotes scripture, it is the Psalms (Q 4:10–11). In Q, the faith of a Roman centurion is used as an example with which to chastise "Israel" (Q 7:9). Q's Jesus is depicted as fulfilling events prophesied in Isaiah (Q 7:22). Q chides disobedient towns by declaring them to be worse off than their foreign counterparts in writings from Israel's past: Sodom, Tyre, and Sidon (Q 10:12–14). Q's listeners are told not to give in to worries and anxieties over material goods, because this is something non-Jews do (Q 12:29–30). Many characters from what would become the Hebrew Bible are invoked, such as Jonah (Q 11:29–30), Solomon (Q 11:31–32), Abel and Zechariah (Q 11:51), Noah (Q 17:26–27), and the Twelve Tribes of Israel (Q 22:30). As well, concepts important across various forms of early Judaism are featured in Q, such as Torah observance (Q 16:17,[73] Q 11:52), the Jerusalem temple (Q 13:34–35), synagogues (Q 12:11), Pharisaism (Q 11:42), and more.[74]

Galilee had a tumultuous past and was often caught in the crossfire of wars both literal and cultural,[75] resulting in its diverse and complex makeup. However, the Jesus community seen in Q indicates that Torah-based Judaism was present and thriving in the Galilee of our time period. The older notion that Galilee was known as "Galilee of the Gentiles" has been dismantled using both archaeological and literary evidence.[76] Dennis Duling, underlining the contemporary consensus, writes that first-century Galilee's population "appears to have been mostly Jewish."[77] Mark Chancey observes that "Gentiles were a small portion of the population" and that "the evidence, both literary and archaeological, corroborates the Gospels' depictions of Jesus as a Jew preaching to and working primarily among other Jews" in a region dominated by Judaism.[78] Kloppenborg calls Q "our rural, Galilean Jewish Gospel."[79] Deriving from Galilee, Q is thus seen as evidence for a more Jewish stage of the Jesus movement, when compared to the increasingly non-Jewish versions of Christianity in later sources or the major Jewish but gentile-fixated contemporaneous source: Paul.[80]

The Jewishness of Q is important for building a clearer picture of the audience for Jesus' sayings and the women in those audiences. Reminding ourselves of Q's Jewishness also helps to counteract a disconcerting habit of New Testament scholarship: namely, the (inadvertently, one hopes) supersessionist claims that Jesus ushered in Christianity, which then provided a glorious "feminist" haven, over and against a rigidly patriarchal (and monolithic) Judaism.[81] Remembering Q's Jewishness helps to properly situate the sayings in their context of inner-Jewish self-definition at a time when there existed a wide spectrum of Jewish diversity. In a sense—and not surprisingly, given Jesus' links to John—Q bears witness to a Jewish reform group or renewal movement like that of John the Baptizer or the Pharisees.[82] In this way, Q is a subversive text.

Countercultural

A final element common to reconstructions of Q People is the view that they were a subversive group who pushed against the boundaries of their social, economic, religious, and political situation, calling for reform and/or renewal. Almost all scholars who attempt to reconstruct the social location of Q describe the contents, and by extension the originary community, as somehow "countercultural."[83] In this view, members of the community in which the sayings emerged and found purchase may have perceived themselves as outsiders, located at the margins of society on a number of levels, such as economic, politico-religious, ethnic, and social.[84] Perhaps in response to this sense of marginalization, there is woven throughout the Q sayings a system of alternative norms—what E. P. Sanders refers to in his classic study of the Historical Jesus as a "reversal of values."[85] More recently, Levine follows Sanders in describing the Q material as "a counter to reigning cultural values."[86]

This countercultural bent makes itself known in a number of ways in the sayings collection. It can be seen in the frequently used trope of diametric reversals, in sayings like, "the last will be first and the first last" (Q 13:30) and "everyone humbling themselves will be exalted, and everyone exalting themselves will be humbled" (Q 14:11). Evidence for this view also comes from the listing as positive of what would normally be understood as negative, such as when poverty, hunger, mourning, and persecution are listed among blessings in Q 6:20–22. Additionally, "woes" against those who don't see things the same way Q does (e.g., some of the Pharisees the residents of various towns) reinforce this redrawing of typical values. Q 11:39–52, for instance, says, "Woe to you Pharisees, for you tithe mint . . . and neglect justice." In these and other ways, the Q sayings participate in their culture subversively by offering a critique of the *status quo*.[87]

Perhaps it is not surprising that countercultural elements might emerge from among first-century Jewish Galileans, who did not enjoy elite status and were marginalized by others.[88] In Jesus' day, there is considerable evidence that Galileans were seen as lesser from both a socioeconomic standpoint, and also an ethnic and religious one; Galilean Judaism was mocked by non-Galileans,[89] and Galilean peasants/artisans were economically disadvantaged[90] in a cycle of "systematic exploitation."[91] If Galilee was typical of other ancient resource-based/agrarian societies, then about 90 percent of the populace worked toward supporting an elite ten percent.[92] The Galileans to whom Jesus spoke, and from whose ranks Jesus came, were disenfranchised socially, economically, religiously, and culturally.[93] Thus, Duling describes Q's "nonconventional wisdom" sayings as "point(ing) to social dislocation."[94]

When Q material was later incorporated into the writings that would come to form part of the Christian Testament, it was re-contextualized and tamed in order to appear less subversive.[95] This tendency would make sense particularly in a traumatized and cautious post-70 context; the shift from a Galilean *milieu* would almost inevitably contribute to such a "taming." We will look more closely at this development when we investigate Luke's incorporation of Q material into his apologetic work.

Q People and Women: General Background

The incorporation of the Q document into two popular gospels firmly indicates its foundational position in the early Jesus movement; it was material that two of the canonical gospel writers deemed worthy of working into their *oeuvres*.[96] It is thus advisable to take Q's significant contribution to our picture of first-century Judaism and Christian origins—and our picture of women in this history—seriously. As is made clear in the following chapters, the Q sayings assume what might in some ways be described as an anomalously positive[97] attitude toward the women in their audience. Q's attitudes toward female membership in the early Jesus movement are most strikingly present in the gendered pairings—a rhetorical strategy that makes women equal to men (although not identical to them). The retention of the gender pairs in the collected sayings is evidence that this awareness of gender was alive in first group of followers who were interested in remembering and perpetuating Jesus' sayings after his death. The reconstructed Q document thus provides a vital lens through which to examine the treatment of women in a group of Jesus people much closer to Jesus' Galilean Judaism than to the largely non-Jewish movement Christianity became in a matter of a century.

In this chapter, I have tried to paint in broad strokes a portrait of how Galilean Judaism is viewed in recent scholarship and how the above descriptors form the general backdrop against which to imagine Jesus' gendered parable pairs. The pairs are first and foremost rhetorical literary devices, but they can also be approached as evidence for the lived experience of real first-century women who heard them and saw themselves featured in them. The above list of categories helps to put a human face on the men and women who first heard and later remembered the gendered pairs. Throughout this book, our imagined recipients of the gendered parallel sayings will be considered in light of first-century Galilean Judaism, a peasant[98] Judaism that shares an interest in Jesus as sage, that does not show interest in auspicious birth narratives or passion accounts, that is enthusiastic about living God's *basileia* here on earth, that relates to both sapiential and apocalyptic modes of communication, that supports itinerant prophets as a way of spreading its message, and that participates in and critiques its surroundings in subversive ways.

NOTES

1. For a brief introduction to Q, see J. S. Kloppenborg, *Q: The Earliest Gospel: An Introduction to the Original Stories and Sayings of Jesus* (Louisville: Westminster John Knox, 2008). For a more in-depth introduction, including a thorough *status quaestionis* and history of scholarship, see Kloppenborg's *The Formation of Q: Trajectories in Ancient Wisdom Collections* (Minneapolis: Fortress, 2007). For a critical history of Q research and critical text, with translation into English, German, and French, see the introductory matter in: Robinson, Hoffmann, and Kloppenborg, eds., *The Critical Edition of Q*.

2. See David B. Sloan, "What If the Gospel according to the Hebrews Was Q?" (paper presented at the Annual Meeting of the SBL, Boston, MA, 18 Nov 2017).

3. Papias as preserved in Eusebius, *Hist Eccl.* 3.39.

4. Although Jesus would have spoken Aramaic, this collection of his sayings had been set down in writing in the Greek language, before they were incorporated into Matthew and Luke. See, for example, Kloppenborg, *The Formation of Q*, 41–88. As Michaud puts it (translation mine): "The agreements between Matthew and Luke, which are sometimes identical to the letter in Greek [. . .] seem to require a written document." J.-P. Michaud, "Quelle(s) communauté(s) derriere la Source Q?" *The Sayings Source Q and the Historical Jesus* (Leuven: Leuven University Press, 2001), 577–578. Particularly convincing is J. Robinson, "A Written Greek Sayings Cluster Older than Q: A Vestige," *HTR* 92 (1999): 61–77, in which a laser-illuminated palimpsest of Sinaiticus reveals a Greek-language typo that must have originated at the level of Q.

5. See P. Vassiliadis, "Original Order of Q: Some Residual Cases," in *Logia: Les Paroles de Jésus—the Sayings of Jesus* (ed. J. Delobel; Leuven: Leuven University Press, 1982), 379–387.

6. Despite having reached widespread acceptance as the *best* hypothesis, Q does remain a hypothesis. For the main formulation of a case against Q, see the work by that title: M. Goodacre, *The Case Against Q* (Harrisburg: Trinity Press International, 2002). Goodacre's book occasioned a variety of painstaking scholarly refutations, including J. Kloppenborg, for example, "On Dispensing with Q: Goodacre on the Relation of Luke to Matthew," *NTS* 49 (2003): 210–236.

7. Robinson, *The Sayings Gospel Q in Greek and English*, 11. This is known as the two-source hypothesis or the two-document hypothesis and was proposed by Christian Weisse in 1838 and, in a cruder form, by Johan Eichhorn in 1794. See C. R. Holladay, *A Critical Introduction to the New Testament* (Nashville: Abingdon, 2005), 55, n.28 for a brief overview of Weiss and Eichhorn's contributions to the Q hypothesis.

8. For a good discussion, see J. Reed, *Archaeology and the Galilean Jesus: A Reexamination of the Evidence* (Harrisburg: Trinity Press International, 2000), 170–196.

For a long list of scholars locating Q in the Galilee, from von Harnack to the present, see S. J. Joseph, *Jesus, Q, and the Dead Sea Scrolls: A Judaic Approach to Q* (Tübingen: Mohr Siebeck, 2012), 75, n.238.

9. Kloppenborg writes that Q was "composed at roughly the same time as the activities of Paul [. . .] during the 50s and 60s of the Common Era." J. S. Kloppenborg, "Discursive Practices in the Sayings Gospel Q and the Quest of the Historical Jesus," in *The Sayings Source Q and the Historical Jesus* (Leuven: Leuven University Press, 2001), 150–151. For a succinct discussion of a range of dates, see J. D. G. Dunn, *Jesus Remembered: Christianity in the Making, Volume 1* (Grand Rapids: Eerdmans, 2003), 159.

10. Kloppenborg points out that, for most of the nineteenth and twentieth centuries, "Q functioned as a kind of algebraic unknown that helped to solve other problems." *Q: The Earliest Gospel*, vii–viii. Mack writes that in the 1920s, "Q was still thought of mainly as part of the solution to the Synoptic problem [. . .] it was defined solely as a source document for the Gospels of Matthew and Luke, not as a text with its own integrity": *The Lost Gospel: The Book of Q and Christian Origins* (San Francisco: HarperSanFrancisco, 1993), 21. Goodacre observes that Q has recently "emerged from the texts of Matthew and Luke, in which it used to be embedded, and onto a stage of its own, no longer simply an aspect of the solution to the Synoptic problem, but now with a distinctive profile and place in early Christianity" (*The Case Against Q*, 3). Goodacre is famously appalled by this shift, but it has otherwise largely taken hold.

11. Now a number of reconstructions of Q exist; these use not only the Synoptics, but also derive support from the epistle of James, and of the gospels of *Thomas* and *Peter*. See Kloppenborg, *Excavating Q: The History and Setting of the Sayings Gospel* (Minneapolis: Fortress, 2000), 2. For a succinct explanation of the way the book of James can function as a confirmation of the two-source hypothesis and assist in the reconstruction of authentic sayings tradition, see Meier, *A Marginal Jew, Volume 4*, 200–202. For a look at the importance of *Thomas* in the search for authentic sayings of Jesus, see J.-M. Sevrin, "Thomas, Q et le Jesus de l'histoire," in *The Sayings Source Q and the Historical Jesus* (Leuven: Leuven University Press, 2001), 461–478. For a good recent discussion of the issues in reconstructing Thomas, see A. D. De Conick, *Recovering the Original Gospel of Thomas: A History of the Gospel and Its Growth* (London: T&T Clark, 2006).

12. Robinson, *The Sayings Gospel Q in Greek and English*, 12.

13. Robinson, Hoffmann, and Kloppenborg, eds., *The Critical Edition of Q*.

14. The Society of Biblical Literature had a Q Seminar from 1985 to 1989, which was established as a permanent section in 1990. A look at the subjects of the papers over the years shows the shift from Q as a text-critical explanation to Q as an object of study in its own right and a source of evidence for the reconstruction of rural Galilean Judaism and for the historical Jesus.

15. Most notably, Adolf von Harnack, *The Sayings of Jesus: The Second Source of St. Matthew and St. Luke* (London: Williams & Norgate, 1908), 185, argued that only the double tradition should be counted as Q. Critiquing von Harnack's minimalist approach is W. C. Allen, "The Book of Sayings Used by the Editor of the First

Gospel," in *Studies in the Synoptic Problem* (ed. W. Sanday; Oxford: Clarendon, 1911), 235–239.

16. J. Kloppenborg, "Introduction," in *The Shape of Q: Signal Essays on the Sayings Gospel* (ed. J. Kloppenborg; Minneapolis: Fortress, 1994), 1–2.

17. See, for instance, S. E. Rollens' *Framing Social Criticism in the Jesus Movement* (Tübingen: Mohr Siebeck, 2014). Unfortunately, the following volume, which compiles such attempts, including Rollens' forthcoming article, "The Kingdom of God is Among You: Prospects for a Q Community," was not available by press time for this book: Stanley E. Porter and Andrew W. Pitts, eds., *Christian Origins and the Establishment of the Early Jesus Movement* (Leiden: Brill, forthcoming).

18. Holladay reminds us that the construction of a profile of Q People is inevitably "controversial." Holladay, *A Critical Introduction to the New Testament*, 50.

19. Mack, *The Lost Gospel*, 245.

20. Mack, *Who Wrote the New Testament*, 47.

21. Richard Horsley with Jonathan A. Draper, *Whoever Hears You Hears Me: Prophets, Performance, and Tradition in Q* (Harrisburg: Trinity Press International, 1999), 150.

22. The idea of discerning a literary development within Q was first discussed by Schulz in the mid-1960s; see S. Schulz, *Q: Die Spruchquelle der Evangelisten* (Zurich: Theologischer Verlag, 1964). Kloppenborg went on to develop this hypothesis, resulting in a quite widely used three-tier stratification of the Q Document; see, *inter alia*, Kloppenborg, *The Formation of Q* and *Excavating Q*. See my section entitled "Sapiential, Apocalyptic, Prophetic" below for a fuller description of the community aspects reflected in Kloppenborg's stratification.

23. For a critique of stratification, see, for example, Holladay, *A Critical Introduction to the New Testament*, 51.

24. Richard Horsley, for instance, places "the Jesus movement that produced Q" in Galilee. See Horsley and Draper, *Whoever Hears You Hears Me*, 102. See Reed, *Archaeology and the Galilean Jesus*, 170–196 for a "social mapping" of Q as a Galilean scribal document that originated in one of the small "cities" in the Galilee.

25. Reed, *Archaeology and the Galilean Jesus*, 171.

26. Dunn, *Jesus Remembered*, 159.

27. For more on a Galilean setting for Q and Jesus' early movement, see, *inter alia*: W. Arnal, *Jesus and the Village Scribes: Galilean Conflicts and the Setting of Q* (Minneapolis: Fortress, 2001); M. A. Chancey, *The Myth of a Gentile Galilee* (Cambridge: Cambridge University Press, 2002); J. D. Crossan, *The Essential Jesus: Original Sayings and Earliest Images* (San Francisco: Harper, 1998); J. D. Crossan, *The Historical Jesus: The Life of a Mediterranean Jewish Peasant* (Edinburgh: T&T Clark, 1991); S. Freyne, *Jesus, A Jewish Galilean: A New Reading of the Jesus Story* (London: T&T Clark, 2004); S. Guijarro, "Domestic Space, Family Relationships, and the Social Location of the Q People," *JSNT* 27/1 (2004): 69–81; K. C. Hanson, "The Galilean Fishing Economy and the Jesus Tradition," *BTB* 27 (1997): 99–111; J. S. Kloppenborg, ed., *Conflict and Invention: Literary, Rhetorical, and Social Studies on the Sayings Gospel Q* (Valley Forge: Trinity Press International, 1995); Kloppenborg, *Excavating Q*; J. S. Kloppenborg, "The Lost Gospel of Q: The Earliest Record

of Jesus' Galilean Followers" (Annual Peter Craigie Memorial Lecture; University of Calgary, 2001); J. S. Kloppenborg, "The Sayings Gospel Q: Recent Opinion on the People Behind the Document," *CurBS* 1 (1993): 9–34; M. Moreland, "Q and the Economics of Early Roman Galilee," in *The Sayings Source Q and the Historical Jesus* (ed. A. Lindemann; Leuven: Leuven University Press, 2001), 561–575; Reed, *Archaeology and the Galilean Jesus*; L. Vaage, *Galilean Upstarts: Jesus' First Followers According to Q* (Valley Forge: Trinity Press International, 1994). For an alternative view, namely, that a Galilean setting does not at all prove a Galilean provenance, see Joseph, *Jesus, Q, and the Dead Sea Scrolls*, esp. 33–93.

28. D. E. Oakman, "The Ancient Economy," in *The Social Sciences and New Testament Interpretation* (ed. R. Rohrbaugh; Peabody: Hendrickson, 1996), 127. Duling writes that "Galilee was a rural farming region" and that the concerns of the Q sayings "imply poverty" (D. C. Duling, "Millennialism," in *The Social Sciences and New Testament Interpretation* [ed. R. Rohrbaugh; Peabody: Hendrickson, 1996], 196). For a succinct description of the shifting sands of debate over how "urbanized" and how "Hellenized" Galilee was, see R. Rohrbaugh, "The Preindustrial City," in *The Social Sciences and New Testament Interpretation* (ed. R. Rohrbaugh; Peabody: Hendrickson, 1996), 117.

29. Rohrbaugh, "Introduction," 6. Rohrbaugh here refers to the situation in first-century Galilee as "systematic exploitation." See further D. E. Oakman, "Jesus and Agrarian Palestine: The Factor of Debt," in *The Social World of the New Testament: Insights and Models* (Peabody: Hendrickson, 2008), 63–84.

30. On the fact that the Q compiler/s could write, and in Greek, the authority is Arnal, *Jesus and the Village Scribes*.

31. R. Redfield, *Peasant Society and Culture* (Chicago: University of Chicago Press, 1956) made an important early contribution to work on peasantry. For a strong argument for Jesus of Nazareth as peasant artisan, see D. E. Oakman, "Was Jesus a Peasant? Implications for Reading the Jesus Tradition," in *The Social World of the New Testament: Insights and Methods* (Peabody: Hendrickson, 2008), 123–140. For an important diversification and nuancing of the concept of peasantry, especially in relation to Q, see Rollens, *Framing Social Criticism in the Jesus Movement*, throughout but esp. pp. 12, 21, and 36. Rollens also questions the sometimes-easy assumptions made about peasants "naturally gravitating" toward the teachings of Jesus (199) and about peasant interests served by Q (142). Rollens builds on the work of Sharon Lea Mattila who demonstrated that the essentializing social scientific category of "peasant" is applied far too easily in New Testament studies and should not be universalized across all time periods and across all socioeconomically disadvantaged peoples as a cultural category. S. L. Mattila, "Jesus and the Middle Peasants?: Problematizing a Social-Scientific Concept," *CBQ* 72 (2010): 291–313. Both Rollens and Mattila argue for a nonessentializing and case-by-case evidence-based treatment of "peasantry" as an ultimately diverse and complicated category.

32. See J. Barr, "Which Language Did Jesus Speak: Some Remarks of a Semitist," *Bulletin of the John Rylands Library* 53 (1970): 9–29 and S. E. Fassberg, "Which Semitic Language Did Jesus and Other Contemporary Jews Speak?," *CBQ* 74/2 (2012): 263–280.

33. For this, see Joseph, *Jesus, Q, and the Dead Sea Scrolls*.

34. The notion that Q was a Jerusalem document emerged in the 1920s, with H. T. Fowler, "Paul, Q, and the Jerusalem Church," *JBL* 43 (1924): 9–14. For a more recent argument against the Galilean hypothesis, see M. Frenschkowski, "Galiläa oder Jerusalem? Die Topographischen und Politischen Hintergründe der Logienquelle," in *The Sayings Source Q and the Historical Jesus* (ed. A. Lindemann; Leuven: Leuven University Press, 2001), 535–560. For a handy summary of the small amount of scholarship that locates Q in Jerusalem as opposed to Galilee, with brief synopses of arguments for and against, see J. S. Kloppenborg, "Q, Bethsaida, Khorazin, and Capernaum," in *Q in Context II: Social Setting and Archaeological Background of the Sayings* (ed. Markus Tiwald; Göttingen: Vandenhoeck & Ruprecht, 2015), 63, n.5.

35. In his enchanting monograph on the oral and textual development of the Gospels, L. M. White explains, "the bulk of the Q material is [. . .] sayings of Jesus with little or no connective narrative. [. . .] What narrative does appear in the Q material usually functions to ground the teaching in a putative life situation that helps to clarify the point of the saying." L. M. White, *Scripting Jesus: The Gospels in Re-Write* (New York: HarperOne, 2010), 189.

36. The *Gospel of Thomas*, itself a collection of sayings, is the notable exception that proves the rule.

37. Martin Kähler, *The So-Called Historical Jesus and the Historic-Biblical Christ* (trans. Carl E. Braaten; Philadelphia: Fortress, 1964), 80, n.11.

38. H. Koester, *History and Literature of Early Christianity, Volume 2* (2nd ed.; Berlin: de Gruyter, 2000), 96.

39. See R. A. Piper, "Jesus and the Conflict of Powers in Q: Two Q Miracle Stories," *The Sayings Source Q and the Historical Jesus* (Leuven: Leuven University Press, 2001), 317–350.

40. Piper, "Jesus and the Conflict of Powers in Q," 319.

41. Kloppenborg, *Q: The Earliest Gospel*, 70. (His emphasis)

42. Dillon writes that apocalypticism "was the locus of the *basileia* vision" in R. J. Dillon, "Ravens, Lilies, and the Kingdom of God (Matthew 6:25-33/ Luke 12:22-31)," *CBQ* 53 (1991): 606, and finds in these *basileia* teachings a "coherence of eschatology and ethics," 626.

43. E. P. Sanders, *The Historical Figure of Jesus* (London: Penguin, 1993), 169.

44. Sanders, *The Historical Figure of Jesus*, 169.

45. Sanders, *The Historical Figure of Jesus*, 174, citing Matt 13:33 // Luke 13:30f.

46. See Stephen Patterson, "An Unanswered Question: Apocalyptic Expectation and Jesus' Basileia Proclamation," *JSHJ* 8/1 (2010): 67–79 for an excellent argument that the tension, at every layer of the Jesus tradition, between John the Baptist's typically apocalyptic future-end-of-world vision and an already-present alternative to Rome's *basileia*, goes back to Jesus' own tension between the two visions.

47. In the minimal critical edition of Q, the term appears at least 17 times. Robinson, Hoffmann, and Kloppenborg, eds., *The Critical Edition of Q*, 567.

48. Temporal aspects of the *basileia*, and the ways that Matthew and Luke deal with the delay of the eschaton, are treated in Guy (who does not treat Q). L. Guy, "The Interplay of the Present and Future in the Kingdom of God (Luke 19:11-44)," *TB* 48/1 (1997): 119–137.

49. Few scholars who treat the *basileia* in the gospels take care to distinguish between its use at the Q level and its use in the gospels. The recent work of Christian Blumenthal on Luke's use of Jesus' *basileia* material is a refreshing exception. See C. Blumenthal, *Basileia bei Lukas: Studien zur erzälehrischen Entfaltung der lukanischen Basileiakonzeption* (Freiburg: Herder, 2016).

50. An important volume outlining the interplay among apocalyptic, wisdom, and prophecy in historical perspective is J. J. Collins' (ed.), *Oxford Handbook of Apocalyptic Literature* (Oxford: Oxford University Press, 2014). For examples of those who discuss the degrees to which Q participates in sapiential and prophetic discourse, see, *inter alia*, S. Schulz, *Q: Die Spruchquelle der Evangelisten* and C. M. Tuckett, *Q and the History of Early Christianity: Studies on Q* (Edinburgh: T&T Clark, 1996).

51. See Kloppenborg, *The Formation of Q*, 96. Kloppenborg's first proposed Q stage is sapiential (Q^1), the second (the main redaction) was updated with sayings of apocalyptic judgement (Q^2), and lastly the narrative passages were added (Q^3).

52. See Mack, *Who Wrote the New Testament?* and also Mack, *The Lost Gospel*.

53. For example, W. Cotter, "Prestige, Protection and Promise: A Proposal for the Apologetics of Q," in *The Gospel Behind the Gospels: Current Studies on Q* (Leiden: Brill, 2014), 117–138; P. J. Hartin, "The Wisdom and Apocalyptic Layers of the Sayings Gospel Q: What Is Their Significance?," *HTS* 50/3 (1994): 556–582; L. Howes, "Whomever You Find, Invite": The Parable of the Great Supper (Q 14:16–21, 23) and the Redaction of Q," *Neotest* 49/2 (2015): 321–350; and L. Vaage, *Galilean Upstarts*.

54. Kloppenborg, *Formation of Q*. But *contra* this, see R. A. Piper, *Wisdom in the Q-Tradition: The Aphoristic Teaching of Jesus* (Cambridge: Cambridge University Press, 1989), 176–178—Piper sees struggles with outsiders across both Q^1 and Q^2.

55. The third stage consists mainly of the temptation narrative and is "an example of a historicizing tendency." R. A. Piper, "In Quest of Q: The Direction of Q Studies," in *The Gospel Behind the Gospels: Current Studies on Q* (ed. R. A. Piper; Leiden: Brill, 1995), 11.

56. B. Mack, "The Kingdom that Didn't Come: A Social History of the Q Tradents," in *SBLSP* 27 (Missoula: Scholars, 1988), 608–635.

57. Mack, "The Kingdom that Didn't Come," 608–635.

58. Mack, "The Kingdom that Didn't Come," 608–635. Duling notes (without necessarily acquiescing to the notion of literary strata) that Q's apocalyptic sayings do imply "a reaction to stressful cultural conditions" and suggest "increasing opposition from outsiders," using Q's condemnation of "this generation" as a key example of this. Duling, "Millennialism," 197.

59. Schüssler Fiorenza, *Jesus, Miriam's Child, Sophia's Prophet*, 141.

60. Dennis Ingolfsland remarks on the popularity of the strata hypothesis, especially in North America, and goes on to collate critiques of stratification and offers some of his own in a reflection piece: D. Ingolfsland, "Kloppenborg's Stratification of Q and Its Significance for Historical Jesus Studies," *JETS* 46/2 (2003): 217–232. On the unhelpfulness of stratification theories, see also C. Tuckett, "Q and the 'Church': The Role of the Christian Community within Judaism according to Q," in *A Vision for the Church: Studies in Early Christian Ecclesiology in Honour of J. P. M. Sweet* (ed. M. Bockmuehl and M. B. Thompson; Edinburgh: T&T Clark, 1997).

61. For an excellent treatment of the complex interrelationships among wisdom, prophecy, and apocalyptic genres in the Second-Temple period, see M. Goff, "Wisdom and Apocalypticism," in *The Oxford Handbook of Apocalyptic Literature* (ed. J. J. Collins; Oxford: Oxford University Press, 2014), 52–68 and H. Najman, "The Inheritance of Prophecy in Apocalypse," in that same volume, 36–51.

62. A. Portier-Young, "Jewish Apocalyptic Literature as Resistance Literature," in *The Oxford Handbook of Apocalyptic Literature* (ed. J. J. Collins; Oxford: Oxford University Press, 2014), 145–162, esp. 146: "(Resistance) was not a necessary function of the genre apocalypse. Resistance literature proves to be an apt category for some apocalyptic literature, but by no means all." Candida Moss has problematized the leap from martyrdom texts and other literary genres to the assumption of sociohistorical realities of widespread Christian persecution in various recent works, such as C. Moss, "Current Trends in the Study of Early Christian Martyrdom," *BSR* 41/3 (2012): 22–29.

63. R. A. Piper, "Wealth, Poverty, and Subsistence in Q," in *From Quest to Q: Festschrift James Robinson* (ed. J. M. Asgeirsson, K. de Troyer, and M. W. Meyer; Leuven: Leuven University Press, 2000), 219–264.

64. To agree with Duling that "the Q material [. . .] implies a community already under some stress" (Duling, "Millennialism," 196) does not necessitate speculation about various "stages." I prefer Duling's description of "stress" and deliberately chose the word "rejection" rather than "persecution" because positing a persecution at this early date is problematic and uncalled for by the evidence. Rejection can mean something as mild as experiencing disappointment that more people were not embracing the *basileia* message. Jervis also mentions that Q needn't be stratified, in an article that perceives in Q's rhetoric a *call* to persecution and suffering as a necessary means of bringing in the eschatological *basileia*. See L. A. Jervis, "Suffering for the Reign of God: The Persecution of Disciples in Q," *NT* 44/4 (2002): 314, n.3.

65. A main proponent of the itinerancy hypothesis is G. Theissen, *Social Reality and the Early Christians* (Minneapolis: Fortress, 1992), 33–59. For an argument against itinerancy in the early Jesus movement and Q, see Arnal, *Jesus and the Village Scribes*.

66. G. Theissen, *Le christianisme de Jésus: ses origines sociales en Palestine* (Paris: Relais Desclée 6, 1978).

67. For an argument against, see Levine, "Who's Catering the Q Affair?" For an argument in favor, see L. Schottroff, "Itinerant Prophetesses: A Feminist Analysis of the Sayings Source Q," in *Current Studies on Q* (ed. R. A. Piper; Leiden: Brill, 1995), 347–360. The main argument in favor is from Theissen, since the 1970s: see Theissen, *Le christianisme de Jésus*.

68. See Arnal, *Jesus and the Village Scribes*, esp. 91–95.

69. Arnal, *Jesus and the Village Scribes*, 11.

70. See Schottroff, "Itinerant Prophetesses."

71. See D. C. Allison, *The Intertextual Jesus: Scripture in Q* (Harrisburg: Trinity Press International: 2000).

72. See Horsley and Draper, *Whoever Hears You Hears Me*, 94–97 for a convincing and nuanced discussion of numerous Israelite traditions in Q. For a full-length

exploration of Q as ethnically Judaean, read M. Cromhout, *Jesus and Identity: Reconstructing Judean Ethnicity in Q* (Eugene: Cascade, 2007).

73. For a look at Q's interpretation of Torah, see Simon J. Joseph, "'For Heaven and Earth to Pass Away?': Reexamining Q 16:16–18, Eschatology, and the Law," *ZNW* 105/2 (2014): 169–188.

74. For an influential set of criteria for deciphering whether something in antiquity is Jewish, see James Davila's *The Provenance of the Pseudepigrapha: Jewish, Christian, or Other* (*JSJSupp* 105; Leiden: Brill, 2005).

75. Jewish Galilee had been "continually subject to outside colonial powers" (such as Assyrians, Babylonians, Persians, Greeks, and Romans), as well as to the recapture and reincorporation into Israel under the Maccabees. Duling, "Millennialism," 196.

76. For a book-length argument, based on exhaustive use of both archaeological and literary evidence, that the population of first-century Galilee was an overwhelming Jewish majority, see Chancey, *The Myth of a Gentile Galilee*. See in particular pages 167–182 for a dismantling of the "Galilee of the Gentiles" as a scholarly myth.

77. Duling, "Millennialism," 196.

78. Chancey, *The Myth of a Gentile Galilee*, 181.

79. Kloppenborg, *Q: The Earliest Gospel*, 69.

80. "Q, since it is almost certainly from Jewish Palestine, gives us a glimpse of a Gospel formulated by Jesus' Galilean followers, quite different in complexion from the diasporic and Gentile Christianities we know from other sources." Kloppenborg, *Q: The Earliest Gospel*, ix.

81. As a typical example of supersessionist feminist analysis, I offer Aida Besançon Spencer's "Jesus' Treatment of Women in the Gospels," which, in its race to highlight moments in the Gospels when women are valued alongside men, dismisses in a single paragraph both "Roman Law" and "first-century Jewish thinkers" as misogynistic across the board, in contrast to a Jesus who, according to Spencer, values faith above gender. A. Besançon Spencer, "Jesus' Treatment of Women in the Gospels," *Discovering Biblical Equality: Complementarity without Hierarchy* (ed. R. W. Pierce and R. Merrill Groothius; Leicester: Apollos, 2005), 126–141, here 139–140.

82. For a discussion of both Pharisees and the Q people as Jewish reform groups, see P. J. Hartin, "The Woes against the Pharisees: (Matthew 23:1–39): The Reception and Development of Q 11, 39–52 within the Matthean Community," in *From Quest to Q: Festschrift James Robinson* (ed. J. M. Asgeirsson, K. de Troyer, and M. W. Meyer; Leuven: Leuven University Press, 2000), 265–284.

83. Racine and Beaumont, "Three Approaches," 101.

84. Duling calls Galilean political, economic, and social conditions "stressful" and outlines the demographics thus: "The vast majority of Galileans were mainly peasants (freeholders or tenant farmers) but the masses also included artisans, slaves, freedmen and freedwomen, and people so marginal that they were expendable." Duling, "Millennialism," 196.

85. See Sanders, *The Historical Figure of Jesus*, 196–204.

86. Levine, "Women in the Q Communit(ies)," 154.

87. On Jesus' program as norm reversal, see, *inter alia*, D. Kraybill, *The Upside-Down Kingdom* (4th rev ed.; Harrisonburg: Herald, 2011); and J. H. Yoder, *The Politics of Jesus* (2nd ed.; Grand Rapids: Eerdmans, 1994).

88. See, for instance, a number of negative references to Galilee in antiquity, such as R. J. Hoffmann's translation of Julian's fourth-century work *Against the Galileans* (Amherst: Prometheus Books, 2004).

89. On being Galilean as a reason for Jesus' nonacceptance in Jerusalem, and on Galileans as outsiders, see G. Vermes, *Jesus the Jew: A Historian's Reading of the Gospels* (Minneapolis: Fortress, 1981), 43–44.

90. "In peasant or agrarian societies, social stratification, best defined as social categorization measured by differences in social wealth and power, is pronounced." Oakman, "The Ancient Economy," 132.

91. Rohrbaugh, "Introduction," 6.

92. Oakman, "The Ancient Economy," 133. See further D. Oakman, *Jesus and the Economic Questions of His Day* (Lewiston: Mellen, 1986) and H. Moxnes, *The Economy of the Kingdom: Social Conflict and Economic Relations in Luke's Gospel* (Philadelphia: Fortress, 1988).

93. This marginalization was not only with regard to external groups but also with regard to the upper classes within Judaism. As Schottroff writes, "the Jewish upper classes' participation in the interests of the Pax Romana" contributed to "internal conflicts within Judaism." Schottroff, "The Sayings Source Q," 510. This is clear from the whole of late Second Temple Jewish history, not least from the various Temple Reform movements.

94. Duling, "Millennialism," 197.

95. See, for example, Duling, "Millennialism," 198.

96. The author of Luke discusses his authorial aims in his prologue (Luke 1:1–4).

97. See Racine and Beaumont, "Three Approaches," 101.

98. But see Rollens, *Framing Social Criticism in the Jesus Movement*, 12, 21, and so forth on the diversity and complication of peasantry, along with Mattila, "Jesus and the Middle Peasants?," 291–313.

Chapter 3

What are They Saying about the Gendered Pairs in Q?

I maintain that there is a substantial difference between looking at the gender pairs in the New Testament and looking at the gender pairs in Q. The pairs were first "discovered" in a Lukan context and discussed with regard to Luke as editor. Yet while the sayings being studied may be similar, the focus of gospel scholarship is quite different from that of Q scholarship. Gender-paired stories discussed in a *gospel* context are focused on the author of each gospel: in David Malick's "The Significance of Three Narrative Parallels of Men and Women in Luke 1, John 3–4, and Acts 9,"[1] we hear about "Luke's choices" (20) and are focused on Luke's authorial project. Likewise, in Moyra Dale's "Dismantling Socio-Sacred Hierarchy: Gender and Gentiles in Luke-Acts," both parable gender pairs and gendered narrative parallels are treated alike as a part of Luke's "inclusive" work.[2] On the other hand, almost all studies of gender-paired parables at the level of Q have naturally been more focused on the first *speaker* of the pairs—the historical Jesus (as in Denis Fricker's study of the Q pairs: *Quand Jésus Parle au Masculin-Féminin*).[3]

Studies of Jesus' habit of teaching in pairs that relate to gender still typically remain centered around Luke's gospel and impervious to considerations of Q. The pairs are usually still treated as a Lukan tendency without reference to the Q hypothesis, and sometimes held up as a contrast to the perceived "worse" treatment of women in the other canonical gospels.[4] I think this is a mistake. To be sure, studying the way each gospel portrays Jesus is a worthy pursuit. But examining the pairs in their Q context, which sometimes means, say, removing Luke's additions and explanations to reveal a rather different saying, is highly rewarding. For one thing, Q offers a unique rural Jewish perspective that the New Testament can otherwise lack. Paula Fredriksen reminds us that for the evangelists, a significant shift had occurred between Jesus' audience and their own. Jesus had taught within the overwhelmingly Jewish context of Galilee and Judea, and most specifically in Jerusalem. His audience was largely Aramaic-speaking Jews. Paul, by contrast, taught within the cities of the western Greek-speaking Diaspora, the most likely setting of the evangelists too.[5]

Thinking about the sayings in their Q context not only helps to show their Jewishness. The Q context also provides a stark difference in genre, which can affect the meaning. Genre is one of the keys to interpretation. As Portier-Young notes, genre can play a "crucial role" in "enabling literature to do its cultural work."[6] In comparison with the narrative context of the Gospels, Q gets straight to the verbal message of Jesus and reveals the concerns of his first followers.

In this chapter, I want to stress the importance of this relocation of the words of Jesus away from the later, urban, increasingly non-Jewish, biographical, and christological Gospels, and toward the earlier, rural, Jewish, sayings collection. We will explore the work of some important authors who have made this shift toward Q in their investigations of the gendered parable pairs.

This examination of the pairs in their Q context is a relatively recent and undeveloped field of research. Rather than reviewing the literature that does exist chronologically, I have arranged the scholarship on Q's gender pairs into categories based on their differing conclusions. There are two conflicting evaluations of what the pairs mean *for women*. A related area of debate centers on the relative comfort or caution with which authors apply the concepts of "egalitarianism" and "feminism" to ancient literature. In what follows, I evaluate this secondary literature. On the whole, these scholars establish the importance of Q as a significant locus of evidence for scholarly understandings of women in the early Jesus movement, in a way the Gospels alone cannot. However, the current debate also demonstrates tension among interpretations of the pairs as seen in Q.

THE PAIRS IN GOSPEL CONTEXT: THE LUKAN GENDER PAIRS AS GATEWAY

The first work on gendered pairs in the teachings of Jesus was in the context of an allegedly Lukan tendency of pairing the genders at both the narrative level (characters in the plot) and the sayings level (characters in parables).[7] One of the most extensive contributions on the so-called Lukan pairs was Turid Seim's 1994 monograph, *The Double Message: Patterns of Gender in Luke/Acts*.[8] As Seim points out, scholars often note that the Gospel of Luke has a habit of "pairing" men and women, and then go on to discuss what this means for Luke's view of women. Scholars who examine these pairs with a view to understanding the role of women in Luke typically do not incorporate the concept of an earlier laying of sayings material into their work at all.[9] Whether or not they would actually support such an assertion, such studies rely on an unexamined assumption that the gender pairs are largely Lukan.[10]

Even when scholars who study the pairs in Luke *do* show an awareness of Q, they do not attribute *all* the Lukan gender pairs to material that derives from Q. Rather, following the cautious *Critical Edition of Q*,[11] they attribute any pairs that do not also occur in Matthew to "special" Lukan Jesus material, often assuming that these pairs are original Lukan creations.

My primary concern here is not to determine the boundaries of Q text critically but rather to question this assumption concerning special Lukan material.[12] There is a strong possibility that some of the so-called Lukan gendered parable pairs also belong among the Q sayings. At the very least, one must acknowledge that the question of Q's boundaries is very much an open one.[13] Later on, I will make a case for a bit of robbing from "special Luke" to widen Q. While the starting point for the current project was *The Critical Edition of Q*[14] as it currently stands, arguments emerged in the secondary literature for the inclusion of some Luke-only parables in Q.[15] In other words, in the course of my research, I have moved from a position of sticking with the cautious critical edition of Q toward a position of openness toward the inclusion in Q of gender pairs for which only one half has come down to us in Luke's gospel and that do not appear in the current minimalist critical edition.[16]

I include some of these "Lukan" parable pairs in my list of Q pairs because I propose, based on Seim's observations in her "Double Message," that the question of whether or not additional gendered parable pairs were created by Luke is an important one for women's history. If Luke's "special" parable pairs differ from an earlier Jesus stratum, this can tell us not only about the place of women but also about the author of Luke. I should be clear that (as we will see in chapter 4), Luke/Acts does have a special Lukan type of *narrative* (historical character) gendered pairing. Here, I am only referring to paired *sayings* in Luke (e.g., parables in the mouth of Jesus) that are not added to Q because they do not occur in Matthew, but am not referring here to the other sort of pairing Luke undertakes at the level of plot. This latter, as we shall see, also occurs in John.

DIVORCING Q'S WOMEN FROM GOSPEL WOMEN

Stripping the sayings away from their (embellished, framed, and occasionally fragmented) placement in the narratives of the canonical gospels provides rather different insights than does examining them in the sayings source.[17]

The gender-paired sayings material in Q reflects rhetorically designed intellectual and religious equality between women and men, while Luke's positioning of women and men cannot be described as equal. Luke may, in the past, have been viewed as a real champion of women[18] among the four canonical gospels, but he has now been re-evaluated quite differently. Dillon rightly notes that both Matthew and Luke "make decisive adaptations of the source text to promote the broader arguments of their books."[19] Jane Schaberg and Sharon Ringe write:

> Because [The Gospel of Luke] contains a great deal of material about women that is found nowhere else in the Gospels, many readers insist that the author is enhancing or promoting the status of women. Luke is said to be a special "friend" of women, portraying them in an extremely progressive and almost modern fashion, giving them a new identity and a new social status. [. . .] Even as this Gospel highlights women as included among the followers of Jesus, subjects of his teaching, and objects of his healing, it deftly portrays them as models of subordinate service, excluded from the power centre of the movement and from significant responsibilities. Claiming the authority of Jesus, this portrayal is an attempt to legitimate male dominance in the Christianity of the author's time. It was successful.[20]

Sometimes even those who explicitly set out to redeem the depiction of women in Luke have to admit that Luke/Acts offers a "mixed message in terms of women's agency and actions."[21] This is partly because women in Luke may be plentiful, but they are also silent; Joanna Dewey's analysis of speech in Luke's gospel shows that its author displays an extreme aversion to women's speech, which adds support to the view that, while Luke may depict plenty of women, he assigns them consistently to "restricted roles."[22] Annette Merz illustrates this glaring lack of women's speech in Luke in the case of Simeon and Anna: "Luke does indeed call [Anna] a prophetess, but he gives only an indirect account of her words—whereas Simeon's are quoted directly."[23]

These observations remind us of the basic historical-critical observation that the Matthean and Lukan literary projects, with their own tendencies, aims, urban *milieux*, and community concerns, provide examples of later literary and community contexts for which material of Jesus' sayings *was used*. Q, on the other hand, is an example of a context in which Jesus' sayings material *emerged*. Or, if that is too optimistic a reading, at the very least, Q provides an alternative context to add to that of the various Gospels, in which we may understand how Jesus' followers used his sayings. This is why an attempt to understand women in the early Jesus movement is incomplete without an examination of these parables and sayings outside their canonical setting in the Matthean and Lukan *oeuvres*.

Luise Schottroff,[24] Denis Fricker,[25] Jean-Francois Racine,[26] Alicia Batten,[27] Kathleen Corley,[28] Amy-Jill Levine,[29] and William Arnal[30] have all worked from the idea that the pairs originate in a stratum of the Jesus movement literature that predates the canonical Gospels, in order to piece together new evidence for Christian origins. Although their methods and starting points may overlap a great deal, their conclusions about women and Q differ sharply. I have clustered their findings into two groups, that I call "Perspective 1" and "Perspective 2," with a complicating, intermediate subgroup called "Perspective 1.5."

As we will see, Schottroff, Fricker, and Racine (Perspective 1) use Q's gendered pairs to reconstruct a highly positive social picture of women in the early Jesus movement, which they attribute (solely?) to the historical Jesus and/or a very early community around Q. Batten and Corley, from the intermediate perspective, also find that the pairs work as evidence for a positive sociohistorical situation for women. However, rather than giving credit for this to the Jesus movement over and against other varieties of Judaism, this moderate approach attributes the positive social situation of women to a wider movement across the period of late Hellenism and the Roman Republic. The third cluster of scholars, such as Levine and Arnal, those I label Perspective 2, do not interpret the gendered pairs as proof of any sociohistorically equal treatment of women and men.

Despite their varied conclusions, the above scholars all accept the methodological stance that studying the gender-focused parables and sayings *as they occur in Q*, and not just through their Christian canonical context in the Gospels of Matthew and Luke, is a necessary shift toward a more precise understanding of the material and of its earliest social backdrops. Examining the sayings in a Lukan or Matthean context may be important for an analysis of how Luke and Matthew incorporate sayings material, but the work of the abovementioned scholars shows that analyzing the gender pairs on their own is also necessary—removed from the narrative frames, tendencies, theologies, and community concerns that form those larger, later texts.

The narrative literary genre that we now call "gospel" established by the author of Mark (c.f. Mark 1:1) had not yet been invented when the Q sayings came into being.[31] Q may be an εὐαγγέλιον in the broadest sense of a "good message,"[32] but as a sayings collection, it differs markedly in interest and style from all the narrative gospels. Of course, genre is always one of the factors in the careful interpretation of a text. Portier-Young writes that "genre is social, political, and historical" and that it "provides a frame for viewing the world as much as it provides a frame for composition and reading."[33] The closest that Q, as a collection of *logia*, might come generically to the narrative gospels is as a "Sayings Gospel," which is indeed how some scholars have chosen to label it, more similar to the *Gospel of Thomas* than the canonical gospels.[34]

Q, as can be reconstructed, holds no narrative framework aside from a mention of John the Baptist in the wilderness at the outset (Q 3:2–3), the temptation narrative in Q 4:1–13, and the briefest setting of the stage here and there, such as "he said to his disciples" (Q 10:2) or "some were demanding from him a sign" (Q 11:16). It is therefore the genre "logia" into which Q is understandably most commonly classified. J. T. Barrera writes that "the sayings of the Q source show generic features of the collections of sayings of the Greek and Roman world."[35] We also see such "sayings lists" in a few other places in early Jewish/Christian antiquity, such as in the collection of parables in Mark 4, as well as in the *Gospel of Thomas*. In fact, the discovery of Thomas was a key turning point in the willingness of many scholars to consider "sayings gospel" as a genre at all:

> The existence of Q was once challenged by some scholars on the grounds that a sayings gospel was not really a gospel. The challengers argued that there were no ancient parallels to a gospel containing only sayings and parables and lacking stories about Jesus, especially the story about his trial and death. The discovery of the Gospel of Thomas changed all that. Thomas, too, is a sayings gospel that contains no account of Jesus' exorcisms, healings, trial, or death.[36]

Thus, the legitimacy of conceiving of a Sayings-based Gospel as a type of text was greatly strengthened with the discovery of the sayings-based *Gospel of Thomas*.[37] Robinson freely links Q and *Thomas* under the shared category of "sayings gospel": "The canonical Gospels are all Narrative Gospels, whereas Q, in this respect more like *Thomas*, is largely a Sayings Gospel."[38]

Perhaps because the Q *logia* lack the more biographically driven narrative of the gospels[39] into which those *logia* became embedded, few scholars before those mentioned above have looked to Q as a separate pool of evidence for women in the Jesus movement, although scores of monographs have addressed the role of women in Matthew and Luke.[40] Yet conceptualizing the Q material as a legitimate ancient genre, worthy of attention apart from Matthean and Lukan contexts, and examining the Q gender parable pairs as distinct from the "Lukan" pairs, opens a window onto an early, entirely Jewish Jesus movement[41] that is largely missing from the increasingly mixed-demographic Jesus movements attested in Christian Testament documents such as Luke/Acts[42] and the Gentile-obsessed letters of Paul.[43] Examining the gendered pairs in their Q setting guides us to women in a Jesus movement that is poorly attested in the Christian Testament.

Not only does Jesus' sayings material move further away from Judaism along the spectrum between Jewish and non-Jewish at the hands of the canonical gospel writers[44] it also moves from a primarily rural background toward a largely urban setting. Leslie Houlden writes that the Gospels filter the sayings "from an originally uneducated Galilean and rural setting to more sophisticated urban settings."[45] Rohrbaugh, too, affirms that "whatever the provenance of Jesus and his earliest followers, the principle writers (and presumably readers as well) of the New Testament were urban persons. [. . .] The Christian movement shifted (almost exclusively) to this urban environment."[46] In addition to these shifts from rural to urban and Jewish to Gentile, the "developing conditions and attitudes in the church" constitute an additional "distorting factor."[47]

In short, if historical accident had left us with only Matthew or only Luke, there would be no reconstructing an earlier layer of sayings material, and the chance to examine the place of women in a distinct and earlier stage of the Jesus movement would have been lost. The fact that both gospels are available to us with clearly separate tendencies and yet verbatim sayings that are often in the same order, allows us, to some extent, to extricate the sayings from their duties in the service of their final narrative resting place. As Amy-Jill Levine reminds us, the parables of Jesus have been reinterpreted and changed, "starting with the Gospel writers themselves,"[48] whereas Q may, as Mack optimistically puts it, "put us in touch with the first followers of Jesus."[49] The more we can extricate Jesus' teaching material from Lukan and Matthean literary aims, the better we can understand how these sayings may have worked for wo/men in their original audiences. In the constant search for what Mack describes as "the movements that regarded Jesus as their founder-teacher,"[50] he advocates that "the picture of Jesus portrayed in the New Testament Gospels be set aside. That portrayal did not occur until Mark wrote his story of Jesus after the Roman-Jewish war."[51] While such a step seems extreme, the exercise of temporarily setting aside preconceptions based on admittedly later moments in the development of the Jesus traditions in order to focus on a snapshot of the sayings material in earlier form is enormously useful. The scholars to follow are doing exactly that work—laying aside the search for women vis-à-vis the Jesus of the Gospels in order to uncover the story of women and the Jesus of the Q sayings.[52]

THE PAIRS IN PRE-GOSPEL CONTEXT:
PERSPECTIVES ON THE Q GENDER PAIRS

Unlike most subjects of New Testament inquiry, there is certainly not a vast body of work needing to be mastered if one wants to ascertain the state of the question on women in the Q pairs. Fricker's *Quand Jésus Parle au Masculin-Féminin* is a rare full-length monograph that focuses exclusively on women and the gender pairs outside of their gospel context.[53] Most of the work to date on women and the Q pairs can, as mentioned above, be divided into two broad camps; indeed, some authors situate themselves as such explicitly. One side of the debate counts the very existence of Q's gender pairs as strong evidence for gender egalitarianism within the early Jesus movement. The other side critiques such readings as overly generous, and instead interprets the pairs in one of two alternative ways: (a) that the pairs *do* indicate a kind of gender equality, but that no credit for this can be awarded to Jesus or the early Jesus movement, and should rather be attributed to the general changes that had been occurring in the society of the day or (b), diverging even further from the first perspective that any findings of gender equality in Q are erroneous—and at times supersessionist—wishful thinking, and that Q is as androcentric a text as any other of its time. My own approach resolves some of the tensions among these perspectives by attempting greater precision in describing the specific aims of the rhetorical work of the pairs vis-à-vis gender.

Perspective 1: Q's Gender Pairs as Evidence for Gender Equality in the Early Jesus Movement

Luise Schottroff

The earliest sustained attention paid to gender in the Q pairs is the work of Luise Schottroff. Throughout the 1990s, Schottroff's work approached the question of women in community around Q using a hermeneutic of feminist liberation theology.[54] Schottroff argues that the Q sayings that reference women—and the gender pairs in particular—demonstrate a deliberate inclusion of women, on equal footing with men, not only in the rhetoric of the teachings but also in the practices of the Jesus movement on the ground. Following Theissen, Schottroff believes that itinerant prophets formed an integral part of the nascent movement,[55] and, that Q contains strong indications that both women and men played this role. She concludes that this practice represents a major and deliberate challenge to patriarchal norms.[56]

Nevertheless, Schottroff does note a generally androcentric worldview throughout Q: "the Christian Testament as a whole, and the Sayings Source in particular, speak in androcentric language and presuppose a patriarchal system of relationships."[57] Schottroff views this androcentrism as something that could hardly be avoided, given the ancient context, and believes it can be hermeneutically stripped away to uncover not only a flourishing of women in the movement, but even a "preferential option for women."[58]

Schottroff's work with women in Q concludes that the medium (the gender pairs), the message (an egalitarian *basileia*), and the method (itinerant prophets and prophetesses) all point to a community and a leader that, although mired in an androcentric context, still managed to deeply challenge certain patriarchal norms around the value of both women and men to this movement and to its God. Such findings are not surprising, given that Schottroff's explicit method as a feminist liberation theologian involves seeking just such points of women's agency in the text.[59] This hermeneutical uncovering of challenges to patriarchy,[60] even within parts of Q that are couched in androcentric language and ideas, has caused Schottroff's critics to reject her conclusions as overly optimistic from a historical perspective, however theologically fruitful they may be.[61]

Denis Fricker

Denis Fricker's 2004 dissertation *Quand Jésus Parle au Masculin-Féminin*[62] was the first book-length work specifically to shine a spotlight on Jesus and gender understood specifically through the gendered pairings as they appear in Q. Examining the pairs from standpoints ranging from sociological to theological to historical-critical to rhetorical, Fricker's work clearly aims to be both exhaustive and precise. Like Schottroff, Fricker also admits at the outset to an overtly feminist and theological goal, relevant to practitioners of Christianity today. At the same time, like Schottroff, Fricker is explicit about his methods and aims for historical rigor. He offers a helpful multilingual literature review and incorporates that existing work into his project exhaustively. His twofold conclusion is that: (1) the Q parable pairs unequivocally represent a deliberate program of equality between men and women and (2) this can be linked directly to the historical Jesus.

Jean-Francois Racine

In keeping with Fricker and Schottroff, Jean-Francois Racine concludes that the gender pairs in Q form admissible evidence not only that women were present in Q's audience but also that treating wo/men as equals was definitely among the rhetorical aims of such sayings. Racine addresses the gender pairs in the context of an article that synthesizes scholarship on women in Q.[63] In reference to the pairs, he states that their deliberate juxtaposition of masculine and feminine can only be seen as "an indication that Q addresses equally men and women."[64]

Racine identifies "an egalitarian social ethos at work in Q,"[65] which he clearly extends to gender and which he believes underlies the practice of gendered pairing. He writes that "Q is addressed as much to women as to men," and that gender pairs show that "women take part along with men in the task of spreading the Jesus movement."[66] For Racine, the likelihood that a gender-egalitarian movement existed on the ground is strongly corroborated by Bernadette Brooten's scholarship on women leaders in early synagogues.[67] It is also supported by Kathleen Corley's juxtaposition of Q material against the backdrop of a burgeoning freedom for women in the late Republic that Augustus worked hard to curtail,[68] as well as Paul's frequent references to women in places of leadership and influence.[69] Racine is thus also positioned in what I have called "Perspective 1," as yet another scholar who sees the gender pairs as evidence for a deliberate move toward gender equality on the part of Q and/or Jesus.

Perspective 1.5: Gender Pairs Show Equality, but in Keeping With the Times

Alicia Batten

In 1994, Alicia Batten published an article in *Biblical Theology Bulletin* focusing on women in Q, and in particular on five gender pairs.[70] In this work, Batten takes a slightly different approach from other scholars; she addresses the implications, for women, of Q's challenges to familial and gender structures. In some aspects, Batten is in direct agreement with Schottroff in the latter's assessment that, despite working within typical androcentric frameworks, Q's rhetoric constitutes "a deliberate challenge to societal norms."[71] Batten's reasons for this conclusion may not be the same as other scholars, but she aligns with "Perspective 1" in her acceptance of the pairs as clear evidence that wo/men were, at least in some ways, on equal rhetorical footing, and possibly equal social footing, with men in the nascent Jesus movement around Q.

Rather than locating Q's challenge to gender norms in its evidence for women's itinerant prophecy, as Schottroff does, Batten instead pinpoints Q's inclusivity more squarely with the pairs themselves; she detects a deliberate social and literary *strategy* in Q's repeated offering of paired masculine and feminine examples.[72] Batten uses the pairs to argue that there were women in the Q audience (whether as itinerant prophets, supportive hosts for itinerants, or both), that these women were included very deliberately in Q's rhetoric, and that, furthermore, the Q community was generally "a group of people who offered a more inclusive environment for women."[73]

Although Batten sides with other "Perspective 1" scholars in her view that the gender pairs provide strong evidence for men's and women's relative equality in the early Jesus movement around Q, she diverges significantly from those others, in that she does not view this equality as spontaneously originating with Jesus or within the Q community, in opposition to everything in the surrounding environment. She instead situates this Q group within its broader socio-historical context in such a way as to suggest that the increased agency offered to women in Q is quite in line with the general situation for women in the late Hellenistic period and at the crossroads of Roman Empire. Batten concludes, after an examination of evidence both textual and material, that "women were increasingly gaining public status throughout the Mediterranean during the Late Republic. Both Jewish and Graeco-Roman women engaged in public activities involving religion, politics, and philosophy."[74] Women in Mediterranean antiquity had generally experienced little to no power over their own lives, but women in the Hellenistic period and late Republic had enjoyed a shift toward greater agency and inclusion.[75]

In other words, Batten does not describe Q's challenge to social hierarchies as an exclusively Christian or Jesus-movement innovation that broke sharply away from Jewish and Roman patriarchies that pushed all women into a "private" realm at all times and allowed all men free reign in the "public realm." Instead, Batten sees Q's treatment of women as participating, alongside many other pockets within Judaism and within the wider umbrella of Hellenism, in a "phenomenon throughout the Hellenistic world" wherein women were already partaking in new opportunities of public participation.[76] Batten writes: "earliest Christianity, often characterized as an inclusive haven for women fleeing from patriarchal Judaism or Graeco-Roman religions, was not unique,"[77] and, further, that

> neither Judaism nor Hellenism needs to be denigrated in order to appreciate the inclusivity discernible in Q [. . .]. It was not necessarily a Christian ideology that promoted such openness, but a wider phenomenon throughout the Hellenistic world, which for some time offered more opportunities for women to participate publicly, as the examples of women benefactors, synagogue leaders, and philosophers solidly illustrate.[78]

Batten has hinted that Augustan marriage reform[79] may be a fruitful context against which to examine Q, pointing to Augustus' concerted focus on women's propriety[80] as an indicator that women at the close of the Roman Republic had been enjoying their new opportunities on a scale that was wide enough to threaten the social and political structures and cause a backlash: "Augustus' laws on marriage are a significant indication that women were becoming too free."[81] In her conclusion, Batten laments the impermanence of this expansion in women's circles of agency and pinpoints Augustus' frequent measures to control women's behavior[82] as the dawn of an era that sought—successfully—to regain tighter control over women's freedoms. She concludes:

> As is commonly known, Christianity later became a patriarchal religion despite these exciting beginnings. Hence, continuing to study its development in light of larger forces will perhaps better enable us to understand why Christianity appears so quickly to have forgotten some of its own origins.[83]

According to Batten, attributing these "exciting beginnings" exclusively to Jesus/Christianity, rather than in the context of a wider societal shift, has highly problematic repercussions, including unhistorical anti-Jewish stereotypes. It is for this important nuance that I have positioned Batten in Perspective 1.5, somewhere in the middle between those who do credit Jesus of Nazareth for the gender pairs (which they evaluate as unequivocally positive), and those who do not evaluate the gender pairs as necessarily positive for women at all. Batten grants the gender-leveling rhetoric of the pairs its due, while looking beyond Jesus to the gendered realities in his surrounding social world as the necessary context from which the impulse for the pairs could spring.

I agree with Batten's approach and findings; she has successfully located the pairs in a wider context, resulting in an important corrective to anti-Jewish analyses, while at the same time recognizing the pairs' rhetorical work as significant for our understanding of the role of women in the Jesus movement.

Kathleen Corley

Kathleen Corley specializes in historical Jesus research with a particular view to the status of women.[84] Meal praxis is central to Corley's analyses of the place of women around Jesus of Nazareth and in the communities that continued and evolved shortly after his death. Corley, like Batten, notices practices mentioned in Jesus material that hint at a newly inclusive place for women, and concludes that the women who enjoyed a strong and valued presence in the Jesus movement "were participants in a larger process of innovation which incorporated the inclusion of women in various social and religious contexts."[85]

As with Batten's findings, Corley's research shows that although the Q material does indicate an emancipation of women, this was part of a larger process then taking place across Mediterranean antiquity. For Corley, Jesus' sayings material is not indicative of any special innovation on the part of Jesus or Q. In fact, Corley essentially finds no qualitative difference between the place of women in Jesus' movement and the place of women in many other movements in other contemporaneous Jewish and Roman groups.[86] Corley thus joins Batten in this middle perspective; for her, the evidence for women around Jesus clearly reveals that they had positions of power and agency, and yet, like Batten, she attributes such gender inclusiveness to wider social changes that had been happening in the previous century and were still happening around the Jesus movement, as elsewhere.

Perspective 2: Gender Pairs not Evidence of Equality at All

The scholars I have clustered in this third and final group diverge from both previous perspectives, in that they simply do not find that Q offers any evidence for an interest in gender, nor for equality between men and women at all. They interpret the pairs in other ways, none of which brings them to the conclusion that gender equality is a force at play in Q.

Amy-Jill Levine

In Amy-Jill Levine's 1990 article, "Who's Catering the Q Affair? Feminist Observations on Q Paraenesis,"[87] she assumes both the existence of "Q people" and the existence of Kloppenborg's two strata in Q, taking the proposed strata as a reflection of two different stages in the social status of the community. Like Schottroff, she views the earlier stage as characterized by mendicant missionaries. However, following Theissen on a point where Schottroff differs, Levine views these wandering prophets as exclusively male. Since these male mendicants are liminal members of society, the role of the female members of the group is to offer much-needed support (such as food, lodging, and finances). She views the "later" stratum (Q2) as reflective of a time after which these missionaries had met, on the one hand, with a measure of success (and therefore a more solid social network was in place) and, on the other hand, with rising opposition from mainstream views (occasioning this layer of Q's more vitriolic rhetoric). In this later stage, the importance of the women's supportive network is, for Levine, more substantial. In Levine's own words, this form-critical analysis thus offers "both confirmation of and qualifications to the popular hypothesis that Q represents a discipleship of equals."[88]

However, in her subsequent article for the *Feminist Companion to the Hebrew Bible in the New Testament*, Levine offers a more exclusively negative interpretation of the gender pairs in Q, in terms of their connection to any sort of equality for first-century women.[89] She sounds an alarm about the dichotomy that much of the scholarship on women in early Christianity has set up between "women in early Judaism" *versus* "women in early Christianity," noting that both are extreme caricatures, with Judaism assumed (*sans* reference to evidence) to be hopelessly patriarchal and restrictive for women and Christianity often depicted as unflaggingly emancipatory.[90] She concludes that the "prevailing hypothesis" remains that "Judaism, however and if ever defined, regarded women as weak-willed, wanton, and, in general, worthless."[91] Judith Plaskow had already noted in the 1970s that feminist New Testament scholarship was emancipating Christian women at the expense of Jews.[92] Plaskow was still lamenting in the 1990s that "the feminist struggle with patriarchal christologies leads back into the trap of anti-Judaism."[93] Levine confirms and laments this trend in Christian scholarship on Jesus and women as an "orientalising of the Jews" that "serves to distinguish them culturally and ethically from Jesus and his followers."[94]

In this later work, Levine deems the Q pairs to be insufficient as evidence of any real difference for women, especially given the continued androcentrism and patriarchy throughout the Jesus movements and early Christianity, and indeed throughout the text of Q; she suggests that analyses that latch onto the pairs as proof of gender egalitarianism stem from bias.[95] In a more recent article, she encapsulates this issue with her typical pith: "negatively categorizing early Judaism as misogynistic and positively categorizing Jesus as proactive on women's rights is both bad history and bad theology."[96] She portrays the Q community as one in which the participation of women is not remarkable:

> Jesus gathered a small but loyal following of fellow Jews who sought to incarnate the *basileia*, the kingdom of heaven, on earth. They preached a joyous attitude toward life, community support and solidarity, and a view of others based on actions, not on pronouncements, birth, or wealth. With this message and this lifestyle, women took their place among Jesus' followers. His association with women, in and of itself, is unremarkable.[97]

Levine's work, like Batten's and Corley's, represents a welcome change of direction in the conversation about women in the Jesus movement, correcting a dismissive lack of attention to early Judaism and its well-known, unflagging diversity, and also working to correct a longstanding tendency toward anti-Jewish assumptions. My work on the Q pairs takes Levine's important caveats against supersessionist readings into account as a strong desideratum; at the same time, building on Corley's and Batten's demonstration of diverse ways in which women were active social and religious participants, I somewhat overturn Levine's ruling on the lack of significance of the Q pairs in terms of what they can tell us about any deliberate inclusion of women on the part of Q. It is possible to have a Jesus who has employed a gender-inclusive tactic without pulling him outside Judaism to pit him against all other varieties of it.

William Arnal

In 1997, William Arnal published an article with a unique thesis on the gendered pairs within Q, namely, "that the phenomenon is more indicative of a penchant for legal and regulatory formulations than it is of an interest in a deliberate critique of patriarchy."[98] According to Arnal, although all work on the pairs to that point had agreed that they indicate deliberate inclusion of women to some degree, "the Q couplets do not in and of themselves serve as any convincing indication of a tendency toward gender inclusiveness."[99] Situating Q, as Arnal does, in a scribal stylistic context,[100] he defines the pairs as "repetitious examples, statements, or arguments" that are typical of scribal activity[101] and concludes that Q, overall, has a "blatantly androcentric character."[102] However, Arnal does admit that the pairs indicate that "the Q program is launched with examples drawn from the world of both male and female experience, and that judgement is proffered to both the men and the women of impenitent Israel."[103] His overall analysis joins Levine's against the conclusions of those who cite the gender pairs as a clear sign of Q's rhetorical inclusivity toward women.

EVALUATION AND CONCLUSIONS

The above collection of thinkers represents a broad shift in the discussion of the gendered pairs, away from their embedded context in the narrative gospels and toward an earlier context within the sayings material itself. The thread of disagreement that runs throughout the above collection of work, and the topic around which I have divided the scholarship into "perspectives," has to do with whether the Q pairs reveal a somewhat gender-egalitarian tendency, or, to the contrary, reaffirm a somewhat patriarchal/kyriarchal and androcentric *status quo*. One point of disagreement involves the extent to which categories like egalitarianism and feminism can be applied to texts from antiquity and whether it is ever appropriate to regard anything in antiquity as either egalitarian or feminist at all. Even among those for whom definitions of feminism and egalitarianism can be sufficiently qualified to avoid anachronism, there is disagreement and discrepancy around how such concepts can and cannot be reliably identified within an ancient text.

Kathleen Corley and John Elliott have taken issue with the use of early Jesus material as evidence for gender equality and/or "egalitarian" social values. Corley views such conclusions as Christian feminist mythmaking,[104] while Elliott views the category of egalitarianism as an historical anachronism.[105] In contrast, Mary Ann Beavis takes issue with those who dismiss the lens of egalitarianism for the study of the early Jesus movement;[106] Beavis' work responds particularly directly to Corley and Elliott, coming to the defense of the "widely held hypothesis" that they had challenged. This narrative, challenged by Corley but held up by Beavis, says that Jesus and his *basileia* movement had been "egalitarian," but that by the time of the deutero-Pauline and Pastoral epistles, the church had already begun reverting to "the non-egalitarian norms of the ancient Mediterranean world."[107] Beavis asserts that critiques like Corley's and Elliott's set up feminist reconstructions of Christian origins in such a selective way as to make them easy to refute.[108] By reference to other ancient utopian writings and movements,[109] Beavis argues that an emphasis on both gender equality and egalitarianism in general—defined appropriately and in context[110]—are not only possible for, but also *clearly* present in the earliest *basileia* movement.[111]

The upshot of all of the above is that interpretation of the pairs and their import for women is complicated. Initial work that saw a remarkable leveling of gender has been challenged due to the bias, the historical inaccuracy, and even the anti-Judaism of Christian feminist interpreters. This book wades into the swirling midst of this discussion. I concur with Beavis in her view that even theological Christian feminist readings that explicitly set out looking to uncover positive moments for women in the text can make contributions to historical questions and cannot be wholly thrown out because of their stated (or unstated) biases. Beavis is correct that these readings have in many cases been described by critics in overly simplistic terms or dismissed wholesale although they vary substantially in nuance and rigor. Schüssler Fiorenza, for instance, while among the loudest and most prolific voices for an egalitarian and woman-positive Jesus of Nazareth who advocated a "discipleship of equals,"[112] is at the same time one of the most systematic laborers against anti-Judaism and supersessionism in Christian scholarship.[113] Schottroff, too, guards mindfully against anti-Jewish reconstructions in her liberation-theological work on women in Q. She writes, for example, that "the Jewish upper classes' participation in the interests of the Pax Romana led also to internal conflicts within Judaism, whose textual expression became, in the later history of Christian interpretation, an instrument of anti-Judaism. As a result, a social-historical contextualization of the texts is also fundamental for the issue of anti-Judaism."[114]

On the other hand, I also agree with Corley and Elliott in their view that the picture of women that we find in the Jesus material is not a clear, uncomplicated one. Whereas Corley and Elliott are rightfully uncomfortable with conclusions such as "Q is feminist" or "Jesus was egalitarian," this work responds to their calls for caution by instead concluding that Q treats women equally *in certain specific ways and not in every way.*

Critics like Elliott complain that allowing current questions and categories to overshadow our investigations of ancient data is a treacherous path for historians to tread; I concur that heading into an investigation of what evidence we have for women in the Jesus movement with our desired conclusions already in hand does a grave disservice to the stories of women in antiquity even as it aims to uplift contemporary women. Furthermore, it teaches us more about modern questions than it does about first-century Judaism. Levine, Arnal, Corley, Batten, and Schottroff are right to note that androcentric language and a patriarchal/kyriarchal worldview mitigate reading Q with rose-colored glasses in terms of the role of women in the earliest Jesus movement versus the role of women in general at the time.

However, all of these cautions present an important *starting point* for investigation into women in Q, but they are not its ending point. The presence of androcentric language is unremarkable in antiquity; it does not negate the fact that a literary pattern exists within Q that is unprecedented in antique literature and that this pattern unmistakably highlights gender in a way that seems to stem from an impulse toward women's inclusion. Scholars on one end of the spectrum are correct to point out that what is happening in the pairs cannot be equated to modern egalitarianism or modern feminism and correct that we ought to be on the lookout for anti-Jewish and anachronistic interpretation. Yet this does not discount the important work of scholars at the other end of the spectrum who highlight a literary anomaly that is of historical importance for the study of women in the Galilean Jesus movement.

Alicia Batten and Kathleen Corley do see gender equality evidenced in the Q pairs, albeit credited not to the Jesus movement alone but also to the *Zeitgeist*. Their work thus falls toward the center of this spectrum I have constructed. It seems to me that in her unique contribution toward situating the Q pairs more carefully in their wider Mediterranean context (and, in so doing, counteracting claims of Christian superiority that can smack of supersessionism), Corley may have downplayed the remarkable innovation that the gender pairs do present. While, as Batten and Corley have demonstrated, the time may indeed have been right to allow for Q's extension of various opportunities to women and its encouragement to community members to challenge traditional familial roles, the particular way in which Q does this is, at least at a rhetorical level, completely unprecedented and should be noted for its creativity. As I will show in chapter 5, the use of the particular rhetorical strategy of the pairs, and the implications of that strategy for its recipients, is undocumented in earlier Hellenistic and Second Temple texts.

The fruit of women's opportunity may indeed have ripened in the late Republic, but the Q material is unique evidence that it was also plucked and enjoyed in a small corner of Galilee. There is no need to dismiss the best research from disparate feminist perspectives on the Q pairs. This present work shares the skepticism of some researchers around how far toward "equality" the Q pairs can be stretched and heeds the sharp warnings against anti-Jewish readings, but it also shares the conviction of feminist scholars who note that something unique is happening in Jesus' rhetoric of gender in Q. The next chapters will demonstrate, through readings that are sensitive to both text and context, that the gendered pairs push against the boundaries of the *status quo* for women in unique and important ways while, in other ways, simultaneously reinforcing gendered social roles.

NOTES

1. D. E. Malick, "The Significance of Three Narrative Parallels of Men and Women in Luke 1, John 3-4, and Acts 9," *Priscilla Pap.* 28/3 (2014): 15–25. The same is true for J. Kopas' article on "Jesus and Women: Luke's Gospel," *Theology Today* 43/2 (1986): 192–202, which deals with gendered pairing, but takes the gospel text as-is without distinguishing between Lukan material and earlier material.

2. Moyra Dale, "Dismantling Socio-Sacred Hierarchy: Gender and Gentiles in Luke-Acts," *Priscilla Papers* 31/2 (2017): 19–23.

3. D. Fricker, *Quand Jésus Parle au Masculin-Féminin: Étude Contextuelle et Exégétique d'une Forme Littéraire Originale* (Paris: Gabalda, 2004).

4. See, for example, a fairly early feminist look at Luke as "the women's gospel" in C. F. Parvey, "The Theology and Leadership of Women in the New Testament," in *Religion and Sexism* (ed. R. Radford Ruether; NY: Simon and Schuster, 1974), 139–146, and see E. H. Maly, "Women and the Gospel of Luke," *BTB* 10/3 (1980): 99–104.

5. P. Fredriksen, *Sin: The Early History of an Idea* (Princeton: Princeton University Press, 2012), 11.

6. Portier-Young, "Jewish Apocalyptic Literature as Resistance Literature," 149.

7. See, for instance, H. Flender in *Heil und Geschichte in der Theologie des Lukas* (Munich: Kaiser, 1965) and J. Klopas, "Jesus and Women: Luke's Gospel," *Theology Today* 43/2 (1986): 192–202.

8. T. Seim, *The Double Message: Patterns of Gender in Luke & Acts* (New York: T&T Clark, 2004), first published in 1994 in the *Studies of the Old Testament and its World* series. Seim's "double message" consists of her thesis that the Gospel of Luke contains mixed messages for women and "cannot be reduced either to a feminist treasure chamber or a chamber of horrors for women's theology" (249). While she finds that the gender pairs in Luke indicate that there were plenty of women in the audience and active in the movement, she notes at the same time a discomfort and ambivalence toward them on the part of Luke and other characters in the gospel, and even a crafted curtailing of women's roles in the broader scheme of Luke/Acts.

9. For example, Flender, *Heil und Geschichte in der Theologie des Lukas*; Klopas, "Jesus and Women: Luke's Gospel"; and Seim, *The Double Message*.

10. The *Women's Bible Commentary* serves as a characteristic example of this scholarly assumption: "The (Lukan) technique called 'pairing' is very noticeable. One version of a story or teaching refers to a man and the other to a woman, reinforcing the message and encouraging women as well as men to identify with the characters. This pairing occurs most often in the discourse of Jesus—for example, the man who plants the mustard seed and the woman who takes the leaven [. . .] Some healings form pairs: the widow's only son and Jairus's only daughter (7:12; 8:42)." J. Schaberg, "Luke," in *The Women's Bible Commentary: Expanded Edition with Apocrypha* (ed. C. Newsom and S. H. Ringe; Louisville: Westminster John Knox, 1998), 366.

11. Robinson, Hoffmann, and Kloppenborg, eds., *The Critical Edition of Q*.

12. For a history of the reconstruction of Q by the International Q Project and the Hermeneia critical edition, including an outline of the key issues, see F. Neirynck, "The Reconstruction of Q and IQP / CritEd Parallels," in *The Sayings Source Q and the Historical Jesus* (ed. A. Lindemann; Leuven, Leuven University Press, 2001), 53–148. For initial work toward widening Q's boundaries by moving material from "Special Luke" into Q, see David B. Sloan, "The τίς ἐξ ὑμῶν Similitudes and the Extent of Q," *JSNT* 38/3 (2016): 339–355. For a fine introduction to the discipline of text criticism as it relates to the Christian Testament, see D. C. Parker, *An Introduction to the New Testament Manuscripts and Their Texts* (Cambridge: Cambridge University Press, 2008).

13. See Sloan, "Extent of Q," 339.

14. Robinson, Hoffmann, and Kloppenborg, eds., *The Critical Edition of Q*.
15. Sloan, "Extent of Q," 342–349.
16. Those who have argued for a wider Q in varying degrees, aside from the aforementioned David Sloan, "Extent of Q," include, but are not limited to: H. Schurmann, *Traditionsgeschichtliche Untersuchungen zu den synoptischen Evangelien* (Dusseldorf: Patmos-Verlag, 1968); E. Schüssler-Fiorenza, *Sharing Her Word: Feminist Biblical Interpretation in Context* (Boston: Beacon, 1998), 150–155; and D. Burkett, *Rethinking the Gospel Sources II: The Unity and Plurality of Q* (Atlanta: SBL, 2009).
17. See J. S. Kloppenborg and L. E. Vaage, "The Sayings Gospel Q and Method in the Study of Christian Origins" in *Early Christianity, Q and Jesus* (Atlanta: Scholars, 1991), 1–4.
18. For instance, Maly writes: "It is a *fact readily acknowledged by all* that in Luke's Gospel not only are women mentioned more often than in the other Gospels but also, and more importantly, are they seen to *play more significant roles*," and goes on to argue that Luke's gospel is a model for the expansion and encouragements of women's roles in church leadership today, in "Women and the Gospel of Luke," 99 and 104 (emphasis mine).
19. Dillon, "Ravens, Lilies, and the Kingdom of God," 610.
20. J. Schaberg and S. Ringe, "Gospel of Luke," *Women's Bible Commentary: Twentieth-Anniversary Edition Revised and Updated* (Louisville: Westminster John Knox, 2012), 493. See further: V. Koperski, "Is 'Luke' a Feminist or Not? Female-Male Parallels in Luke-Acts," in *Luke and His Readers: Festschrift A. Denaux* (ed. R. Bieringer, G. Van Belle, and J. Verheyden; Leuven: Peeters, 2005), 25–48.
21. F. S. Spencer. *Salty Wives, Spirited Mothers, and Savvy Widows: Capable Women of Purpose and Persistence in Luke's Gospel* (Grand Rapids: Eerdmans, 2012), 4.
22. Luke's women are not given speaking roles at all. See Joanna Dewey, "Women in the Synoptic Gospels: Seen But Not Heard?," *BTB* 27/2 (1997): 58.
23. A. Merz, "How a Woman Who Fought Back and Demanded her Rights became an Importunate Widow: The Transformations of a Parable of Jesus," in *Jesus from Judaism to Christianity: Continuum Approaches to the Historical Jesus* (ed. T. Holmen; London: T&T Clark, 2007), 84.
24. See Schottroff's "Itinerant Prophetesses"; "The Sayings Source Q"; and *Lydia's Impatient Sisters: A Feminist Social History of Early Christianity* (London: SCM, 1995).
25. See D. Fricker, *Quand Jésus Parle au Masculin-Féminin* and "La femme, la famille, et la communauté dans la source des *logia*," *RevScRel* 79/1 (2005): 97–116.
26. See Racine and Beaumont, "Three Approaches."
27. See Batten, "More Queries for Q."
28. See Corley, *Private Women, Public Meals* and *Women and the Historical Jesus*.
29. See Levine, "Yeast of Eden," 302–331 and "Women in the Q Communit(ies) and Traditions," 150–170.
30. See Arnal, "Gendered Couplets in Q," 75–94.

31. Q has been dated anywhere from the 30s to the 70s of the first century, with the majority opinion falling in the 60s. (See E. Boring, *Introduction to the New Testament* [Louisville: Westminster John Knox, 2012], excursus 3.5, "The Sayings Source Q"). However, the earliest of the less sayings-based, more biographical works about Jesus that came to be known as "gospels" seem to have been set in writing beginning no earlier than 70. (See Boring, *Introduction to the New Testament*, section 21.4, "Interpreting Mark: Date, Occasion.") The first known use of the term "gospel" (*euangelion*) to refer not only to the general "good news" about Jesus but also to a literary genre is by Justin in his *First Apology* (dated c. 155 C.E.) See L. Wills, *The Quest of the Historical Gospel: Mark, John, and the Origins of the Gospel Genre* (London: Routledge, 1997) for an excellent discussion of the origins of the Gospel genre that includes frequent references to the history of scholarship and incorporates fruitful comparisons with Greek Hero Cult. For an argument for the complex and multivalent use of the term εὐαγγέλιον from very early in the Jesus movement, see S. Guijarro, "La Coexistence de différents sens du terme *euaggelion* aux origines du christianisme," *RTL* 45 (2014): 481–501.

32. See Kloppenborg, *Q: The Earliest Gospel*, 60–61 for a discussion of the ways in which Q can be considered an εὐαγγέλιον in the sense that Paul had a gospel and *Thomas* called itself a gospel, but not in the sense of the biographical literary genre innovated by "Mark."

33. Portier-Young, "Jewish Apocalyptic Literature as Resistance Literature," 149.

34. See, for instance, Kloppenborg, "Discursive Practices in the Sayings Gospel Q," 149–190 and *Excavating Q*. See also J. Robinson's *The Sayings of Jesus: The Sayings Gospel Q in English* (Minneapolis: Fortress, 2002).

35. J. T. Barrera, *The Jewish Bible and the Christian Bible: An Introduction to the History of the Bible* (transl. W. G. E. Watson; Leiden: Brill, 1998), 34.

36. R. W. Funk, R. W. Hoover, and the Jesus Seminar, *The Five Gospels: What Did Jesus Really Say? The Search for the Authentic Words of Jesus* (New York: HarperOne, 1997), 12.

37. See Kloppenborg, *Q: The Earliest Gospel*, 73 for a brief summary of the ramifications of the discovery of *Thomas* for scholarly attitudes and nomenclature for Q. For a good book-length argument for *Thomas* as an independent witness to original Jesus traditions, see S. J. Patterson, *The Gospel of Thomas and Jesus* (Sonoma: Polebridge, 1993). For the notion that *Thomas* contains elements that have been handed down orally from a very early point in the Jesus movement, which can thus help in the reconstruction of original Jesus sayings, see, *inter alia*, L. M. McDonald, *The Formation of the Christian Biblical Canon: Revised and Expanded Edition* (Peabody: Hendrickson, 1995), 139, esp. n.5.

38. Robinson, "The Critical Edition of Q and the Study of Jesus," 28.

39. I here call the Gospels "biographically-driven" rather than straight "biographies" quite deliberately. I am aware that generic issues prevent the Gospels from fitting easily into existing Greco-Roman "Lives" (βίοι). At the same time, in comparison to Q, the most obvious difference between the Gospels and Q is the presence or lack of focus on biographical moments in Jesus' life, such as passion narratives, birth narratives, career description, encounters with others, and actions (such as accounts of healings and miracles). See R. A. Burridge, *Four Gospels, One Jesus?* (2nd ed.;

Grand Rapids: Eerdmans, 2005), 6–7 for a very brief summary of how viewing the Gospels as biography has come in and out of vogue and is now in favor once again, with limitations.

40. For example, in the last two decades alone, the following studies are among many that purport to analyze women in the context of Matthew and/or Luke, and yet do not differentiate between women in the Synoptic Gospels and women in the Sayings Gospel: R. Bauckham, *Gospel Women: Studies of the Named Women in the Gospels* (Grand Rapids: Eerdmans, 2002); S. J. Binz, *Women and the Gospels: Friends and Disciples of Jesus* (Grand Rapids: Baker, 2011); Dale, "Dismantling Socio-Sacred Hierarchy: Gender and Gentiles in Luke-Acts"; E. V. Dowling, *Taking Away the Pound: Women, Theology, and the Parable of the Pounds in the Gospel of Luke* (London: T&T Clark, 2007); F. Gench, *Back to the Well: Women's Encounters with Jesus in the Gospels* (Louisville: Westminster John Knox, 2004); A.-J. Levine, ed., *A Feminist Companion to Luke* (London: Sheffield Academic, 2002); A.-J. Levine, ed., *A Feminist Companion to Matthew* (Sheffield: Sheffield Academic, 2001); B. E. Reid, *Choosing the Better Part? Women in the Gospel of Luke* (Collegeville: Liturgical Press, 1996); Spencer, *Salty Wives, Spirited Mothers, and Savvy Widows*; and B. B. Thurston, *Women in the New Testament: Questions and Commentary* (New York: Crossroad, 1998). One notable exception to this trend is the volume *Women and Christian Origins*, edited by R. S. Kraemer and M. R. D'Angelo, in which one chapter is devoted to "Representations of Women in the Gospel of Matthew and Luke/Acts" and a separate chapter treats "Women in the Q Communit(ies) and Traditions" (Oxford: Oxford University Press, 1999).

41. Indeed, many scholars such as L. M. McDonald date Q "well before" a Pauline corpus of writings. See McDonald, *The Formation of the Christian Biblical Canon*, 253, n.9.

42. Robinson points out that "the Q People, that is to say, the few who still identified themselves with Jesus in Galilee, have largely been lost from sight, as has always been the case since Luke almost completely bypassed Galilee in Acts." Robinson, "The Critical Edition of Q and the Study of Jesus," 27–28.

43. On the juxtaposition of the earliest Jesus movement as Jewish and the Christianity represented in the canon Christian Testament as Gentile, see, *inter alia*, Vermes, *Jesus the Jew*, esp. 42–57.

44. "The hypothesis of a Jewish Q is firmly supported by recent scholarship," writes Joseph in *Jesus, Q, and the Dead Sea Scrolls*, 47. By the time of Luke/Acts, however, the material has been incorporated into an urban document whose "implied author claims to be an authentic part of the heterogeneous population of the Roman Empire." V. K. Robbins, "The Social Location of the Implied Author of Luke-Acts," *The Social World of Luke-Acts* (ed. J. H. Neyrey; Peabody: Hendrickson, 1991), 332.

45. L. Houlden, "Introduction to the New Testament," *Oxford Bible Commentary* (ed. J. Barton and J. Muddiman; New York: Oxford University Press, 2001), 840.

46. Rohrbaugh, "The Preindustrial City," 107.

47. Houlden, "Introduction to the New Testament," 840.

48. A.-J. Levine, *Short Stories by Jesus: The Enigmatic Parables of a Controversial Rabbi* (New York: HarperCollins, 2014), 3. Cf. L. Houlden's comment that "Jesus is never encountered 'neat' in the New Testament" but is instead subject to

"all the inevitable distortion that goes with subjectivity." Houlden, "Introduction to the New Testament," 840.

49. Mack, *Who Wrote the New Testament*, 47.

50. Mack, *Who Wrote the New Testament*, 47.

51. Mack, *Who Wrote the New Testament*, 47.

52. It should be noted that by wishing to remove the sayings material from its gospel dressings and studying it in the Q collection, I do not imply that I can study it "raw." As Robinson notes, Q, "as a text [. . .] would inevitably have its own way of shaping the material it took over from the tradition." Robinson, "The Critical Edition of Q and the Study of Jesus," 27. Likewise, Kloppenborg states that "Q, no less than Mark, has a definite editorial perspective" and that "its selection and arrangement likely reflects the situation of its framers (in the late 50s or 60s or even 70s) rather than Jesus in the 30s." Kloppenborg, "Discursive Practices in the Sayings Gospel Q," 163.

53. This French-language work is Fricker's *Quand Jésus Parle au Masculin-Féminin*. Fricker has a thorough *état de la question* (21–47) as well as an excellent multilingual bibliography (391–413). Any citations of Fricker in English herein are my own translations from his original French. In addition to Fricker's book-length work, there is also M. Johnson-Debaufre's, *Jesus Among Her Children*. Debaufre, however, does not specifically direct her focus to the pairs, but rather to women in Q in relation to Christian origins in general, with a focus on Woman Wisdom.

54. Luise Schottroff's first work on women in Q ("Itinerant Prophetesses: A Feminist Analysis of the Sayings Source Q") arose as part of the SBL Q seminar. It was translated by J. Reed of the Institute for Antiquity and Christianity at Claremont and published as one of their Occasional Papers (21) in 1991. The work was republished with the same title in *The Gospel Behind the Gospels: Current Studies on Q* (ed. R. A. Piper; Leiden: Brill, 1995), 347–360. In 1994, Schottroff also contributed "The Sayings Source Q," also from the perspective of feminist liberation theology, along with *Lydia's Impatient Sisters*.

55. See Schottroff, *Itinerant Prophetesses*, throughout. Theissen formulates a picture of early Jesus communities relying on both itinerant prophets and stationary hosts in *Le christianisme de Jésus*, but attention is not paid to gender here as it is in Schottroff. For additional arguments for the inclusion of women followers of Jesus among itinerant prophets, see J. D. Crossan, "Itinerants and Householders in the Earliest Kingdom Movement," *Reimagining Christian Origins* (ed. E. Castelli and H. Taussig; Valley Forge: Trinity Press International, 1996), 113–129.

56. See Schottroff, "The Sayings Source Q," throughout.

57. Schottroff, "The Sayings Source Q," 509.

58. "Despite its intensely androcentric language and its patriarchal horizon of imagination, this sayings tradition encourages us to develop visions of a better world, a world that, through a preferential option for women who are tormented by poverty, sexual exploitation, and ignorance, we can begin to envision and to achieve." Schottroff, "The Sayings Source Q," 531.

59. When discussing her method, Schottroff is candid about the questions asked of the text: "An analysis of patriarchy in the Christian Testament implies a critical examination of patriarchal structures at several levels: (1) Where in the Christian

Testament texts do we find patriarchal power structures uncritically maintained? (2) Where in the Christian Testament are there initiatives toward a critique of patriarchy? (3) Where, even in androcentric texts, is it possible to bring to light the history of women that has been rendered invisible? (4) Where does the Christian Testament contain options from which a feminist theology of liberation can draw inspiration?" Schottroff, "The Sayings Source Q," 509.

60. See, for example, Schottroff, *Itinerant Prophetesses*, 9–10.

61. Examples of such critiques are outlined in the "Perspective 2" section below. Approaching a text with Schottroff's feminist hermeneutic of liberation does predict that the outcome is more likely to be a favorable one for women. That said, Schottroff's analysis is nonetheless meticulous, as she is explicit about her method, and she thoroughly combs the text of Q for both its androcentric and its "liberating" aspects.

62. Fricker, *Quand Jésus Parle au Masculin-Féminin*.

63. Racine and Beaumont, "Three Approaches."

64. Racine and Beaumont, "Three Approaches," 114.

65. Racine and Beaumont, "Three Approaches," 114.

66. Racine and Beaumont, "Three Approaches," 116.

67. Bernadette Brooten, *Women Leaders in the Ancient Synagogue: Inscriptional Evidence and Background Issues* (Chico: Scholars, 1982).

68. It is well-known among Augustan-period scholars that his legislation and his hardline changes to various Roman practices "can claim major responsibility for the notable changes that occurred in women's legal, political, and social circumstances during his principate." Judith P. Hallett, "Women in Augustan Rome," in *A Companion to Women in the Ancient World* (ed. S. L. James and S. Dillon; Chichester: Wiley Blackwell, 2012), 373. See also, for a connection between (women's) sexual freedom and civil and financial ruin, Alison Keith, "Women in Augustan Literature," in *A Companion to Women in the Ancient World* (ed. S. L. James and S. Dillon; Chichester: Wiley Blackwell, 2012), 385–399.

69. Racine and Beaumont, "Three Approaches," 116.

70. Batten, "More Queries for Q," 44–51.

71. Batten, "More Queries for Q," 47.

72. Batten, "More Queries for Q," 47.

73. Batten, "More Queries for Q," 49.

74. Batten, "More Queries for Q," 46–47.

75. See Batten, "More Queries for Q," 44. On the changing and ameliorating situation of women in a cosmopolitan context (i.e., the Hellenistic and Republican periods), see Sharon L. James and Sheila Dillon, eds., *A Companion to Women in the Ancient World* (Chichester: Wiley Blackwell, 2012), especially 229–354.

76. Batten, "More Queries for Q," 49.

77. Batten, "More Queries for Q," 47.

78. Batten, "More Queries for Q," 49. On this, she sides with Corley, *Private Women, Public Meals* (see below).

79. See Hallett, "Women in Augustan Rome," 372–384.

80. See Hallett, "Women in Augustan Rome," 372–384, as well as Keith, "Women in Augustan Literature," 385–399.

81. Batten, "More Queries for Q," 49.

82. In both his legislation (see L. F. Raditsa, "Augustus' Legislation Concerning Marriage, Procreation, Love Affairs and Adultery," *ANRW* 2/13 [1980]: 278–339) and his state-commissioned literature (see Keith, "Women in Augustan Literature," 385–399).

83. Batten, "More Queries for Q," 49.

84. Corley's key works that touch on women and the Q document are: *Private Women, Public Meals* and *Women and the Historical Jesus*.

85. Corley, *Women and the Historical Jesus*, acknowledgements, n.p.

86. Corley, *Women and the Historical Jesus*.

87. Levine, "Who's Catering the Q Affair."

88. Levine, "Who's Catering the Q Affair," 146.

89. Levine, "Yeast of Eden," 302–331.

90. Levine, "Yeast of Eden," 307.

91. Levine, "Yeast of Eden," 303.

92. J. Plaskow, "Christian Feminism and Anti-Judaism," *Cross Currents* 33 (1978): 306–309.

93. J. Plaskow, "Feminist Anti-Judaism and the Christian God," *JFSR* 7/2 (1991): 106. See also Plaskow's "Anti-Judaism in Christian Feminist Interpretation," *Searching the Scriptures: A Feminist Introduction* (ed. E. Schüssler Fiorenza; New York: Crossroad, 1993), 7–29.

94. Levine, "Second-Temple Judaism, Jesus, and Women," 303. I agree wholeheartedly with Levine's critique of early feminist scholarship on women in Christianity as highly problematic with regard to its oversimplification of Judaism in its rush to uncover gender equality at the roots of the Christian tradition. Schüssler Fiorenza's afore-mentioned 1995 work *Jesus, Miriam's Child, Sophia's Prophet* is a refreshing corrective, as it addresses Christian anti-Judaism around Jesus and women directly.

95. See also Levine's 2002 article, "Matthew, Mark, and Luke: Good News or Bad?" in *Jesus, Judaism, and Christian Anti-Judaism* (ed. P. Fredriksen and A. Reinhartz; Louisville: Westminster John Knox, 2002), 77–98, which argues broadly that both modern interpretive biases and incomplete/conflicting ancient evidence work to complicate the issue of anti-Judaism in early Christian texts, although the article does not reflect on Q per se.

96. A.-J. Levine, "The Word Becomes Flesh: Jesus, Gender, and Sexuality," *The Historical Jesus in Recent Research* (ed. J. D. G. Dunn and S. McKnight; Winona Lake: Eisenbrauns, 2005), 516.

97. Levine, "The Word Becomes Flesh," 523.

98. Arnal, "Gendered Couplets in Q," 77.

99. Arnal, "Gendered Couplets in Q," 92.

100. See Arnal, *Jesus and the Village Scribes*, esp. 168ff.

101. Arnal, "Gendered Couplets in Q," 77.

102. Arnal, "Gendered Couplets in Q," 92.

103. Arnal, "Gendered Couplets in Q," 93.

104. Corley, *Women and the Historical Jesus*.

105. See Elliott, "Jesus was not an Egalitarian," 75–91 for a critique of scholars who, in Elliott's view, paint too rosy a picture of early Christianity at the expense of

historicity. Elliott calls, rightly, for a definition of "egalitarian" by any who choose to use the term (76).

106. M. A. Beavis, "Christian Origins, Egalitarianism, and Utopia," *JFSR* 23/2 (Fall 2007): 27.

107. Beavis, "Christian Origins," 27.

108. Beavis, "Christian Origins," 27.

109. Beavis, "Christian Origins," 46.

110. Beavis, "Christian Origins," 49.

111. Beavis, "Christian Origins," 27.

112. See, for example, Schüssler Fiorenza, *Discipleship of Equals*.

113. See, for example, E. Schüssler Fiorenza, *Jesus and the Politics of Interpretation* (New York: Continuum, 2000), 128, as well as *Jesus, Miriam's Child, Sophia's Prophet,* esp. 67–96.

114. Schottroff, "The Sayings Source Q," 510.

Chapter 4

Gendered Pairs in Q

Taxonomy and Analysis

DEFINITIONS

The literary devices in Q of particular interest to us consist of an equal juxtaposition of masculine and feminine concepts and/or masculine and feminine characters within parables[1] or short sayings. Whatever their various conclusions, all of the scholars mentioned in the previous chapter note this tendency of Q to remember Jesus as a teacher who deliberately positioned male and female genders side by side in his parables and sayings. According to Schottroff, Fricker, Racine, Batten, and Corley, this gendered juxtaposition functions to plant—and/or perhaps to mirror—a notion of parity among female and male recipients of the sayings material. This question of whether the presence in Jesus' *logia* of these rhetorically crafted references to the masculine and the feminine is as a *result* of women already existing in the movement or is as a *catalyst* or invitation to women to join the movement may not be answerable, but is certainly captivating. Either way, everyday Galilean women's experiences are reflected in these parables, from carding wool and spinning it into cloth, to sweeping the floor, to kneading bread dough.

This chapter sets out a taxonomy and description of the primary ancient texts[2] that are at stake in the debate over what gendered pairing in Q might mean for women. For clarity, I have separated the texts into two major generic categories: examples where the gender-pairing tendency in Q is expressed in binary sets of parables (short narratives with two levels of meaning) and other times when it is shown in briefer binary phrases.

In the first instance—sets of parables—two highly similar short narratives that teach an identical lesson are reiterated in succession, once using feminine examples and once using masculine examples. In one half of each pair (sometimes the first half and other times the second), the protagonist is a woman or women or the subject is some task[3] that is related to first-century women's daily lives. In the other half of each pair, the protagonist is a man or men or the subject is some task or object that is related to first-century men's daily lives. In each set of repeated lessons, key lines are repeated verbatim.

In addition to the frequent verbatim similarities in the wording of the two successive parables, and their generally parallel narrative structures (each parable is essentially the same story, with different characters and setting), a few elements of the parable are set up as variables or variations. The variables represent a different example with which to illustrate the same lesson. *The main variable in the pairs is always gendered* (e.g., the man who loses the sheep, the woman who loses the coin). The gendered variables stand in the same symbolic location within each teaching pericope. Given that each half of the pair of parables teaches the same lesson, the gendered portions do not have the effect of setting the genders apart from each other[4]—quite the opposite. I argue that the parallel didactic contents of the juxtaposed pairs have the effect of *equating* the genders.

In addition to these gendered narrative/parable sets, there is a second type of gendered pairing that also occurs in Q. In this secondary type of pairing, a brief *phrase* including both a masculine and a feminine element such as "sons and daughters" is used, when the masculine element alone (such as "sons") would normally be allowed to suffice. These briefer pairs again signal an attempt to mention women alongside men. The simplest inference we can make from these repeated cases of pairing is that these sayings mean to include women as intended recipients, and in doing so acknowledge women as preexisting community members.

Throughout this book, I refer to the former sort of pairing (twinned stories) using terms such as "full pairs," "parable pairs," or some similar label. The latter, briefer sort (e.g., "sons and daughters") will be referred to as the "shorter pairs." Terms like "gender pairs" or "the pairs" can refer to either type of pairing. Immediately below, all the pairs are laid out, grouped into categories, and analyzed. At the end of this chapter, we will see how both sides of the debate discussed in the previous chapter can be reconciled—with the introduction of greater precision around *what sort of equality* is (and isn't) present in the texts.

Full Pairs

In what I call the full pairs, the gendered variable can be present either literally or figuratively. In other words, gender is sometimes conveyed in the plain sense of the text (i.e., a male protagonist in one parable and a female protagonist in the other), while, at other times, gender is only indirectly implied by the content and context (i.e., a male-associated activity or topic in one and a female-associated activity or topic in the other). In some cases, the concept of gender is reinforced in both of these ways within the same pair.

My definition of a full parallel parable pair includes each component from letters (a) to (d) in the following list. Complete gender pairs

a) are a set of two short parables that
b) teach the same lesson
c) in a verbally parallel manner
d) wherein one parable highlights masculinity and the other femininity, either:
   i. literally (i.e., a male protagonist and a female protagonist), or
   ii. indirectly (i.e., a male-associated activity or topic and a female-associated activity or topic), or
   iii. both literally and figuratively (i.e., a male protagonist is also performing a masculine task and a female protagonist is also performing a feminine task).

By way of illustration, we can take a brief look at the twin Q parables of the lost sheep and the lost coin (Q 15:4–5a and 7–9):

> Which man[5] is there among you who has a hundred sheep, on losing one of them, will not leave the ninety-nine in the mountains, and go hunt for the lost one? And if it should happen that he finds it, I say to you that he rejoices over it more than over the ninety-nine that did not go astray.
>
> Or what woman who has ten coins, if she were to lose one coin, would not light a lamp and sweep the house and hunt until she finds? And on finding she calls the friends and neighbors, saying: Rejoice with me, for I found the coin which I had lost. (Q 15:4–5a, 7–9)

In this example, the parable about a man who has a hundred sheep and loses one is coupled with the parable about a woman who has ten coins and loses one. In both cases, what has been lost—although a small portion of the whole—is diligently sought and is recovered in the end, and rejoicing ensues. These two parables, taken together, fill all of the criteria required to form a full parallel pair, gendered in both form and content (i.e., gender is both overt and implied):

- They both teach the same lesson (about valuing what is lost, even if what is lost is but a minority of the whole);
- They are largely verbally parallel (which man/what woman, who has a hundred sheep/who has ten coins, losing/lose, will not . . . hunt/would not . . . hunt, he finds it/on finding, rejoicing/rejoice);

- The *variable* in each parable has to do with gender, both literally, as the first protagonist is a man and the second a woman, and indirectly, as shepherding is a task undertaken in a typically masculine realm,[6] while caring for the home is a typically feminine task.[7]

Thus, the companion parables about the lost sheep and the lost coin form a "full pair."

I have developed a further taxonomy for referring to the various configurations of these full pairs, based on *how* the text conveys gender. According to my analysis, there are eight full parable pairs in Q. In three cases, the gender is mentioned overtly. An example of this is Q 11:31–32, where the protagonist is a foreign woman from Israel's literary past in one half of the parable pair (i.e., "The Queen of the South") and a group of foreign men from Israel's literary past in the other (i.e., "Ninevite men"). In two cases, the gender is not overtly mentioned, but is only indirectly implied by the contents of the parables, such as in Q 12:24 and 27, where sowing crops is juxtaposed with spinning wool in the parable pair of the ravens and the lilies. There, no human protagonists exist; instead the female-associated topic of spinning is juxtaposed with the male-associated activity of farming. Finally, in three cases, the gender is both overt *and* implied, such as in the parables of the lost coin and the lost sheep (Q 15:4–5a, 7–9), where the male protagonist also performs the masculine task of shepherding and the female protagonist also performs the feminine task of housekeeping. I have described these differences among the full parallel parable pairs with the following subcategories: (a) the full pair, gender overt; (b) the full pair, gender implied; and (c) the double full pair, gender overt and implied.

Shorter Pairs

The other literary devices present in Q—the shorter pairs—also juxtapose gender in such a way as to include both feminine and masculine. These shorter pairs may be less complex, but they still merit mention. Such mini-pairs in the sayings material are stand-alone phrases that mention male and female counterparts, such as "brothers and sisters" or "fathers and mothers." In these cases, the masculine alone would normally have sufficed, according to typical usage in the literature of the day (in any language). Referring to groups of people in the plural in the ancient Mediterranean world does not require the feminine at all. The masculine plurals of words like "Jews," "brothers," "sons of Israel," or "disciples" generally suffice and can be interpreted as either including women without having to mention them or as simply excluding women altogether.[8] The several instances in Q where phrases appear that take care to include both the feminine and the masculine noun are unusual. They reinforce the notion that there is an interest in gender behind the sayings material of Jesus, especially when these minor examples are taken together with the more concerted juxtapositions of gender seen in the full pairs.

In an effort to be exhaustive, I include in my analysis some *potential* gendered Q pairs. Potential pairs include those that are not overtly gendered, but for which an argument in favor of gender parallelism can be made. In addition, I have included some pairs that are outside the critical edition of Q because they have survived only in one witness. Given that the critical edition reconstructs Q with a highly cautious approach that errs on the side of minimalism, it is highly probable that gender pairs that occur only in one Gospel may nonetheless go back to Q (just as Markan pericopes that only occur in one Synoptic Gospel nonetheless originate in Mark). Where other scholars have argued for the inclusion of a gender pair in Q, and I agree with their arguments, I have included that pair here too. (This is the case with the parables of the persistent friend and persistent widow, found in Luke 11:5–8 and Luke 18:1–8.)

Taxonomy: Full Pairs

It should by now be clear that all of the scholars in the conversation agree on the importance of extricating the discussion of the paired gender sayings from their Christian Testament context, and instead approaching them in their context in the sayings source. Among these researchers, two in particular have made concerted attempts to collect and classify all of the full parable Q pairs, namely, Arnal in his 1997 article,[9] and Fricker in his 2004 monograph.[10] Additionally, Dieter Roth has produced a monograph on Q parables in general.[11] Arnal and Fricker have laid the groundwork for the following taxonomy of pairs, but I have expanded it and clustered the pairs according to my own categories of whether the gender is implied, overt, or both implied and overt (see table 4.1).

Taxonomy: Shorter Pairs

In addition to the above full parallel parable pairings are a number of the aforementioned short phrases in Q that include parallel male and female examples. As mentioned, these brief pairings are not complete didactic pericopes, with one lesson having a male example and the other a female example, rather they are short phrases that nonetheless make a point of mentioning a masculine component and a feminine component. As such, they provide an additional example where the inclusion of a male and a female example is not seemingly integral to the sense of the passage in Q, and yet some sort of care is taken to include both. The following table includes the shorter pairs

Table 4.1   Full Pairs

Q 12:24, 27	Ravens, lilies	Full parallel parable pair	gender implied
Q 11:11–12	Bread, fish	Full parallel parable pair	gender implied
Luke 4:25–27	Widows, lepers	Full parallel parable pair	gender overt
Luke 11:5–8/ Luke 18:2–5	Persistent friend, persistent widow	Full parallel parable pair	gender overt
Q 11:31–32	Queen of the south, Ninevite men	Full parallel parable pair	gender overt
Q 13:18–21	Mustard seed, yeast	Double-full parallel parable pair	gender both overt and implied
Q 15:4–5a, 7–9	Lost sheep, lost coin	Double-full parallel parable pair	gender both overt and implied
Q 17:34–35	Two men, two women	Double-full parallel parable pair	gender both overt and implied

Table 4.2   Shorter Pairs

Q 7:29–30	Tax collectors and prostitutes
Q 7:32	Fluting and wailing
Q 12:53	Division in the household
Q 14:26	Parents and children

roughly in the order in which they may have appeared in the sayings source (see table 4.2).

TEXT AND ANALYSIS OF EACH FULL PAIR

Gender Implied

The two full pairs wherein the gender is only implied are the parables of the ravens and lilies and the parables of the bread and the fish. In these pairs, the gendered variables are not indicated literally by the gender of the protagonists, but are rather implied indirectly by the presence of other elements associated with gender, such as tasks normally undertaken primarily by either the men or the women of the day.

Q 12:24, 27 Ravens/Lilies

> Consider the ravens: They neither sow nor reap nor gather into barns, and yet God feeds them. Are you not better than the birds?
> Consider[12] the lilies, they neither card[13] nor toil nor spin; yet I tell you: Not even Solomon in all his glory was arrayed like one of these. (Q 12:24, 27)

The paired parables of the ravens and the lilies appear in Schottroff's list of Q pairs, but Arnal does not include them as a gendered pairing. He writes that, because Solomon is a man, Schottroff "incorrectly adduces" that this is a pair.[14] Arnal is clearly mistaken; his mistake lies in his assumption about which part of the parable constitutes the gendered variable. The gender-variable component of the pair is not in the part about Solomon. Instead, it is the *tasks* of sowing and reaping, versus carding and spinning, that make up the parable's gendered parts. Dillon explains, "in complementary parallelism, the labors of which birds and flowers are spared, agriculture (sow, reap, etc.) and needlework (toil, spin), are the occupations of men and women respectively."[15] Sowing and reaping are types of work associated with the male gender in Mediterranean antiquity,[16] whereas the association between spinning and the female gender for this period could not be stronger.[17] Solomon, on the other hand, is an incidental character in a secondary part of the lesson—a descriptive detail rather than a major variable. In other words, this pair is a full parable pair, but with the gender implied rather than overt.

That both a woman's work of spinning and a man's work of sowing are mentioned in the parallel pair shows an awareness on the part of the author/editor/speaker of the concerns of both male and female audience members. The lesson of the parable is that labor, whether it is the work of women or of men, is not to be credited as the source of provision and blessing in the world of the *basileia*. Instead, the listener is meant to acknowledge that blessings and provisions ultimately come from God, as do the meals of the birds and the garments of the flowers. In this way, the pair of parables accomplishes a double rhetorical goal: it lifts up women's tasks as equally worthy of mention as men's tasks while simultaneously pointing beyond the earthly work of both women and men and calling both women and men to acknowledge God as provider. Additionally, God, too, performs both masculine and feminine tasks in this parable pair, providing both clothing and crops.[18] Both the feminine role of spinning cloth and the masculine role of sowing crops are imbued with value by having been taken over by God on behalf of those who do not worry.

It should be noted at the same time, that this pair of parables works within the parameters of existing first-century gendered occupations. The pairs do not seem to suggest a social equality that would, for instance, see women sowing and men spinning cloth. That is, rather than functioning to transform gender roles on a social level, the way in which the pairs imply gendered equality is on a spiritual and/or religious level. Both the women who spin and the men who sow are individuals who are beholden to an attitude of piety that acknowledges God as provider, and thus both have agency in their own religious lives in the *basileia* community. Still, as Johnson and Tannehill point out, there is nevertheless an element of social change being supported by the rhetoric of the pairs: although neither gender is called away from their socially gendered occupational roles, both men and women, together, are encouraged to be less concerned about economic endeavors and everyday needs.[19]

Q 11:11–12 Bread/Fish

> What person[20] of you, whose son[21] asks him for bread, will give him a stone?
> Or again when he asks for a fish, will give him a snake? (Q 11:11–12)

I posit that this pair, which occurs in both Matthew (7:9–10) and Luke (11:11–12), with small variations, may constitute another Q pair in which the gender is implied, rather than overt. The repetitive nature of the saying "asks for x . . . will give him y // asks for c . . . will give him d" indicates that parallelism is at play. Because bread-making was a task associated with women,[22] and fishing a task associated with men,[23] an argument can be made for including this parallel parable pair among the gendered pairs originating in Q. Although this paired saying is very brief, I include it here rather than among the shorter pairs, since despite its brevity it is nonetheless a little lesson—symbolic and didactic. The two parallel lines, one evoking a first-century man's task and one evoking a first-century woman's task, both ask a rhetorical question in which the elements, in addition to their literal meaning, stand in metaphorically for some aspect of life among members of the *basileia* movement. Although the reference to gender is subtle—only the parallel terms "bread" and "fish" have any connection to gender roles—the fact that other instances of parallelism in Jesus' sayings material often refer to gender strengthens the possibility that this is true here as well, in the case of this Matthean and Lukan paired saying of Jesus.

Gender Overt

The pairs in this second section, unlike those just examined, do not rely on a knowledge of gender-based divisions of labor in first-century Palestine. Instead, their references to gender are direct. Here a specifically female widow (Zarephath) is juxtaposed with a specifically male leper (Naaman), a pestering woman is paired with a pestering man, and a foreign Queen from Israel's literary past is doubled by a group of foreign (masculine) Ninevites from the book of Jonah.

Luke 4:25–27 Many Widows including Zarephath/ Many Lepers including Naaman

> But in truth, I tell you, there were many widows [πολλαὶ χῆραι] in Israel in the days of Elijah, when the heaven was shut up three years and six months, when

there came a great famine over all the land; and Elijah was sent to none of them but only to Zarephath, in the land of Sidon, to a woman who was a widow.

And there were many lepers [πολλοὶ λεπροὶ] in Israel in the time of the prophet Elisha; and none of them was cleansed, but only Naaman the Syrian. (Luke 4:25–27 RSV)

This full parable pair makes overt reference to gender. "Widows (feminine plural πολλαὶ χῆραι) in Israel" are juxtaposed with "lepers (masculine plural πολλοὶ λεπροὶ) in Israel." Both are traditionally disadvantaged groups—in antiquity, in general, and in the texts that came to form the Hebrew Bible, specifically.[24] In each lesson, only one individual from the greater group is the recipient of prophetic blessing: Elijah is sent to Zarephath, one widow out of many, in Sidon, to help her during a time of famine, and Elisha is sent to Naaman of Syria, one leper out of many, to cleanse him from his leprosy.

The plot twist in both cases is that the disadvantaged individual who receives divinely sanctioned assistance from Israel's God is an "outsider" to Israel. The parable thus implies that blessing in the *basileia* is not automatically bestowed on the merit of being an insider, since a Sidonite and a Syrian are the beneficiaries here. More importantly for our purposes, the pairing of these parables indicates, with equal force, that both women and men are eligible for this type of help; the effect of the rhetoric is that being of a certain gender is not a relevant prerequisite for privilege and blessing. One's gender neither guarantees nor precludes divine assistance.

The lesson in this pair is similar to that of the pair that will be discussed below—that of the Queen of the South and the Ninevite men (Q 11:31–32). In that text, in a similar way, possessing a privileged status within the people of Israel does not guarantee blessing; instead, there are other criteria at play by which even non-Jews/outsiders can achieve high status in God's *basileia*. Of course, the function may be less a welcome of outsiders into the *basileia* and more an antidote to smug self-confidence of insiders, as foreigners often function as chastising examples to insiders in Hebrew Bible and early Jewish writings. In any case, by employing the figures of both poor Sidonite widows and high-class Syrian lepers, both royal Southerners and average Ninevites, these sayings are showing that insider/outsider status, socio-economic status, geography, and gender are *all* irrelevant as criteria of eligibility for divine notice.

Both halves of this parable pair of the widows and the lepers occur in Luke; neither portion occurs in Matthew. Because of its commitment to caution, and its minimalist methodology, the critical edition of Q does not include this pair.[25] Thus, this pair with the widow from Sidon and the leper from Syria are included in Brice Jones' handy collection of material unique to Luke; however, Jones is careful to state that his "inclusion of these particular passages is not meant to suggest that some of the material cannot possibly be assigned to Q."[26] I include it here because its absence from Matthew by no means indicates conclusively that it was not present in Q, especially given its Q-like format. My proposal to include this pair in Q is based on the not-implausible premise that Matthew and Luke would have used the sayings source in much the same way that they used their other source, Mark. About 90 percent of Mark appears in *either* Matthew *or* Luke.[27] However, if we did not have Mark, and had to reconstruct it—as we do Q—from Matthew and Luke alone, we would lose 44 percent of it if we only preserved the bits of Mark that appear in both gospels. David Sloan has calculated our loss of Markan verses if it were reconstructed using only the double tradition, as was the critical edition of Q:

> 290 of Mark's verses (44%) are unparalleled in either Matthew or Luke. [. . .] Note that these statistics do not reflect verses that are partially paralleled in Matthew or Luke. Even more of Mark is omitted in one gospel or the other if we consider Mark's gospel at a clausal level.[28]

It stands to reason that if the Matthean and Lukan methods for the incorporation of Q sayings are similar to their methods for incorporating Mark (and we have no reason to assume they would treat one source drastically differently from the other), it then becomes much more likely that the paired gender parable of the widows and the lepers goes back to Q, even if Matthew, in this case, did not see fit to use this pair. Further, given the fact that in the grand scheme of Luke/Acts, the authorial effect overall is to weaken Q's gender-leveling,[29] it does not seem necessary to assume Luke coined one or both parables to create a new gender pair. I therefore believe it to be quite possible that the widows/lepers pair belongs among the authentic sayings of Jesus, as remembered in Q.

Luke 11:5–8/Luke 18:2–5 Persistent Friend/Persistent Widow

> And he said to them [πρὸς αὐτούς], "Which of you who has a friend [φίλον] will go to him at midnight and say to him, 'Friend, lend me three loaves; for a friend of mine has arrived on a journey, and I have nothing to set before him'; and he will answer from within, 'Do not bother me; the door is now shut, and my children are with me in bed; I cannot get up and give you anything'? I tell you, though he will not get up and give him anything because he is his friend, yet because of his importunity he will rise and give him whatever he needs." (Luke 11:5–8 RSV)

> He said, "In a certain city there was a judge who neither feared God nor regarded man; and there was a widow [χήρα] in that city who kept coming to him and saying, 'Vindicate me against my adversary.' For a while he refused;

but afterward he said to himself, 'Though I neither fear God nor regard man, yet because this widow bothers me, I will vindicate her, or she will wear me out by her continual coming.'" (Luke 18:2–5 RSV)

Matthew's Gospel does not contain this set of parables; again, both are known to us only through Luke. For this reason, they were not included in the critical edition of Q. However, they were nevertheless granted a blank page in the text; obviously, at least one editor suspected they went back to the early sayings tradition. (The page for Q 11:5–8 exists in Q, but is virtually blank, save the brief and honest footnote: "Is Luke 11:5–8 in Q?")[30] Since then, Sloan has argued convincingly (because the use of the phrase "τίς ἐξ ὑμῶν" is virtually exclusive to Q and to those who use Q in all of Greek antiquity) that for text-critical reasons this pair should be included in the original sayings tradition.[31] In addition to Sloan's impressive text-critical arguments, many other scholars have also pushed, on other grounds, for the inclusion of these parables among early (authentic) sayings material.[32] Merz asserts that "the overwhelming majority of exegetes are right" to view the parable of the widow and the judge as "an evolved text which displays clear traces of a series of interpretations" between their original context in Jesus' teaching and their setting in Luke.[33]

The two lessons clearly form a full parallel parable pair, gender overt, as they both teach the same lesson and contain a feminine and a masculine example. The widow, the gender variable in the second parable, is specifically feminine (χήρα), whereas the friend, who is the gender variable in the first parable is specifically masculine (φίλον). For the same redaction-critical reasons given for the previous Lukan pairing—the widows and the lepers (Luke 4:25–27)—I include this as a probable Q pair as well. If the passages were unique to Luke and he had deliberately crafted such a parallel pair, one would be hard pressed to explain why they are not recorded together in the Lukan text. Why would Luke have created a pairing, only to separate it?

Elisabeth Schüssler Fiorenza also highlights these two texts—the persistent widow and the persistent friend—as a gender pair original to Q/Jesus.[34] Schüssler Fiorenza views the parables proper as original Jesus material, but maintains that this authenticity definitely does not extend to their book-ended lead-up and commentary in Luke's Gospel. According to her, the bookends attached to the pair in the present gospel context are Lukan additions that *alter the meaning significantly, and deliberately*. In Luke, the parable of the persistent friend is sandwiched between discussions of prayer, forcing the reluctant sleeping character to become a symbol for God. Likewise, Lukan additions to the parable of the "Persistent Widow" similarly force the uncaring judge into God's position, a difficulty which was also noted by Herzog.[35] Schüssler Fiorenza regards Luke 18:6–8 as a Lukan framing—and taming—of the original parable pair:

> And the Lord said, "Hear what the unrighteous judge says. And will not God vindicate his elect, who cry to him day and night? Will he delay long over them? I tell you, he will vindicate them speedily. Nevertheless, when the Son of man comes, will he find faith on earth?" (Luke 18:6–8 RSV)

Both Merz[36] and Schüssler Fiorenza argue that the addition of verses 6 to 8 innovates a connection of the uncaring friend and unjust judge with God, not only depicting God in a surprisingly negative light but also giving those unsavory characters all the power. The message in Luke becomes, in Schüssler Fiorenza's words, "pray harder, but don't mess with the system."[37] According to Merz, the Lukan addition of verses 6 to 8 "can be plausibly explained as toning down" what was originally a "politically explosive message."[38]

Remove this guiding frame, though, and the meaning of these parables becomes quite different, and consistent with other parts of Q. The parables without the bookends are not about prayer at all, but rather about demanding justice, even if it makes one appear disruptive or annoying. Indeed, I would argue that the statement that the judge "has no fear of God" makes the Lukan rendition, where the character of the judge is meant to be a stand-in for God, acutely problematic, as it is highly unlikely that Jesus would have depicted God so negatively and with such convoluted self-reference. Luke's framing of the parables goes against their internal grain, in order to force a different reading (perhaps a reading more palatable to an elite post-destruction audience)—a reading that carefully deflects possible associations with subversion and uprising and encourages political inaction except in the form of prayer.

Amy-Jill Levine agrees that this widow has been "domesticated" by Luke.[39] Levine demonstrates that the trope of the widow in the Hebrew Bible and other earlier Jewish literature most often reverses the expected widow's role of helplessness and instead epitomizes strength and cleverness.[40] She contrasts this literary norm against the "importuning widow" as portrayed in Luke (as opposed to Q), who is "more 'woman on her knees' than 'woman with a fist.' Luke nicely tucks the widow of the parable within other conventional images of poor, dependent, or powerless widows."[41] When we look at the pared-down pair as it may have appeared in Q, the message is markedly different. There, the fact that both a male and a female example are given indicates emphatically that agents of the *basileia* come in both male and female packages, and that both men and women can effect positive changes by persistently speaking up about their needs, whether for bread or for justice.

As in the case of the son asking for bread and fish in Q 11:11–12, there is some grammatical androcentrism at play here, insofar as a masculine third-person plural is used to describe the listeners in the first parable: "And he said to them [πρὸς αὐτούς]." This, of course, is quite standard for the Greek language (or, for that matter, for many languages both antique and modern) and cannot be used to argue that no women were present. Yet despite its unremarkable nature, this grammatical usage still speaks to an inherently male-centered worldview in the text. The androcentric language at the outset of this parable pair means that even if we agree with Schüssler Fiorenza and Levine that the emphasis on prayer, which downplays women's agency in the parable, is entirely Lukan, and that the emphasis of the original sayings was likely a gender-equal call to persistence in pursuing justice in the face of an unjust system, that this unjust system is not gender inequality. The androcentrism throughout Q serves to remind us that the patriarchy is not the system against which *basileia* members are being encouraged to fight in these parables.

This instance of male-centered language in the pair supports the position of what I earlier termed "Perspective 2," but the example of the widow/friend pair also supports the positions of the other two groups. It does so because of its insistence on having both a male and a female protagonist teach the same lesson. The widow functions, as with the other gender pairs, in such a way as to imply that women are included as important agents of the *basileia* movement, even as this particular pair at the same time excludes them in some of its typically androcentric grammar.

Q 11:31–32 The Queen of the South and the Ninevite Men

> The Queen of the South will be raised at the judgment with this generation and condemn it, for she came from the ends of the earth to listen to the wisdom of Solomon, and look, something more than Solomon is here!
>
> Ninevite men [ἄνδρες] will arise at the judgment with this generation and condemn it, for they repented at the announcement of Jonah, and look, something more than Jonah is here! (Q 11:31–32)

This pair, taken directly from the critical edition of Q (and found in both Matthew and Luke), is another full parable[42] pair, gender overt. The strong parallelism in Q 11:31–32 is visible at a verbal level, in the near-exact repetition of the following phrases: "will be raised/will arise," "at the judgment with this generation and condemn it, for" and "and look, something more than Solomon/Jonah is here." The sections that stray from verbatim repetition are, as usual, the alternately male and female protagonists, and the briefest of summaries of their earlier narrative contexts, the famous Queen from the books of 1 Kings (10:1–13) and 2 Chronicles (9:1–12) and the Ninevite men from the tale of Jonah (3:5, etc.).

In addition to the careful verbal parallelism is the parallel *content* of the lessons. The characters in both parables are foreigners from Israel's literary past, one a woman and the other a group of men (their maleness specifically noted by the word ἄνδρες). Although these characters are not from among the people of Israel, the parables nonetheless have them being "raised at the judgment with this generation and [they] condemn it." The foreigners, alternately male and female, are used in the double parable as a didactic device to shame "this generation" and presumably to generate apocalyptic awareness. That is to say, even though these figures from texts that would come to form the Hebrew Bible were not the expected heroes in their stories, because of their outsider status, they behaved in such a way as to merit praise and to raise their standing with the God of Israel. In the case of the Queen of Sheba, she listened to and acted upon Solomon's wisdom, and in the case of the men of Nineveh, they listened to and acted upon Jonah's prophecy. In both cases, it is assumed that "this generation," unlike the male and female examples being held up in the parables, is behaving incorrectly by not listening to the wisdom/prophecy of the day, that is, "something even bigger than" Solomon and Jonah. Pairing these two parables, which teach an identical lesson, but one of which features the Queen and the other the Ninevite men, functions to indicate that no matter one's Jewish status and no matter one's gender, one can achieve high status in the *basileia* movement by listening to, and acting upon, Jesus' wisdom.

Gender Both Overt and Implied

Q 13:18–21 Mustard Seed/Yeast

> What is the *basileia* of God like, and with what am I to compare it? It is like a seed of mustard, which a man[43] took and threw into his garden. And it grew and developed into a tree, and the birds of the sky nested in its branches.
> And again: With what am I to compare the *basileia* of God? It is like yeast, which a woman [γυνὴ] took and hid in three measures of flour until it was fully fermented. (Q 13:18–21)

Unlike the rest of the parable pairs covered in this book, one half of this pair occurs in Mark! The mustard seed is in Mark 4:30–32. Both Luke and Matthew have it as well and add the yeast immediately following it. Zeba Crook has covered the ramifications for the Synoptic problem of this Markan appearance, and concludes, after weighing each explanation for the three-way overlap, that the two-source hypothesis remains the least problematic, although all hypotheses are imperfect.[44]

In these two short lessons on the nature of the *basileia* of God as they appear in Matthew and Luke, the parallelism is evident. In both cases, the teacher presents a simile with which to illustrate God's rule: "It is like *x*, which (someone) took and *y*." In each case, the item of comparison is something that begins tiny—almost imperceptible—and grows into something not only noticeable, but useful and positive—shelter and food. The minuscule mustard seed grows into a large plant, which houses the birds, and the teeny amount of yeast aids in the bread-making process causing dough to grow large and ready to be baked into bread.

These two stories again follow the over-riding characteristic of the gender pairs, which is that a marked variable in two otherwise largely parallel accounts is gender. The lesson of the yeast features a woman (γυνή), and the lesson of the mustard seed features a man. In this case, the two characters' genders are reinforced by their activities: sowing is a task that was traditionally performed by men,[45] while baking was traditionally performed by women,[46] making this a double full parable pair, with the gender being both overt and implied.

In some ways, the gender pairs imply a certain inclusivity for women by their very existence; this one, though, has an added feature that makes it especially attractive for feminist readings. Levine grants that, in Q's depictions of women baking bread or grinding at a flour mill, "women's work is acknowledged."[47] And added to this simple recognition of tasks normally performed by women is the fact that, in these particular parables of the yeast and the mustard seed, the concept for which the gendered variables stand in is an unequivocally positive one; the man's sowing and the woman's kneading make them agents of the *basileia*. As Schüssler Fiorenza has pointed out, the fact that a woman appears as an active participant in the spread and growth of the *basileia* lends itself to a highly positive interpretation of her intended agency in the text, from a feminist-theological point of view.[48] A similar example of the activities of a woman or women being likened to the activities of God occurs in the parable of the lost coin (below).[49] Schottroff, too, points out the positive feminist implications of a task so closely associated with women in the household, and here performed by a woman, being explicitly associated with God's actions.[50] Such an illustration serves to value women as potentially equal spiritual and religious agents of the Jesus movement. These pairs are good illustrations of why I take a middle position in the scholarship on women and the gender pairs: the actions of women in these two cases are undoubtedly positive and serve to show God's (here woman-positive) actions in the *basileia*. At the same time, since the woman is not sowing and the man is not kneading, socially gendered roles do not disappear altogether in Q's world.

Q 15:4–5a, 7–9 Lost Sheep and Lost Coin

Which man[51] is there among you who has a hundred sheep, on losing one of them, will not leave the ninety-nine in the mountains, and go hunt for the lost one? And if it should happen that he finds it, I say to you that he rejoices over it more than over the ninety-nine that did not go astray.

Or what woman who has ten coins, if she were to lose one coin, would not light a lamp and sweep the house and hunt until she finds? And on finding she calls the friends and neighbors, saying: Rejoice with me, for I found the coin which I had lost. (Q 15:4–5a, 7–9)

Here we have another set of parallel parables. While the parable of the sheep appears in both Luke and Matthew, the parable of the coin only appears in Luke. Nonetheless, pairs scholars and other Q scholars agree that it is original to Q and not Luke, and it appears in the critical edition.[52] Arnal concurs that "there are good grounds for regarding it [the coin parable] as having been derived from Q and omitted by Matthew"[53] and points out that Luke introduces *both* parables with the singular την παραβολην ταύτην, "an indication that he regarded them, and received them, as a single unit."[54] The arguments I have made previously for considering material outside the critical edition of Q, when it comes to parallel parable pairs, seem supported by this particular example's wide-spread acceptance.

In this pair of parables, both characters lose a small portion of their complete wealth: the man has a hundred sheep and loses one, and the woman has ten coins and loses one. In each case, the protagonist considers the relatively small loss to be of great importance nonetheless and goes out of his/her way to scour the surroundings until what was lost has been recovered. In each case, the small percentage that is lost is the focus of the parable, rather than the larger balance of the wealth that remains safe. This is evidenced by the great rejoicing, once the lost element has been located and returned. As with the mustard seed/yeast parable, in this pair of stories there is also an additional reinforcing layer of genderedness, beyond the simple juxtaposition of τίς ἄνθρωπος with τίς γυνὴ, since the man is out with the sheep in the traditionally male[55] arena of the field, and the woman is keeping house, in the traditionally female arena of domestic life.[56] This example therefore constitutes another double full parable pair, with the gender being both overt and also reinforced by the gendered task and setting.

These two parables, as they have come down to us in this case, are not strictly verbally parallel. When the man retrieves the sheep, he "rejoices more over it than the ninety-nine that did not go astray." For literary balance, we might expect the woman's found money to result in her "rejoicing more over it than the nine that were not lost" or some such. The woman indeed rejoices, but she prefers to do so collectively; the text reports that she "calls the friends and neighbors, saying 'rejoice with me.'" The fact that this gender pair is not carefully parallel actually militates against Arnal's argument that the reason these pairs exist has nothing to do with gender and more to do with a penchant for stylistic variations on a theme in connection with Galilean Jewish scribal culture.[57] If the author/s or editor/s of this pair were interested more in wordplay around gender than in actual gender diversity in the text and its audience, then the wordplay could easily have been more artfully consistent.

Again, this is a pairing in which the woman and the man both function in the same variable location in the parables; while not interchangeable in terms of societal roles (i.e., they are performing typically gendered social tasks), they are certainly equal variables in the rhetorical and didactic world of the parables in which they stand. In this way, this pair reinforces the notion that the same religious or intellectual lesson can be applied equally to all wo/men, whereas, yet again, no similar attempt is made toward a leveling of social expectations in terms of gendered tasks.

Q 17:34–35 Two Men/Two Women

> I tell you, there will be two men [δύο] in the field; one [εἷς] is taken and one [εἷς] is left.
> Two women [δύο] will be grinding at the mill; one [μία] is taken and one [μία] is left. (Q 17:34–35)

Despite their relative brevity, these two texts nonetheless represent a full pair. In fact, they are a double full pair, with the gender both overt and implied. The two men of the first situation are juxtaposed with two women in the second,[58] signifying overt gendering, while additional implied gendering is presented through the sowing, which can be connected with "men's work,"[59] and the grinding of grain, which can be connected with "women's work."[60] In the Lukan version, the two men are in bed at night rather than in a field, but they work better as a pair in the Q version, where having the men in the field strengthens the gendered nature of the variables, and the parallelism is more balanced as each line represented an important social and economic task, whether sowing/harvesting crops or grinding flour.

In both cases, one of the two characters is "taken," while the other is "left behind," in the presumable context of apocalyptic judgment. This implies that one of the men and one of the women will be rewarded, while the other man and the other women will miss out. Or, conversely, one of the men and one of the women will be punished or destroyed, while the other man and the other woman will be spared. Either way, the fact that examples of both women and men are depicted as being somehow accountable for their own divine assessment at the time of judgment works to sustain my argument that the pairs imply an equality between the genders on a religious level. Even Arnal concludes from this saying that "the people responsible for Q quite self-consciously count women among culpable outsiders and hence imagine the judgment to pertain to them as well as to men. This would in turn be indicative of the presence of culpable or laudable women among 'insiders' as well."[61] Women are here depicted as being responsible for their own spiritual destinies in the same way as men. In the world of the text, both men and women are accountable for their own actions vis-à-vis eschatological salvation. The two women grinding at the mill are presented alone, unconnected in the text to any men, and yet one woman has behaved in such a way as to avoid eschatological destruction while the other has not.

TEXT AND ANALYSIS OF THE SHORTER PAIRS

In addition to the above companion parable pairs, with their carefully balanced male and female counterparts, there exists, as previously mentioned, a second type of gender-paired literary device in Q. As described above, I have dubbed these second, abbreviated versions of gender pairs the "shorter pairs." The shorter pairs consist of phrases that, despite their brevity, are nevertheless notable for including one male and one female component. Sons are mentioned alongside daughters, mothers alongside fathers, (male) tax collectors alongside (female) prostitutes, and so on.

Q 7:29–30 Tax Collectors and Prostitutes

For John came to you, and the tax collectors [τελῶναι] and [prostitutes?][62] responded positively, but the religious authorities rejected him.

In this saying, the unsavory group/s of characters in the first line are contrasted with the supposedly respectable and laudable group in the second line, but the unexpected has occurred yet again. These examples of socially marginalized male and female groups have responded correctly to John, but the religious leaders (referred to as Pharisees in Luke 7:30) responded incorrectly. The now-familiar Q theme of a reversal of expectations for what can happen to those who self-identify as Israel's insiders in the *basileia* recurs in this verse. If my tentative reconstruction is correct, then the two unsavory groups (male tax collectors and female prostitutes) could represent a small, but not insignificant, gender pair.

However, it is not at all certain whether these masculine plural tax collectors were matched by masculine plural sinners and/or feminine plural prostitutes in an earlier version of the saying or not, which makes a difference as to whether or not this saying ever took the form of a shorter gender pair. Many reconstructions of Q from the members of the International Q Project, including the critical edition, leave the second part of the pair blank; most Q texts merely read "tax collectors and . . ." since the reconstruction is not straightforward,[63] implying that they suspect the saying predates Matthew and Luke but are not able to reconcile its substantial variants. Matthew 21:32 has (male) tax collectors (τελῶναι) and (female) prostitutes (πόρναι)"[64] but its counterpart in Luke 7:39 has only the tax collectors. An argument similar to that made for Q 15:4–5, 7–9 above could be made here, but the critical edition does not do so. Perhaps this is because of other variants between Matthew and Luke's versions of the underlying Q text. Matthew does not have the second part of the saying, where Luke (7:30) chastises the Pharisees (φαρισαῖοι) and lawyers (νομικοί). Instead, Matthew 21:32 chastises the "you" of the implied audience: "you did not believe [John] but the tax collectors and prostitutes did."

There is a similar verse in Q that has been reconstructed more confidently because it appears the same in both Matthew (11:19) and Luke (7:34). There, the phrase is "tax collectors and sinners." It reads: "The son of humanity came, eating and drinking, and you say: Look! A person who is a glutton and drunkard, a chum of tax collectors and sinners!" (Q 7:34). However, this does not help to clarify the situation of our potential short gender pair where the stark difference between the Matthean and Lukan versions seems to block the reconstruction of the Q antecedent.

Corley argues that Matthew's "tax collectors and prostitutes" (Matt 21:32) is the more likely reading, precisely *because* it would make Q 7:29–30 a gender pair.[65] If this short pair were originally gendered, then Jesus is here associated with two groups of gendered sinners: male tax collectors and female prostitutes. This juxtaposition of two frowned-upon occupations, tax collection performed by men and sex work performed by women (as πόρναι is used), does fit well with the tendency to pair gendered tasks elsewhere in Q.

In a situation where such a form-critical decision must be made, the work presented so far in this book leads to a useful principal for the reconstruction of Q. In such a case, it is reasonably likely that if, as has been shown, there is a general tendency within Q toward such gendered pairings, and if, when Matthew and Luke vary, one possible reconstruction is a parallel gendered pair, then, I argue, that reconstruction may be preferred, if all else is equal. Each gospel writer has simply dropped one half of the example and has substituted a group of sinners that fits better with his gospel's aims. In the case of Luke, the function of the saying was to chastise Pharisees and lawyers, whereas Matthew was concerned with chastising the chief priests and elders, the Jerusalem leadership being a group well-known to be singled out for scorn in his gospel. (Matthew 21:23 situates Jesus' delivery of this string of parables in the temple.) If this is the case, then, as I suggest, it demonstrates that the earlier reading pays attention to the inclusion of female examples whereas the Gospel writers share an interest in using the saying, but disregard its gender pairing in favor of their own rhetorical goals. Even though the examples in this pair are socially negative examples, the inclusion of both genders would still indicate a measure of attention to the inclusion of women. Both men and women play an active role in their own deliverance by being capable, even eager, to respond to John. Although both can be held responsible for sins or at least for tasks perceived as socially unsavory such as tax collection and sex work, both can also be lauded for overcoming negative expectations and acknowledging wisdom when they see it.

Q 7:31–32 Fluting and Wailing

> To what am I to compare this generation and what is it like? It is like children seated in the marketplace who, addressing the others, say: We fluted for you, but you would not dance; we wailed, but you would not cry. (Q 7:31–32)

Although Fricker is of the opinion that this section of Q also follows the pattern of a *paire mixte* (his term for gendered parable pairs),[66] its format is a little different from what I call a full parable pair; rather than two separate parables, this segment could either be considered a single parable that contains a male and a female element within it (i.e., a shorter pair that happens to occur within a didactic pericope) or else two parables that are extremely short. The masculine and feminine elements are not overt, but rather are implied by the juxtaposed gendered concepts "fluting" and "wailing." Whether one views these verses as a single parable with two parts or as two tiny parables, the passage uses two adjacent comparisons to describe "this generation." The tentative allusion to gender would be easy enough to miss. However, the fact that Q is prone to gendered pairs, coupled with the fact that wailing is a component of mourning practices assigned to women in Greco-Roman antiquity[67] is enough to suggest that the pairing may have been intentionally gendered. However, although flute-playing *can* sometimes be connected with men, and this is attested in both literary and material evidence,[68] the presence of flute-girls (*auletrides*) in Greco-Roman antiquity is well-known as well.[69] Thus, despite Fricker's suggestion, and despite the proclivity of Q to gender-pairing, we cannot with confidence count this passage among the short Q sayings that pair masculine and feminine examples.

Q 12:51–53 Division in the Household

> Do you think that I have come to hurl peace on earth? I did not come to hurl peace, but a sword. For I have come to divide son against father, and daughter against her mother, and daughter-in-law against her mother-in-law. (Q 12:51–53)

In this passage, we see a list of three pairs: a parent–child bond between two male family members (son and father), a parent–child bond between two female family members (daughter and mother), and an in-law parent–child bond between women (daughter-in-law and mother-in-law). From a strictly literary angle, the pairs are not a perfectly balanced parallelism. For that to be the case, one more pair would be required—that of son-in-law and father-in-law. Of course, the reason for the lack of this fourth pairing is simple: these are examples drawn from daily life, and in daily life the relationship between father-in-law and son-in-law essentially did not exist. A son-in-law and father-in-law pairing would not have made sense to the audience and may not even have occurred to the author, due to its meaninglessness; marriage in a patriarchal society meant that a daughter would leave her father's household to join her husband's household,[70] making relationships between sons-in-law and their fathers-in-law much less important, or even altogether unlikely, in comparison with their corresponding female relationships. Mothers-in-law and daughters-in-law, on the other hand, were almost inevitably thrust into close proximity. Most would lead highly intertwined lives. Thus, the relationship permutations within this passage only reflect relationships that actually existed in the social world in which the audience lived.

The inclusion of these three relationships in a saying that refers to the potentially tumultuous consequences of discipleship to Jesus implies the active membership of both men and women in the movement.[71] In ancient Mediterranean society, where anthropologists speak of people as "embedded" in the family, severed family ties were no small matter.[72] Schottroff argues that the inclusion in this verse of all three core family relationships as loci of division indicates that the rifts "affect both genders in the same way."[73] She not only interprets the saying as evidence for the involvement of women in discipleship and itinerant prophecy, but takes it as indicating a deliberate attempt to overthrow the patriarchal household structure. She juxtaposes Q against a previous saying from early Jewish scriptures that also details the breakdown of the patriarchal family, found in Micah 7:5–6. Whereas, in Micah, the destruction of patriarchy is viewed as going against the will of God, this same destruction in Jesus' sayings ushers in that will, in the form of the *basileia*: "In Mic 7:5–6, the collapse of the patriarchal family expresses the disorder of the whole society, an anarchy raised against good order. In the Sayings Source what we find is a terrible—but by the will of God *necessary*—event."[74] In other words, Schottroff not only interprets this short gender pair as evidence that the social reality for Jesus' earliest followers included both male and female leaders but also as evidence for the programmatic dismantling of patriarchy on the part of Jesus or the first compilers of his sayings material. Schottroff is clearly right that the obvious attention paid to including both genders in this saying does imply female membership in the *basileia* movement—and that such involvement might bring about disruption of familial relationships for women as well as men. However, I believe she goes too far in reading this disruption as somehow necessary to the movement or at the core of the movement's message. It is possible for a controversial movement to result in the disruption of its members' patriarchal family structures *without* having as its goal the destruction of patriarchy. It is clear that the saying acknowledges women and men equally, but it is not as clear that the saying declares—or intends to implement—women's and men's societal equality. As Merz notes, the "non-family ethos" of the Jesus movement is well attested,[75] but this is more likely a byproduct of apocalyptic urgency than a plan to smash the patriarchy.

Q 14:26 Parents and Children

> The one who does not hate father and mother cannot be my disciple; and the one who does not hate son and daughter cannot be my disciple. (Q: 14:26)

Here is a straightforward and balanced set of pairs: a father and a mother, along with a son and a daughter, with the rest of the pairing being verbally identical. The call to place discipleship to Jesus as a priority that surpasses family bonds mentions two hypothetical familial relationships: that of the parent and that of the child. Once more, in the pattern that I have identified throughout the pairings, for each of the two relationships, one male and one female example is given. Each set of people (male and female parents and male and female children) is called upon to place *basileia* loyalty above even loyalty to family. What's more, these radical *basileia* expectations are the same for both women and men.

It is noteworthy that the passage is quite different in its later Lukan form: "If any one comes to me and does not hate his own father and mother *and wife/woman and children* and brothers and sisters, yes, and even his own life, he cannot be my disciple" (Luke 14:26 RSV, emphasis mine). The critical edition of Q excludes the phrase "wife/woman and children" as a Lukan interpolation. Even before the publication of the critical edition, scholars of women in the early Jesus movement had already noted that adding "wife/woman and children" to the list of groups to be left behind not only destroys the balanced parallelism of the saying but also craftily excludes women from itinerancy by implying that those called by Jesus for his movement had wives (i.e., were men).[76] This is further evidence of an overall Lukan tendency to narrow the acceptable social roles of women in the early Jesus movement.

CONCLUSIONS

Based on the pair-by-pair analysis above, I argue, along with Schüssler Fiorenza, Schottroff, Corley, and Batten that we see emerging in Q a real tendency, not only toward gender *inclusivity* (i.e., including women as well as men as subjects and implied audience members) but also toward gender *equality*. This is not an unqualified equality. As Levine and Arnal, from the "no gender implications of Q pairs" perspective, and also Schottroff (Perspective 1) have pointed out, the androcentrism generally present in Q's worldview and language mitigates against any idealistic discipleship of women and men as complete equals in a twenty-first-century sense. However, the unsurprising presence of androcentric language in first-century sayings is not reason enough to throw out the challenging implications of these unusual rhetorical pairings.[77]

That said, their significance for first-century women and men in the Jesus movement can certainly be made more precise and nuanced than some of the more extreme or oversimplified options. It is true that while women and men are both appealed to and valued in the countercultural *basileia* of Q, they are not conceived of as indistinguishable from one another in most aspects. A gendered division of labor, for instance, seems to remain intact,[78] as does the general androcentrism typical of first-century Palestinian and Roman society. The Q pairs, however, do imply that gender is simply not a relevant criterion when it comes to inclusion in the *basileia* movement. The pairs may also indicate that both men and women are sometimes called *out of* their regular social roles, gendered and otherwise, into the same new role of apocalyptic itinerant prophet, even if this disrupts traditional family roles.

Q is unique. These specific types of gender equality that emerge from close readings of the sayings of Jesus in Q do not match results that emerge when those same sayings are analyzed as found in the Gospels. The study of the sayings in Q is not the same project as studying the material around women in Luke, for instance. Although both Q and Luke seem to have female audience members in mind, the Lukan author seems to be rhetorically shaping his burgeoning movement in a very different direction than that inferred from Q material. Schaberg and Ringe explain:

> The author of Luke is interested in the education of women in the basics of the Christian faith and in the education of outsiders about Christian women. The Gospel attempts to meet various needs such as [. . .] controlling women who practice or aspire to practice a prophetic ministry in the church. One of the strategies of this Gospel is to provide female readers with female characters as role models: prayerful, quiet, grateful women, supportive of male leadership, forgoing the prophetic ministry.[79]

Whereas Luke's plentiful female characters serve as role models for women who, although valued, are decidedly subordinate and (literally) silent,[80] the female role models in Q's gender pairs are not subordinated to men in the *basileia*.

Of course, identifying specific sorts of rhetorical gender-leveling in the Q sayings is not the same as arguing that "Jesus was an egalitarian" nor that the primary aim of his movement was a feminist or gender-egalitarian revolution. Elliott states clearly why such claims are problematic. In his sharp response to Schüssler Fiorenza, Crossan, and others who reconstruct the earliest Jesus movements as a "discipleship of equals," Elliott concludes:

> An anachronistic imputation of modern notions to the biblical authors should be challenged and resisted in the name of historical honesty wherever and however it occurs. To be sure, let us expend every ounce of energy it takes to reform the ills of society and church. But let us do so with historical honesty, respecting the past as past and not trying to recreate it with modern constructs or re-write it with new ideological pens.[81]

Elliott rightly calls for "historical honesty" over what he considers to be revisionist wishful thinking. The gender pairs are clearly not breaking out of their historical context to suggest that women and men should be indistinguishable in every social setting nor advocating that socially gendered roles become interchangeable on principle. Nor are the pairs overtly addressing or even acknowledging a situation that is now described as patriarchy or androcentrism. That is, it is not within the rhetorical aims of the sayings, of Q as a whole, or of the historical Jesus to encourage women to burn their aprons, follow their dreams, and become shepherds, and to encourage men to get in touch with their housekeeping side and learn to spin wool into cloth. Reading them this way and imagining that one is attaining historical accuracy is an extreme form of uncritical retrojection. This is not to say that a theologian mightn't legitimately come to exactly such a reading, using a different set of (non-historical) methods. While historians must attempt to be loyal to the past, the theologian's first loyalty is to the contemporary practitioner. Elliott may be failing to distinguish between historical work and theological work in an area where we can see the two—at times competing—modes intersecting.

And yet, while the sayings cannot, in a first-century context, be expected to push for a complete societal equality based on the eradication of gender discrimination, they certainly do imply specific types of equality. These seem to have to do with each individual's inner intellectual abilities and outward religious participation, regardless of gender. The rhetorical use of the pairs implies that both women and men are expected to wrestle with the meaning of the parables. The pairs clearly imply that both women and men are held eschatologically responsible for properly interpreting and acting on them. Even when such a vocation involves societal disruption, the pairs call both women and men to be willing to travel and endure hardship to spread and model the parables' message. Moreover, both women and men seem to be expected to undergo the social, familial, and economic disruptions that will occur in families where some, but not all, are convinced by the *basileia* message. The rhetorical device of pairing sayings in this way, with gender as the notable variable, suggests that wo/men are seen as equally worthy of hearing Jesus' message and equally eligible to participate in the *basileia*, and that their sufferings within, and also their contributions to, that religious community are equally important.

These findings further our understanding of the role of women in Q and around the historical Jesus and help to differentiate this stage in the early Jesus movement from the various later stages to which the gospels bear witness, each one in its own way. But they do not support historical claims that Jesus was more or less "feminist." His use of gendered pairs as a didactic technique indicates that, for him, women and men were considered equally able on a cognitive and spiritual level to understand and discern metaphorical teaching and equally invited to participate in the enactment of the Jesus movement's lifestyle and the spread of its message. The rhetorical function of the pairs is to treat men and women equally—even identically—at the level of their capacity to receive and interpret the teachings and also to invite both men and women to the role of itinerant prophecy for the *basileia*, explicitly (Q 12:51–53) asking both men and women to break away from familial duties despite immense social pressure if these duties impede the work of the movement.

This observation resolves some of the tension between the "divided" Q-pairs scholars, half of whom insist that the pairs point to a more or less "feminist" Jesus, while the other half caution that any utopia in the earliest Jesus movement is too good to be true. In effect, both perspectives make important contributions. What I have done is to describe more precisely where the pairs imply, condone, or promote equality, as well as what types of equality are implied, along with where and what type of equality the pairs do not promote—a nuancing of the scholarship that I hope will help to clarify this debate and move it forward. This distinction is my own contribution to the conversation around women in the Q pairs, and it helps to reconcile the polarized voices in the discussion.

The limited and specific equality between the genders that can repeatedly be found in the paired sayings does serve to level the playing field for first-century wo/men in the Jesus movement in some senses, by ignoring gender as a criterion for exclusion and inclusion. At the same time, it is (as is to be expected in the ancient Mediterranean world) entirely apathetic to the deconstruction of socially constructed gendered tasks, except when the *basileia* disrupts—equally—the social lives of both its women and men adherents.

Addressing both male and female audience members with an identical message through the use of these parallel gender pairs may indeed demonstrate to both male and female audience members their intrinsic value to the movement, but it does not tackle patriarchy programmatically nor imply a targeted attempt to throw off an androcentric worldview. These latter tasks may be completely appropriate for theologians using the words of Jesus to guide communities to reflect on how they want to follow Jesus today—but they are not accurate historical analyses of the first-century context of the sayings, not least because Jesus is sometimes sloppily held up as the first ancient feminist example over and against a flattened, un-diverse Judaism's orientalized patriarchy.

Corley, Batten, and Levine all work against such dismissive portrayals of early Judaism by correctly pointing out that Q's gender-leveling enterprise, such as it is, did not arise out of thin air in an otherwise abysmally patriarchal Jewish setting. On the contrary, this limited gender-leveling is only made possible by a relaxing of societal restrictions upon women that had already been happening all over the late Republic throughout diverse pockets within Judaism and Hellenism.[82] Supersessionism in Christian feminist scholarship is a serious ill; unargued assumptions among researchers about a Christian "breath of fresh air" sweeping through a stale and stagnant Judaism deserve a swift and permanent denial. Corley, Batten, and Levine have all done their part in correcting against such (mis)interpretations of the early Jesus movement.

Having said this, the precise rhetorical treatment of wo/men seen in these paired Q sayings—within the context of this general relaxing of restrictions for women—must nevertheless be recognized as a rhetorical innovation. Acknowledging that a phenomenon like the pairs did not arise out of a vacuum does not diminish their gender-leveling implications, circumscribed as they are. The next chapter is dedicated to exploring the rhetorically novel aspect of Jesus' gendered pairs; examining previously posited precedents for gendered parable pairs in Greco-Roman literature serves to illustrate the pairs' rhetorical uniqueness in Hellenistic/Jewish antiquity. Uncovering a variety of additional kinds of Jewish and Roman gender-pairing in the first century (Chapter 6) both elucidates and complicates matters.

NOTES

1. The classic work of Julicher on the parables of Jesus and their literary and cultural heritage remains in many ways influential to the present day. A. Julicher, *Die Gleichnisreden Jesu* (Freiburg: J. C. B. Mohr [Paul Siebeck]), 1888. For a reflection on the ongoing relevance of Julicher's parable classifications and a report on the state

of the investigation in the last century, see M. A. Beavis, "Parable and Fable," *CBQ* 52 (1990): 473–498 and Roth, *The Parables in Q*, 6–12.

2. Throughout, quotations from the primary text in Greek are from the *Hermeneia* critical edition: Robinson, Hoffmann, and Kloppenborg, eds., *The Critical Edition of Q*. In the instance that a Greek passage does not occur in the critical edition, quotations are from the twenty-eighth edition of the Nestle-Aland *Novum Testamentum Graece* (NA[28]). Translations into English are those of the critical edition of Q. In the instance that a Greek passage does not occur in the critical edition, translations are from the Revised Standard Version (RSV). When translations are my own, they are noted as such.

3. For more on this, see the section entitled "gender implied" below.

4. A handy example of how a saying that juxtaposes genders might instead set them apart can be found in Ephesians 5:22–25: "Wives, submit to your husbands [. . .] Husbands, love your wives."

5. Q reads τίς ἄνθρωπος and translates it as "which person" in keeping with a standard translation choice toward inclusive language throughout the critical edition, but I argue that in cases like paralleled pairs, where τίς ἄνθρωπος stands in literary opposition to τίς γυνή in the parallel verse, it stands to reason that "man" is the translation that better captures what is happening rhetorically.

6. Sheep are "distinctively under male control" in the ancient Mediterranean world. B. J. Malina, "Understanding New Testament Persons," *The Social Sciences and New Testament Interpretation* (ed. R. Rohrbaugh; Peabody: Hendrickson, 1996), 50. See also C. Osiek and D. L. Balch, *Families in the New Testament World: Households and House Churches* (Louisville: Westminster John Knox, 1997), 138. As a rule, men in Graeco-Roman antiquity were socialized to perform most outdoor tasks such as shepherding, whereas women were socialized to remain largely indoors; women were "in the house, weaving, veiled, guarding the stores" and men, both upper class and peasant, were "outside, fighting, farming, and winning goods to store." J. J. Winkler, *The Constraints of Desire: The Anthropology of Sex and Gender in Ancient Greece* (New York: Routledge, 1990), 160.

7. H. Moxnes, "Honor and Shame," *The Social Sciences and New Testament Interpretation* (ed. R. Rohrbaugh; Peabody: Hendrickson, 1996), 21. Although, as Neyrey puts it: "the ancients construed the world as gender divided: males in the 'public' and females in the 'private' world." J. H. Neyrey, "What's Wrong with this Picture: John 4, Cultural Stereotypes of Women, and Public and Private Space," *A Feminist Companion to John: Volume 1* (ed. A.-J. Levine; London: Sheffield Academic, 2003), 100, and Malina writes that "some places are distinctively female: for example, the inside of a house," in "Understanding New Testament Persons," 50, it should be noted that the simplicity of this dichotomy has recently been questioned, namely because spaces were multi-purpose depending on the time of day or the people using them. As Cynthia Baker cautions, "houses were often fluid space" and "'inside' and 'outside,' 'public' and 'private' are problematic categories when applied to domestic spaces," C. Baker, *Rebuilding the House of Israel: Architectures of Gender in Jewish Antiquity* (Stanford: Stanford University Press, 2002), 41. Although the ancient Mediterranean world may have broadly relegated women to the private realm

while men functioned primarily in public, there are nuances and exceptions related to class in addition to the abovementioned fluidity of homes. Amy-Jill Levine writes: "Studies of the early Christian household have modified any strict reconstruction of public versus private geographical divisions. It may be more accurate to see public and private space as determined not only by location (e.g., market and home), the male 'without' (εχω) and the female 'within' (ἐν), but also by time. That is, the upper-class house has a public function during the day and a private function at night. In like manner, the assignment of men to the agricultural, commercial, and civic realms and the female to the domestic space of home, well, and oven must be tempered by notions of class. There were women who worked in the market and men who served in the home. The 'women's quarters' were an attribute only of the elite." A.-J. Levine, "Introduction," in *A Feminist Companion to John: Volume 1* (ed. A.-J. Levine; London: Sheffield Academic, 2003), 8.

8. See Polaski's discussion of how to determine whether women are meant to be included in masculine plurals, such as ἀδελφοὶ (brothers) in the writings of Paul, in S. Polaski, *A Feminist Introduction to Paul* (Danvers: Chalice, 2005), 16–17. The same questions arise from biblical Hebrew, as if even one male is present in a group, it is the masculine plural form that is used; for a feminist reading of exceptions to this rule in the Hebrew Bible, see A. R. Davis, "The Literary Effect of Gender Discord in the Book of Ruth," *JBL* 132/3 (2013): 495–513.

9. Arnal, "Gendered Couplets in Q," 77–82.

10. Fricker, *Quand Jésus Parle au Masculin-Féminin,* Chapter 1.

11. Roth, *The Parables in Q.*

12. I have chosen to begin both sayings with "consider" in English, in the interest of greater parallelism, as I believe this is the translation that makes the most sense. However, the critical edition, which does not seem to have had the gender pairs in mind at all when considering English renderings, translates the first instance as "consider" and the second instance as "observe." Both reconstructions in the critical edition are conjectural; in the first parable, "consider" is reconstructed from [κατανοήσ]ατε and in the second parable, "observe" is reconstructed from κατα[[(μάθε)]]τε. Since the portions within square brackets signify conjecture, and portions within double square brackets signify extreme conjecture, there is no reason not to reconstruct both parables as beginning with κατανοήσατε—"consider," and thus enjoy parallel beginnings for these parallel lessons.

13. I have here modified the text from the Q translation in the critical edition, which reads "Observe the lilies, how they grow: They do not work nor do they spin" (which is how the verse also appears in the gospels). As the text-critical note in the critical edition notes, there was already a scribal error here at the level of Q: "The original reading οὐ ξαίνει ("do not card") is, already in Q, corrupted by a scribal error into αὐξάνει." Robinson, Hoffmann, and Kloppenborg, eds., *The Critical Edition of Q,* 344. I have thus translated the verse as it likely originally circulated, since the original version of the saying is in a more parallel form. The scholarship that went into this decision is highly informed by a palimpsest of this text in Codex Sinaiticus, discovered under ultraviolet light, which confirms that the original version of the pair contains superior literary parallelism. In the underlying text—a rendering that is also preserved in saying 36 of the *Gospel of Thomas*—the lilies and the ravens are each

connected to a trio of negative verbs: ravens neither sow nor reap nor gather into barns, and lilies neither *card* nor toil nor spin (as seen above, the difference in Greek between "they grow," αὐξάνει, and "they do not card," οὐ ξαίνει, is very slight); this was uncovered by T. C. Skeat in 1938, who also confirmed its reinforcement in *Thomas*. See H. J. M. Milne and T. C. Skeat, *Scribes and Correctors of the Codex Sinaiticus* (London: Trustees of the British Museum, 1938). James Robinson pointed out the importance of this discovery as a proof that Q was a written Greek text. See J. Robinson, "The Nag Hammadi Gospels and the Fourfold Gospel" in *The Earliest Gospels* (London: T&T Clark, 2004), 84–85, as well as his earlier "A Written Greek Sayings Cluster Older than Q," 61–77 and his "The Pre-Q Text of the (Ravens and) Lilies: Q 12:22–31 and P. Oxy 655 (*Gos. Thom.* 36)," in *Text und Geschichte* (Marburg: Elwert, 1999), 143–180.

14. Arnal, "Gendered Couplets in Q," 78, n.15.

15. Dillon, "Ravens, Lilies, and the Kingdom of God," 619.

16. Neyrey, "What's Wrong with this Picture?," 105.

17. See J. Peters, "Gendered Activity and Jesus's Saying Not to Worry," *Neotest* 50/1 (2016): 35–52, esp. 44–45 and Neyrey, "What's Wrong with this Picture?," 105.

18. See Lee A. Johnson and Robert C. Tannehill, "Lilies Do Not Spin: A Challenge to Female Social Norms," *NTS* 56/4 (2010): 480.

19. Johnson and Tannehill, "Lilies Do Not Spin," 490.

20. In this case, I have let ἄνθρωπος stand as "person" as is the custom in the critical edition, since it is not juxtaposed with another character and does not form part of the gender pair in this saying.

21. I have taken the translation of this whole saying directly from the Q critical edition, except for changing "child" to "son" here. As the Greek is υἱός, this is really the best choice here. This single point of conflict between my translation and that of the critical edition does not have any bearing on the gendered or paralleled parts of the saying, but it does show that Q's language is generally, if not always, male-centered, outside of the specific instances of the gendered parallels, which is important for the purposes of this study.

22. Says Neyrey, "What's Wrong with this Picture?," 105. Athenaeus of Atteneia writes that a woman can "get good exercise" by "wetting the flour and kneading the dough" (21.6–8).

23. For example, all named fishers in the Canonical Gospels are male. Simon, Andrew, James, and John are fishing when Jesus calls them in Matt 4:18 (cf. Mark 1:16), and John 21:1 has Simon, Thomas, Nathanael, and the sons of Zebedee heading out to fish. See Hanson, "The Galilean Fishing Economy and the Jesus Tradition," 99–111. While it seems that men were universally the fishers in Mediterranean antiquity, women could be involved in the making of fishing nets: see A. Marzano, *Harvesting the Sea: The Exploitation of Marine Resources in the Roman Mediterranean* (Oxford: Oxford University Press, 2013), 296.

24. See R. A. Simkins, "The Widow and Orphan in the Political Economy of Ancient Israel," *Journal of Religion & Society Supplement* 10 (2014): 20–33 and G. T. Sheppard, "Poor," in *Mercer Dictionary of the* Bible (ed. W. E. Mills; Macon: Mercer University Press, 1990), 700–701.

25. Robinson, Hoffmann, and Kloppenborg, eds., *The Critical Edition of Q*.

26. B. Jones, *Matthean and Lukan Special Material: A Brief Introduction with Texts in Greek and English* (Eugene: Wipf and Stock, 2011), 13.

27. "(M)ore than 90 percent of Mark was copied by either Matthew or Luke or both." Kloppenborg, *Q: The Earliest Gospel*, 98.

28. Sloan, "Extent of Q," 340.

29. This is argued extensively in Schaberg and Ringe, "Gospel of Luke," 493–511. It is also the most important premise of that seminal work on Lukan gender pairs, Seim's *The Double Message*. B. Reid goes so far as to say that Luke "is intent on restricting [women] to silent, passive, supporting roles." Reid, *Choosing the Better Part?*, 53.

30. Robinson, Hoffmann, and Kloppenborg, eds., *The Critical Edition of Q*, 212.

31. Sloan, "Extent of Q," 342–343, 345–348.

32. For a variety of angles of argumentation for the inclusion of both these parables in pre-Lukan sayings material, see D. R. Catchpole, *The Quest for Q* (Edinburgh: T&T Clark, 1993), 201–28; B. S. Easton, *The Gospel According to St. Luke* (Edinburgh: T&T Clark, 1926), 177; A. Kirk, *The Composition of the Sayings Source: Genre, Synchrony, and Wisdom Redaction in Q* (Leiden: Brill, 1998), 176–82; J. Schmid, *Matthäus und Lukas: Eine Untersuchung des Verhältnisses ihrer Evangelien* (Freiburg: Herder & Herder, 1930), 241–242.

33. Merz, "Woman Who Fought Back," 49–50.

34. The material from this paragraph is from my notes from Schüssler Fiorenza's keynote address at the Bible and Social Justice Conference at St. Ambrose University, Davenport, Iowa, in 2013.

35. W. R. Herzog II, *Parables as Subversive Speech: Jesus as Pedagogue of the Oppressed* (Louisville: Westminster John Knox, 1989), 220.

36. Merz, "Woman who Fought Back," 49–86.

37. E. Schüssler Fiorenza, keynote address, Bible and Social Justice Conference, St. Ambrose University, Davenport, Iowa. 2013.

38. Merz, "Woman who Fought Back," 85.

39. See A.-J. Levine, "This Widow Keeps Bothering Me," in *Finding a Woman's Place: Essays in Honor of Carolyn Osiek* (ed. D. L. Balch and J. T. Lamoreaux; Eugene: Pickwick, 2011).

40. Levine, "This Widow," 124.

41. Levine, "This Widow," 124.

42. This pair may not technically be a parable in that, rather than telling a story with a double meaning, it may be making a statement that might very well have been meant literally. I include it because, as Dieter Roth shows in *The Parables in Q*, 14–15, ancient definitions of parables were less strict than our own, and this pair, as a short didactic narrative, is participating in the same illustrative gendered pairing as the other examples.

43. The critical edition has "person" here, as is its consistent translation custom for the Greek ἄνθρωπος. However, as argued above, I suggest that in this context of gender-pairings, the word is not inclusive but is clearly functioning in opposition to the γυνή in its parallel saying.

44. See Z. Crook, "The Synoptic Parables of the Mustard Seed and the Leaven: A Test-Case for the Two-Document, Two-Gospel, and Farrer-Goulder Hypotheses," *JSNT* 22/78 (2000): 23–48.

45. As has been addressed above, "males, whose proper gender space is the 'open air,' do tasks appropriate to that space: 'plowing, sowing, planting, and grazing are all such open-air employments.'" Neyrey, "What's Wrong with this Picture?" 105. The only time in Greco-Roman antiquity that one hears of women working in fields is in texts that are describing ways in which the culture of an Other is "barbaric." P. Garnsey, *Food and Society in Classical Antiquity* (Cambridge: Cambridge University Press, 1999), 110.

46. "Females, whose proper gender place is 'covered,' do the basic tasks that support the household [. . .] cover is needed for the making of corn into bread." Neyrey, "What's Wrong with this Picture?," 105.

47. Levine, "Women in the Q Communit(ies)," 150.

48. Schüssler Fiorenza, *In Memory of Her*, 131.

49. Schüssler Fiorenza, *In Memory of Her*, 131.

50. Luise Schottroff, "Feminist Observations on the Eschatology of the Sayings Source" (paper presented at the 1992 annual meeting of the SBL, San Francisco, November 1992), 6.

51. As mentioned above, this translation is from the critical edition of Q, with the exception of my translation "man." Q translates τίς ἄνθρωπος as "which person" in keeping with the typical inclusive translation choices throughout the critical edition, but in cases where τίς ἄνθρωπος stands in literary opposition to τίς γυνὴ in a parallel verse, it stands to reason that "man" better captures what is happening rhetorically.

52. For an outline of some of the scholarship behind this decision, see J. S. Kloppenborg, *Q Parallels: Synopsis, Concordance, and Critical Notes* (Sonoma: Polebridge, 1988), 176.

53. Arnal, "Gendered Couplets in Q," 82.

54. Arnal, "Gendered Couplets in Q," 82. See further on that page: "[The Lost Coin's] strong formal and thematic affinities with the lost sheep parable make it unlikely that the parable could have circulated in Luke's 'L' traditions independently of the lost sheep. The parable must either have been formulated along with the lost sheep or have been modelled after it."

55. Malina, "Understanding New Testament Persons," 50. It can be generalized across Greco-Roman antiquity that women did not work in fields. Garnsey, *Food and Society in Classical Antiquity*, 110. The only exception would be in times of dire need in peasant communities when "all hands had to be mobilised." Garnsey, *Food and Society*, 111.

56. As mentioned above and elsewhere, "women occupied the . . . domestic sphere." Moxnes, "Honor and Shame," 21. Although some exceptions were forced by class, in general non-elite rural females were expected to match everything that was expected of elite, urban females, as far as their wealth permitted. Levine, "Introduction," 8.

57. This is the argument throughout Arnal, "Gendered Couplets in Q" and is a small part of his important monograph *Jesus and the Village Scribes*, esp. 168ff. Arnal's solid argumentation for Galilean scribes behind the Q document do not at all hinge significantly on what I consider to be the sole error in his otherwise top-notch contribution, namely, not granting any connection between the women in the gendered pairs and possible women on the ground in the early Jesus movement. Arnal's

arguments against any deliberate inclusiveness toward women in Q are discussed and refuted in greater detail in the following chapter.

58. There is no noun specifying that the "two" in the field are male and the "two" at the mill are female at the outset of each line. The Greek in both cases simply uses δύο. However, in the second part of each line, the reason why these are always translated as "two men" and "two women" in both Q and the gospel passages becomes clear. The "ones" are gendered. Those in the field are the masculine εἷς and those at the mill are the feminine μία.

59. Garnsey, *Food and Society*, 110; Malina, "Understanding New Testament Persons," 50.

60. See T. Takaoglu, "Archaeological Evidence for Grain Mills in the Greek and Roman Troad," *Vom Euphrat bis zum Bosporus: Kleinasien in der Antike* (Bonn: Dr. Rudolph Habelt, 2008), 673–679, esp. the discussion of the importance of simple domestic hand mills on page 678. Homer also makes reference to a woman grinding flour and twelve maids grinding flour: Hom.*Od*, 20, 117–121.

61. Arnal, "Gendered Couplets in Q," 85. Even while Arnal admits this, he goes on to note (85) that the social status of these female insiders is not clear. This is because he is attempting to argue that Q does not necessarily have women in the audience, so that he can connect the gender pairs to a scribal context. The two, however, are not mutually exclusive: there is no reason why scribes cannot have been involved in the composition or compilation of Q while also reflecting a group that had women as active participants who were thus addressed deliberately in many of the sayings.

62. The word in square brackets is my reconstruction, as the critical edition of Q leaves a lacuna in the place of "prostitutes." The text-critical notes leave the question open as to whether the Lukan or the Matthean version appeared in Q. Robinson, Hoffmann, and Kloppenborg, eds., *The Critical Edition of Q*, 138.

63. See Kloppenborg, *Q: The Earliest Gospel*, 129.

64. The phrase, with paired gender, occurs twice in Matthew 21:31–32: Jesus said to them, "Truly I tell you, the tax collectors and the prostitutes are going into the kingdom of God ahead of you. For John came to you in the way of righteousness and you did not believe him, but the tax collectors and the prostitutes believed him; and even after you saw it, you did not change your minds and believe him."

65. See Corley, *Private Women, Public Meals*, 157–58 as well as "Jesus, Egalitarian Meals, and Q" (paper presented at the annual meeting of the SBL, San Francisco, November 1992), 1–11.

66. Fricker, *Quand Jésus Parle au Masculin-Féminin*.

67. See D. Good, "Beyond the Canon," *Women's Bible Commentary Twentieth Anniversary Edition: Revised and Updated* (ed. C. A. Newsom, S. H. Ringe, and J. E. Lapsley; Louisville: Westminster John Knox, 2012), 633–639, here 635 for a list of places in the Christian Testament and other early Christian literature where women's oral funerary lament traditions are mentioned. See also T. Gamliel, "Textual Categories and Gender Images in a Women's Wailing Performance," *Social Analysis* 51/3 (2007): 23–54.

68. See C. A. Evans, *Matthew* (New York: Cambridge University Press, 2012), 207. See also Josephus *J.W.* 3.437. Male flute-players also appear often in sacrificial processions on reliefs.

69. Horace mentions a "college of female flute players" in *Satire* 1.2.1. A flute-girl is also mentioned in *Acts of Thomas* 1.5, and in Philo, *Contempl.* VII. 58.

70. "Both versions of the saying [i.e., in both Matthew and Luke] presuppose a patriarchal household structure in which a daughter, a married son, and his wife live with the parents." Schottroff, "The Sayings Source Q," 511.

71. Schottroff, "The Sayings Source Q," 511.

72. "The line between personal identity and family identity [in the ancient Mediterranean world] tended to disappear." Moxnes, "Honor and Shame," 21. For a specific look at kinship in this context, see K. C. Hanson's "Kinship," *The Social Sciences and New Testament Interpretation* (ed. R. Rohrbaugh; Peabody: Hendrickson, 1996), 62–79 as well as his "All in the Family: Kinship in Agrarian Roman Palestine," *The Social World of the New Testament* (ed. J. H. Neyrey and E. C. Stewart; Peabody: Hendrickson, 2008), 25–46.

73. Schottroff, "The Sayings Source Q," 511.

74. Schottroff, "The Sayings Source Q," 512.

75. Merz, "Woman who Fought Back," 76.

76. See Schüssler Fiorenza, *In Memory of Her*, 145–146; Schottroff, "Sayings Source Q," 515. Arnal, in "Gendered Couplets in Q," 78, n.12, writes: "Note also in support of this conclusion that the 'children' referred to in Luke are described with the word τέκνα, which is consistently used in Q as a positive designation for the Q people themselves, whereas here, in contrast, it is used of those left behind."

77. Arnal tries to argue against a connection between women in the gender pairs and actual women in the audience by saying, "were women sufficiently active to ensure the composition of such couplets, we can hardly account for the preponderance of androcentric language." However, this is hardly an argument; androcentric language can certainly co-exist alongside some elements of gender equality, just as it frequently does to this day. "Gendered Couplets in Q," 86.

78. This is no surprise for first-century Mediterranean society: "Societies with kinship as the focal point invariably have a moral division of labour based on gender." Malina, "Understanding New Testament Persons," 50.

79. Schaberg and Ringe, "Gospel of Luke," 493.

80. Dewey, "Women in the Synoptic Gospels," 58.

81. Elliott, "Jesus Was Not an Egalitarian," 90.

82. For an excellent synthesis of the complex, overlapping, and reciprocal interaction between Judaism and Hellenism in the spirit of Hengel, as it pertains to women and sexuality in Judaism in the Greco-Roman period, see the concluding chapter of W. Loader, ed. *The Pseudepigrapha on Sexuality: Attitudes toward Sexuality in Apocalypses, Testaments, Legends, Wisdom, and Related Literature* (Grand Rapids: Eerdmans, 2011), 490–513.

Chapter 5

Were There Gendered Parable Pairs before Jesus?

This chapter takes a comparative look at the ancient literary record to reveal that although Jesus' gendered twin parables participate in various tropes and genres of ancient Mediterranean literature (such as parallelism, parable, and even other occasions of the juxtaposition of gender), they are at the same time a rhetorical first. The knowledge that Q's gender pairs are at once both unique and well anchored in their contexts provides an important supplement to the work of Batten and Corley. They are quite right to highlight the indispensable role of the *Zeitgeist* in making women's participation and value in movements like the *basileia* group around Jesus possible. By doing so, they complicate and combat supersessionist readings of the Jesus movement's earliest context. Demonstrating that the pairs participate in this *Zeitgeist*—yet in their own unique way—repositions early Jesus-following women within a world of far greater gender complexity.

To substantiate the literary uniqueness of the Q gender pairs, this chapter lays out prior literature, such as the earlier Jewish texts that came to be collected into the Hebrew Bible, along with other Jewish and Hellenistic writings that predate Q. This first section of this chapter looks in particular at specific writings that have been mentioned by others as possible direct literary ancestors to the Q gender pairs. These comparisons include parallelism in Hebrew poetry (Fricker) and scribal/rabbinic culture (Arnal).

The following chapter then looks at the pairs in relation to other contemporaneous or post-Q texts that also pair gender. In some of these texts, I think the Q pairs can be said to have an afterlife; comparisons with early Christian literature immediately following Q underscore a connection between Jesus of Nazareth and gendered pairing. In addition, comparisons with gender-paired examples from non-Jesus-following varieties of Judaism (such as Philo), or ambiguously provenanced examples (such as *Joseph and Aseneth*) help to properly situate Jesus within first-century Judaism.

Applying some of the criteria for authenticity that are typically used in historical Jesus research across these first-century writings corroborates my findings that specifically pairing parables by gender in a way that implies and empowers a mixed-gender audience is a rhetorical invention original to Jesus of Nazareth. (Such pairs did not exist before Jesus, but they seem to proliferate in various ways in multiple independent texts connected to him.) As such, they are a precious addition to our evidence for the rhetoric around—and the role of—women in the earliest Jesus movement. At the same time, the presence of different types of gender pairing in *Joseph and Aseneth* and Philo's *De Vita Contemplativa* pushes back against the notion that Jesus ushered in an egalitarian feminist vision that had nothing whatsoever in common with the Judaism of his day.

SUMMARY OF CHAPTERS 3 AND 4

Before we continue, it will be helpful to sum up the book so far. As demonstrated, Q contains a number of verbally parallel parable duos that appear alongside one another and that highlights first one gender and then another. Additionally, Q has various instances of shorter phrases that also contain gendered pairs. Although one or two cases of attention to gender might be seen as coincidence, several repeated occurrences throughout Q strengthen the likelihood that they flag gender as a special focus; the full parallel parable pairs work in conjunction with shorter paired phrases to indicate that there is a crafted emphasis on male–female pairing in the sayings of Jesus. Specifically, there exists throughout Q a tendency, not only toward general gender *inclusivity*, that is including women as subjects and implied audience members, but also toward a particular gender *equality*, that is, modeling gender inclusion as a norm in the *basileia* group. Up until this point, my findings have confirmed an ongoing consideration for women in the text of Q, most commonly in the form of a specific rhetorical attempt (gendered pairings) to recognize and validate female audience members.

As mentioned, those scholars who argue that this tendency toward gendered pairing within Q points to social "egalitarianism" or "a discipleship of equals"[1] in the early Jesus movement have sometimes erroneously used "patriarchal Judaism" as a foil against which to measure the relative freedom offered to women by the early movements around Jesus of Nazareth.[2] They have been rightly called to task[3] for anti-Judaism in Christian feminist scholarship. This critique is especially apt given the widespread relaxation of many strict societal expectations upon women that occurred throughout diverse Hellenistic and Jewish groups during the late Republic, as Corley and Batten have pointed out.[4] This relaxation helped make women's involvement in movements such as the one around Jesus possible, but also ultimately gave rise to redoubled restrictions on women's behavior, such as the Augustan marital reforms. (Augustus is famous for his "preoccupations with marital fidelity and female fecundity."[5] For instance, Augustan-era laws like *the Lex Iulia de maritantibus ordinibu*s in 18 B.C.E. and *Lex Papia Poppaea nuptialis* in 9 B.C.E. made marriage non-optional precisely to limit women's growing emancipation as a result of their participation in banquets.[6]) My approach yields some precision that, I hope, may better articulate in which ways the pairs can claim to be egalitarian or gender-leveling and in which ways they cannot, as well as to clarify appropriate backdrops against which to view them.

In this chapter, I wish to showcase the literary uniqueness of the pairs, and thus rescue the proverbial baby from the bathwater. It is possible to highlight what is exceptional about the pairs' gender-leveling work in the early Jesus movement, without denigrating other varieties of Judaism, while recognizing that this gender equality did not arise in a vacuum. As evidenced by the systematic attempts at curtailing women's freedoms by Augustus,[7] Hellenistic women, including Jewish women, were indeed enjoying unprecedented social mobility and freedom in the decades leading up to the time of Jesus.[8]

That said, this chapter confirms that the particular literary structure, and rhetorical argument, of the parallel parable gender pairs *is not extant prior to Q* in earlier Jewish or Hellenistic literature. In other words, *contra* Arnal, who locates the work of the pairs in repetitive scribal tendencies unrelated to social gender,[9] and *contra* Fricker, who locates (at least the formal) rhetorical ancestry of the pairs in the Hebrew poetic tradition,[10] and building on Corley[11] and Batten,[12] who locate the gender equality of the pairs in the aftermath of Hellenistic Republican culture, I demonstrate that the rhetorical work of these sayings vis-à-vis gender is a rhetorical innovation that acknowledges female audience members. The time was ripe for women's welcome engagement in some intellectual and spiritual/religious movements in a relatively new way at the close of the Republic and the dawn of the Roman Empire, and the pairs take advantage of this possibility in a demonstrably creative way.

If gendered parable pairing is a Q innovation, it represents an important piece of evidence in the study of first-century Galilean Judaism and Christian origins. If this unique literary signal for paying equal attention to women and men recipients does not occur prior to Q, which I will demonstrate, then it is highly plausible that it is a literary form that originated with Jesus of Nazareth, the ostensible speaker of the sayings. This is not to say that the Jesus movement can be credited with innovating female leadership, participation, or social agency in general. Rather, it is to say that this particular literary device of gendered pairing must be credited as original to the early Jesus movement at the pre-Gospel stage and can take its place *among other* varying forms of innovative gender-leveling taking place across the Mediterranean world at the time.

Below, we will see that others have suggested possible literary ancestors for the gender pairs of Jesus' sayings material, but I engage with them to demonstrate that no evidence of this rhetorical tool is extant before Q. No precise literary precursor to the Q gender parallels can be identified; no text from antiquity prior to Q performs the particular work that the Q pairs do. After reviewing the Apocrypha, Pseudepigrapha, Hebrew Bible, and various works of didactic or sayings literature in Greek that could possibly form a background to Q, including Greek works and bodies of works ranging from the fables of Aesop, to the Homeric corpus, to the poets contemporaneous with Q, to the range of other Greek language works that are searchable using the *Thesaurus Linguae Graecae*, I cannot report having found anything resembling the literary genre of a parallel parable pair that uses gender as its variable, to impart an identical lesson to women and men.

The work of the below scholars who have attempted to connect Q with different possible precursors remains useful for comparison, yet decidedly unconvincing as direct ancestry. Examining those texts which, according to these scholars, have come the closest to the parallel gendered parables only serves to highlight, through their generic and thematic distance from the pairs, the uniqueness of the gendered parable pairs as remembered in Q.

NO DIRECT LITERARY ANCESTRY FOR THE Q PAIRS: CLOSE CALLS

This section will examine the textual background in which one might reasonably expect to begin a search for literary ancestors for the Q pairs, if ancestors existed. Pre-Christian Jewish texts—some of which came to be collected in the Hebrew Bible and others of which are now collected in the Apocrypha, Pseudepigrapha, Dead Sea Scrolls, and beyond—include many texts with which Jesus and his early followers were attestably familiar. And perhaps non-Jewish pre-Christian Hellenistic literature, such as the fables of Aesop, the works of philosophers, novels, and drama might have provided inspiration for Jesus' rhetorical moves. I have not found such precedent in any of these bodies of work, though, although there are a few cases where connections have been posited. This next section outlines some of these "close calls."

Close Calls in the Hebrew Bible and Apocrypha

The context that may seem the most obvious in which to search for literary precedent for the gendered pairs of Q is in prior Jewish literature, including those books that were later collected in the Apocrypha and Hebrew Bible,[13] and canonized as Jewish and Christian scripture.[14] It is beyond doubt that Jesus and his earliest Jewish followers knew, or knew of, many of these texts.[15]

Of course, two key features of Jesus' pairs are also recurring features in Hebrew literature. These are the genre of small teaching stories such as parables and the device of parallelism. Both parable and parallelism are quite common in Hebrew, and they even sometimes occur *together* in the Hebrew poetic tradition.[16] This is why Denis Fricker pinpoints Hebrew poetry as the inspiration for Jesus' parallel pairs.[17] Importantly, though, Hebrew poetry never employs parable and parallelism deliberately as a unit in order to address both masculine and feminine topics and audience members identically.

Parables and Parallelism in the Hebrew Bible and Apocrypha

Short fictional teaching stories can certainly be found in a variety of places within the Hebrew Bible.[18] For instance, in Judges 9:8–15, Jotham recounts the parable of the trees, wherein the most noble and deserving trees decline ruling over the other trees, but the low-class bramble jumps at the chance to rule—and rule violently. In 2 Sam 12:1–7, the prophet Nathan bravely regales David with the condemnatory parable of the ewe lamb. The didactic form of the short teaching story was quite common in Hebrew writings. It would have been known by those who were familiar with such texts, including Jesus,[19] and is, of a certainty, a favored teaching mode of Jesus. So Jesus' didactic methods as found in Q certainly echo the Hebrew scriptures; however, those ancient Hebrew parables certainly do not come in pairs where gender is the main variable.

The other element of the Q pairs also found within the Hebrew Bible and Apocrypha—and sometimes, although far less often, even within the *parables* of the Hebrew Bible and Apocrypha—is parallelism.[20] Parallelism or "the repetition of an idea in slightly different terms"[21] is a well-known marker of Hebrew poetry.[22] The parallelism at work in Hebrew literature has been divided into a variety of sub-types.[23] The most basic and overarching categories of parallelism relevant to our purposes are synonymous parallelism and antithetic parallelism.[24] Within these devices are "parallel lines" and "parallel terms," the former referring to an entire structural half of the pair of texts in question and the latter referring to the individual paralleled terms within those lines[25] (something akin to what I refer to as the "variables"). To illustrate,

Prov 1:20 reads, "Wisdom cries out in the street; she raises her voice in the public squares." In this case, "Wisdom cries out in the street" and "she raises her voice in the public squares" are the parallel lines. "Cries out" and "raises her voice" are parallel terms, as are "the street" and "the public squares." This is an example of *synonymous* parallelism, which uses the second line to reinforce or expand upon the ideas in the first line.[26]

In Isaiah 60:2, "darkness will cover the earth; thick darkness [will cover] the peoples." Sandra Gravett explains that the second half of synonymous cases like this serve in the text both as emphasis as well as for poetic/aesthetic purposes: "Darkness" and "thick darkness" are different Hebrew words that convey the same idea, as are "earth" and "peoples"; thus the ideas are emphasized through reinforcement.[27] Similarly, Amos 5:24 reads "But let justice roll down like waters, and righteousness like an ever-flowing stream." Here, the concept of justice is reinforced by the concept of righteousness, which stands in the same position in the second phrase. The "waters" in the first phrase are echoed by the "ever-flowing stream" of the second. Both of the lines in the parallel convey approximately the same message, through repetition of synonyms or near-synonyms. Ben Sira frequently does the same; Sirach 14:20 reads, "blessed is the man who meditates on wisdom, and who reasons intelligently" and 14:26 continues, "he will place his children under (Wisdom's) shelter, and will camp under (Wisdom's) boughs." Of course, Q uses synonymous parallelism too. Q 11:11–12 reads, "Which of you, whose son asks him for bread, will give him a stone? Or again when he asks for a fish, will give him a snake?" The nourishing bread in the first line is reiterated with the nourishing fish in the second, as the inedible stone is reiterated in the decidedly unpalatable snake.

By contrast, *antithetical* parallelism is where the two lines, still similar in structure, show contrasting ideas.[28] Much like synonymous parallelism, antithetical parallelism also reinforces the same idea in the second line. However, it does so by using a negative inversion of the first line, rather than a repeated echo of it. Antithetical parallelism is frequent throughout Proverbs[29] (e.g., Prov 12:1, "Whoever loves discipline loves knowledge, but those who hate to be rebuked are stupid"). It can also be found in Sirach (e.g., Sirach 21:22, "The foot of a fool rushes into a house, but an experienced person waits respectfully outside" and Sirach 21:26, "The mind of fools is in their mouth, but the mouth of wise men is in their mind.") Like synonymous parallels, antithetical parallels also ultimately convey the same message, but do so by reiterating the concept using two opposite ways of saying the same thing, rather than using synonyms or closely related concepts. Antithetical pairs are not a preferred device in Q.

Virtually all of the Q parable pairs are a kind of synonymous parallelism. This similarity in form between the Q gender pairs and the synonymous parallels of Hebrew poetry brings Denis Fricker to the conclusion that the Q pairs owe their formal ancestry (although not the ancestry of their content) to the Hebrew poetic tradition. (Fricker believes that the *theological* function of the pairs is an innovation of Jesus, but that the *format* of the pairs takes its cues from Hebrew parallelism.[30]) I concur with Fricker that the literary device is similar at a *formal* level and also agree with him that the gender-leveling didactic aims of the parables in Q are quite unique from the contents of Hebrew parables. Although synonymous parallelism is abundant throughout the Hebrew scriptures as well as throughout Q, at no point prior to Q do *two parallel parables or sayings* occur in the Hebrew Bible (nor, for that matter, in the apocrypha and Pseudepigrapha), where an identical lesson is clearly geared toward both male and female audience members. Nor is there any such occurrence in which a male example and a female example are used in synonymous fashion to convey an identical teaching. In this regard, Q is decidedly divergent from this earlier device. In other words, the gender pairs of Q reflect the Hebrew traditions of parallelism and of parabolic teaching, but they join these traditions into a pioneering usage that makes use of human gender as a linking factor between two parables that communicate the same message.

Grammatical Gender and Parallelism in Hebrew Poetry

In the 1970s, Adele Berlin and Wilfred Watson made the case that ancient Hebrew makes deliberate use of components of grammar as part of its poetic parallelism, including grammatical gender.[31] Because, at times, the two parallel terms in Hebrew couplets alternate between masculine and feminine grammatical gender, then Hebrew poetry could be explored as an ancestor of the gender-based parallelism in Q. Psalm 85:11, for instance, reads:

> Faithfulness will spring up from the ground (אֶרֶץ), and righteousness (צֶדֶק) will look down from the sky (שָׁמַיִם).

Here, the two nouns in the first line (faithfulness and ground) are grammatically feminine, while their two parallel nouns in the second half (righteousness and sky) are grammatically masculine.[32] Watson referred to this as "gender-matched synonymous parallelism."[33] Because, at times, the two parallel terms in Hebrew couplets alternate between masculine and feminine grammatical gender, it might be tempting to see a connection with Q's gender pairs. But this hypothetical Hebrew poetic device, which is said to rely on grammatical gender as one of the elements in parallel, is tenuous. It is well-known in the field of linguistics, and borne out by common experience, that grammatical gender does not extrapolate to human social gender.[34] Although grammatical gender may sometimes correlate in nouns like "lion" and "lioness" that refer to beings with implied social gender, grammatical gender certainly does not correlate to human gender in nouns like "righteousness," "songs," "pride," and "mountains," which are the kinds of terms far more likely to form parallel elements in Hebrew poetry. Therefore, even if it could be shown that the author was deliberately juxtaposing masculine nouns with feminine nouns, it would make no sense to assume a correlation between this use of grammatical gender and the socialized gender we see addressed in Jesus' paired sayings.[35] Furthermore, there is no way of determining that the cases where parallel terms in Hebrew happen to use a masculine noun and then a feminine noun are deliberate. Chances are naturally statistically high that, in some of the cases, the terms in one line of the parallel would randomly be grammatically masculine and the other randomly grammatically feminine, since Hebrew only has the two options for grammatical gender, masculine and feminine.

Even if it *were* a good idea to equate grammatical gender with human gender in analysis, which it is not, and even if we assumed that the psalmists juxtaposed male with female grammatical gender deliberately some of the time, which we cannot, there would still not be a clear ancestral literary path between this hypothetical device in Hebrew poetry and the much more specific and directly audience-appropriate rhetorical enterprise undertaken in the parable pairs of Q. To understand a rhetorical project in the likely accidental grammatical gender of Hebrew parallelism requires a maximalist optimism that is not required for Jesus' paired parables, in which the use of gender is quite obvious. In other words, even if Q is drawing on the parallelism tradition of the Psalms, Sirach, and other Hebrew poetic texts, I put it that Q addresses gender at a different level entirely and with strong evidence of intentionality. Q's Jesus innovates in that his use of parallelism focuses on human gender in human social community.

In short, no text from the Hebrew poetic tradition deals with human social gender in intentional parallel. Although there is precedent within Jewish scriptures for the use of parables, on the one hand, and for literary parallelism, on the other, it is clear that the precise literary device found within Q—that is, the gendered parallel parable pair, employed for inclusive purposes, is something different.

Close Calls in the Pseudepigrapha

Another group of early Jewish texts in which one might search for precedent for the gender doublets is the Pseudepigrapha. The books known by scholars under the name "Old Testament Pseudepigrapha"[36] were not a collection in antiquity, but the grouping is rather a modern academic construct.[37] However, there is no question that many of the books within this category were known by Christian Testament authors as well as by Jesus.[38] Many of the texts of the

Pseudepigrapha[39] also employ parallelism.[40] However, neither human gender nor a rhetorical attempt to be inclusive to female audience members using paired parables feature in any of the Pseudepigrapha's parallels, synonymous or otherwise, with one exception. According to my findings, *Joseph and Aseneth* contains a single passage that repeats the same instruction twice—once for men and once for women.

However, *Joseph and Aseneth*, although set in the time of Joseph, cannot be said with certainty to predate Q. In Davila's *The Provenance of the Pseudepigrapha*,[41] he does not come down firmly on a date for the work, instead offering an even-handed discussion of various hypotheses, noting that the work has been tentatively dated anywhere between the second-century B.C.E. and the second-century C.E. John J. Collins's article on its provenance says that the majority of recent research narrows the composition to between 100 B.C.E. and 100 C.E.[42] Notably, Kraemer's recent book-length treatment argues that a Christian provenance is at least as likely as a pre-Christian one, in which case the work's composition would obviously post-date Q.[43] Given its contested and potentially late date, *Joseph and Aseneth* it is not a good candidate as an ancestor of Jesus' gender pairing. Its one marvelous example of gendered pairing will be discussed in the following chapter, alongside other literature contemporaneous with Q.

Close Calls in Other Hellenistic Literature

A detailed search through other Hellenistic literature in the centuries leading up to the common era, focusing mainly on didactic genres, such as fables, as the realms most likely to be fruitful for comparison with Q's parallel parable pairs, also reveals that no earlier Greek text can be said to clearly address a mixed audience of men and women while offering them repeated parables that provided an identical lesson with an example of each gender.

Parables and Fables in other Hellenistic Writings

Scholar Klyne Snodgrass has written a sourcebook for the Hellenistic background to Jesus' parables.[44] Unlike many scholars, Snodgrass commendably searches for parallels to the parables of Jesus not only throughout early Jewish books but also throughout wider Hellenistic writings, and also compiles handy appendices for everywhere the Greek word *parabole* and the Hebrew word *mashal* occur, throughout the Hebrew Bible, the LXX, other early Jewish literature, and beyond. Within this sourcebook, which extends as far back as the fables of Aesop, Snodgrass has not reported a literary structure comparable to that of the gender pairs of Q.[45]

Fables are fictional stories that display a truth—the definition given in Aelios Theon's *Progymnasmata* 3 in the first century. Fables, then, share traits with the parables in the full gender pairs of Q. They were also in circulation around the time of Jesus—for instance, Aesop and Stesichorus, among the most famous fabulists before the Common Era, were still in circulation in the first century. We know this because, for example, Aesop's stories merit a mention in the work of the first-century philosopher Apollonius of Tyana. Therefore, fables might seem like an apt place to search for gender-paralleled tales. However, the manner in which they are collected and circulated precludes this possibility, as each fable is a separate entity; they are not paired. Furthermore, none are doubled and parallel, let alone doubled and paralleled with gender as the main variable. Thus, although fables might be related to parables in general, they do not provide a precursor to the device that is found in the gendered parallel parable pairs of Q.

Close Calls in Rabbinic Literature: Scribal Wordplay

As mentioned earlier, William Arnal has argued for the location of the gender pairs as they appear in Greek translation in Q within the patterned legal repetitions of early rabbinic scribes.[46] Although the texts Arnal uses as evidence for this are generally later than Q,[47] he sees the common legislative scribal culture from which both emerged as a possible explanation for the presence of gender juxtaposition in the Q pairs and likens them to civic codes and contracts, such as marriage and divorce documents,[48] and thus I include him in this chapter. Arnal points to wordplay elsewhere in Q as a clue that the parable pairs do not have to do with gender, but rather have to do with a proclivity toward repetition and variations on a theme. (Examples for this from Q might include things like: "Foxes have holes, and birds of the sky have nests; but the son of humanity does not have anywhere he can lay his head" (Q 9:58) and "you, Capernaum, up to heaven will you be exalted? Into Hades shall you come down!" (Q 10:15). Because of this, Arnal asserts that "the Q couplets do not in and of themselves serve as any convincing indication of a tendency toward gender inclusiveness."[49] In other words, Arnal argues that the author/s or translator/s of Q, which he describes as a scribe or scribes, had no intention of commenting on gender, or reaching out to female audience members, or acknowledging existing community members, but rather that these scribes simply had a tradition of employing parallelism and enjoying wordplay with variables: "a specific identification of Q's tradents with legal administration, presumably at the village level, serves only to reinforce the impression already gained that these couplets are in fact patterned after legal or quasi-legal formulas."[50]

Arnal's thesis, however, is flawed in one respect. He argues that the parallel parables in Q have *nothing* to do with gender and are rather *all* about variable wordplay, on the basis that Q can be connected with scribal culture.

Arnal's hypothesis that Q's sayings were curated in a scribal context is practically undeniable and makes more sense than any other current theory. His problematic arguments that the Q gender pairs do not have to do with gender[51] are not integral to his otherwise impeccable work on Galilean scribal culture. That is, his fruitful connection of Q with scribal culture is by no means mutually exclusive to the presence of attention to gender. From an argument that other wordplay exists in Q, it does not logically follow that the gendered pairs are therefore meaningful *only* as wordplay, and not relevant to a discussion of social/historical gender. When we encounter close verbal parallels in Q where the only variable in the otherwise parallel parable is gender, gender is what should rise to the fore as the key to narrative analysis of those pairs.

My argument that gender is a key element in Q's parallel parables is strengthened by the fact that the parallelism in Q is somewhat uneven and verbally imperfect—literary parallelism alone cannot possibly be at the forefront of the significance of these passages or else it would be more carefully and evenly done. Many of the Q gender pairs, while they parallel one another in a general way and in the theme and content, do not show any evidence of being rigidly verbally parallel nor do they address content that is particularly legal. The parables of the lost sheep and the lost coin (Q 15:4–5a, 7–9), for instance, with the shepherd rejoicing on his own and the woman calling her neighbors to rejoice as a group, serve to highlight the fact that the pairs are clearly not *pedantically* parallel as one might expect if legal or artistic permutations were the concern. Indeed most of the parallel gender pairs are *imperfectly* parallel at the verbal level and show stronger parallelism at the level of *content*. These pairs might be symmetrical in terms of their lesson and their juxtaposition of gender, but if the whole point were legislative permutations of a theme, then it is likely that this feature would be more obvious in the text of Q and occur with more frequency and consistency throughout the text, and, most importantly, occur with many other variables besides masculinity and femininity. Likewise, Arnal's claim that Q tends toward parallelism in general would be stronger if Q exhibited more verbal play, but as this feature is fairly infrequent, it becomes likely that gender is a driving force in the parallelism of these twinned parables. If the gender pairs could be explained away by a tendency toward parallelism in general, as Arnal claims, then one would expect to see far more verbal play throughout Q and to see a variety of repeated parable pairs that do not relate to gender.

To restate my critique of Arnal's position, it can by all means be argued as he does that Q was curated in a scribal context. Who else in Jewish Galilee could not only write, but also translate from Aramaic? But it does not follow that the presence of scribes precludes attention to gender, particularly when these pairs so often consistently offer one masculine and one feminine example. Arnal claims that Q's general androcentrism indicates that "these administrators were exclusively male" and that "the Q traditions and the various layers were composed by, transmitted by, and preserved by men."[52] Both of these things may well be true and still not be cause for dismissal of the rhetorical work of the pairs, which seems to go back to Jesus; Arnal's work does not consider the distinct possibility that a rhetorical valuing of women audience members may coexist simultaneously with male-dominated scribal culture, androcentric language and a patriarchal/kyriarchal worldview. There are thus significant problems with Arnal's attempt to move the pairs into a discussion of scribal culture *at the expense* of a discussion of gender. This is a discussion that by no means needs to take on an either/or character. If there is a tension between the gender-leveling content of the pairs and the overall androcentrism of Q, it may reflect a difference in the aims of the historical Jesus and the aims of those who curated his sayings collection, rather than a lack of any gender-leveling work whatsoever.

SUMMARY OF CLOSE CALLS: GENDER PAIRS AS INNOVATION

The above "close calls" are really not so close after all. These literary comparisons, whether the poetic synonymous parallelism in Hebrew literature, the double injunction in the pseudepigraphon *Joseph and Aseneth* that cannot be dated prior to Q, or the posited wordplay of scribes, do not provide convincing origins for Q's gendered pairing. It is clear that synonymous parallelism in Hebrew poetry, even when its variables may sometimes seem to correlate with grammatical gender, does not approach the rhetorical project at work in the Q pairs with socialized gender. Neither can Q's rhetoric be wholly explained away as wordplay. When we do encounter close verbal parallels in Q, and the only variable in the otherwise parallel parable is gender, an approach that is guided by the primary texts themselves dictates that *gender is what should rise to the fore as the key to analysis.*

In light of the results of this search for precedents and close calls throughout the Hebrew Bible and Hellenistic/Jewish writings prior to Q, it becomes likely that Q's gendered parallels can be described as an innovation. The same device—that is, synonymous parallelism in twin-lessoned parables, having masculinity and femininity as the parallel terms—does not appear in previous early Jewish and Hellenistic writings. Even those of us who work with Jesus' sayings material don't often think of him in terms of a particularly savvy rhetorician. However, his innovative gendered pairing reveals him to be a sophisticated—and evidently effective—rhetor indeed. He had an ability to craft audience-appropriate teaching material and demonstrates a rare antique acknowledgement of gender as a social category while, at the same time, making a theological statement that gender is not a criterion of inclusion or exclusion in the *basileia* of God. As an effective orator, Q's Jesus seems to have very deliberately geared his teaching to relate to his mixed-gender audience, effectively delivering identical messaging to both men and women, drawing from the immediate surroundings to include both positive and negative examples of women and men with individual agency, in a way that no one else before him had done. This finding has important ramifications beyond simply understanding the origins of the pairs themselves but also for understanding the historical Jesus and his earliest followers.

NOTES

1. See, for example, Schüssler Fiorenza's "Jesus of Nazareth in Historical Research," 29–48.
2. This problem is addressed in Batten, "More Queries for Q," 47–49.
3. By, *inter alia*, Batten, "More Queries for Q," 47–49 and Corley, *Women and the Historical Jesus*, 1–6.
4. Batten, "More Queries for Q," 46–47; Corley, *Women and the Historical Jesus*.
5. See Hallett, "Women in Augustan Rome," 372.
6. Corley, *Private Women, Public Meals*, 53–65.
7. In order to encourage relationships deemed "appropriate," Augustus introduced financial "baby bonus" laws, which only applied to "approved" marriages (e.g., marriages between individuals of "appropriately matched" class), not only rendering the children of non-approved marriages illegitimate but even making their parents liable for penalties for being "unmarried" and "childless." Raditsa, "Augustus' Legislation Concerning Marriage," 281. For more on Augustus' "moral renewal" program, see R. Horsley, "The Gospel of Imperial Salvation: Introduction," in *Paul and Empire* (ed. R. Horsley; Harrisburg: Trinity Press International, 1997), 10–24, esp. 15.
8. For examples of flexibility for Republic-era women juxtaposed with attempts to curtail them, see L. E. Mitchell, "Codes of Law and Laws: Ancient Greek and Roman Law," *The Oxford Encyclopedia of Women in World History* (ed. B. G. Smith; Oxford: Oxford University Press, 2008), 422–426, esp. 425.
9. Arnal, "Gendered Couplets in Q."
10. Fricker, *Quand Jésus Parle au Masculin-Féminin*, Chapters 3 and 4. See esp. 120ff for Hebraic parallelism.
11. Corley, *Women and the Historical Jesus*.
12. Batten, "More Queries for Q."
13. The terms "Hebrew Bible" and "Apocrypha" are anachronistic at the time of Q, but are a convenient way to highlight the group of ancient and Hellenistic Jewish texts in Hebrew and Greek that came to be canonized in various configurations by both Jews and Christians and that existed as individual writings in the background for Jews at the time of Q. I avoid the use of the term "Old Testament" entirely, as it is a

Christian theological construct that is meaningless for the first century and can serve to obscure the Jewishness of all of the texts under discussion. At the time of Q, aside from the five books of Torah, which comprised a single scroll, the Hebrew Bible and Apocrypha were not canons in the way we think of them today. The texts therein were in circulation separately or in smaller, idiosyncratic collections. Different communities appreciated and held dear different small groups of texts. Only centuries after Q did closed collections such as the Hebrew Bible and Apocrypha begin to be conceived of. See Lee Martin McDonald and James A. Sanders, eds., *The Canon Debate* (Peabody: Hendrickson, 2002); see also Eva Mroczek, *The Literary Imagination in Jewish Antiquity* (Oxford: Oxford University Press, 2016), which re-conceptualizes how early Jews understood sacred writing if we admit that the terms "bible," "book," and "canon" are anachronistic for the Second Temple period.

14. See S. Z. Leiman, *The Canonization of Hebrew Scripture* (Hamden: Archon, 1976) for a history of the collection process of the Hebrew Bible and McDonald, *The Formation of the Christian Biblical Canon*, for a history of the same for the Christian Testament, "Old" Testament/LXX, and Apocrypha/Deuterocanon. See also Barrera, *The Jewish Bible and the Christian Bible*.

15. On the presence of earlier Jewish literature in the Gospels and the sayings of Jesus, see W. Adler, "The Pseudepigrapha in the Early Church," in *The Canon Debate* (ed. L. M. McDonald and J. A. Sanders; Peabody: Hendrickson, 2002), 211–228; J. R. Edwards, *The Hebrew Gospel and the Development of Synoptic Tradition* (Grand Rapids: Eerdmans, 2009); D. J. Harrington, "The Old Testament Apocrypha in the Early Church and Today," in *The Canon Debate* (ed. L. M. McDonald and J. A. Sanders; Peabody: Hendrickson, 2002), 196–210; M. Hengel, *The Septuagint as Christian Scripture* (London: T&T Clark, 2002); and S. Moyise, *Jesus and Scripture: Studying the New Testament Use of the Old Testament* (Grand Rapids: Baker Academic, 2011). See also G. Oegema, "Non-Canonical Writings and Biblical Theology," in *The Changing Face of Judaism, Christianity, and Other Greco-Roman Religions in Antiquity* (ed. I. Henderson and G. Oegema with S. Parks; Gutersloh: Gutersloher Verlagshaus, 2006), 491–512.

16. The definition of *mashal* (לָשָׁמ) (the closest Hebrew approximation of the English "parable") connects parable with parallelism in its main definition: a "proverb, parable (of sentences constructed in parallelism)." F. Brown, S. R. Driver, and C. A. Briggs, A *Hebrew and English Lexicon of the Old Testament* (Oxford: Oxford University Press, 1907).

17. Fricker, *Quand Jésus Parle au Masculin-Féminin*, 120, 236.

18. See the section entitled "The Parables in Israel's Scriptures" in Levine, *Short Stories by Jesus*, 4–6. *Mashal* (לָשָׁמ) is considered the closest Hebrew counterpart to the English "parable" and Greek *parabole* (παραβολη).

19. See Levine, *Short Stories by Jesus*, 4.

20. For a concise overview of the use of parallelism as a poetic device in Hebrew, see J. C. Dancy, *The Divine Drama: The Old Testament as* Literature (Cambridge: Lutterworth, 2001), 21–24.

21. S. L. Gravett, "Literature, Old Testament As," in *Eerdmans Dictionary of the Bible* (ed. D. N. Freedman; Grand Rapids: Eerdmans, 2000), 813.

22. R. Lowth's still oft-cited work of more than two centuries ago, *De sacra poesi Hebraeorum praelectiones academicae (Lectures on the Sacred Poetry of the Hebrews)* (Oxford: Clarendon, 1753), remains surprisingly influential on the subject of Hebrew poetry, and it is in Lowth's commentary on Isaiah that he declares parallelism to be its defining characteristic: R. Lowth, *Isaiah: A New Translation, with a Preliminary Dissertation and Notes, Critical, Philological, and Explanatory* (Boston: Pierce, 1834). For a recent overview of the discussion, see F. W. Dobbs-Allsopp, "Poetry, Hebrew," *The New Interpreter's Dictionary of the Bible* 4 (ed. K. D. Sakenfeld; Nashville: Abingdon, 2009), 550–558. For a good general introduction to the field, see D. L. Petersen and K. H. Richards, *Interpreting Hebrew Poetry* (Minneapolis: Fortress, 1992).

23. See M. A. Powell, ed. *Harper Collins Bible Dictionary: Revised and Updated* (New York: HarperCollins, 2011), 718 and J. M. LeMon and B. A. Strawn, "Parallelism," *Dictionary of the Old Testament: Wisdom, Poetry, and Writings* (ed. T. Longman III and P. Enns; Downer's Grove: InterVarsity, 2008), 502–515 for taxonomies of the numerous categories of poetic parallelism in Hebrew.

24. See Lowth, *Isaiah*, as well as W. C. Kaiser, Jr. and M. Silva, *Introduction to Biblical Hermeneutics: The Search for Meaning* (Grand Rapids: Zondervan, 1994), 90.

25. Lowth, *Isaiah*, ix.

26. K. Dell, "Proverbs," *The New Oxford Annotated Bible, New Revised Standard Version with Apocrypha* (fully revised 4th ed.; Oxford: Oxford University Press, 2010), 896.

27. Gravett, "Literature, Old Testament As," 813.

28. J. B. Gabel and C. B. Wheeler, *The Bible As Literature: An Introduction* (New York: Oxford University Press, 1986), 38; J. L. Resseguie, "Literature, New Testament As," in *Eerdmans Dictionary of the Bible* (ed. D. N. Freedman; Grand Rapids: Eerdmans, 2000), 815.

29. Gravett, "Literature, Old Testament As," 813.

30. Fricker, *Quand Jésus Parle au Masculin-Féminin*, 236.

31. See, for example, A. Berlin, "Grammatical Aspects of Biblical Parallelism," *HUCA* 50 (1979): 17–43.

32. LeMon and Strawn, "Parallelism," 511.

33. See W. G. E. Watson, "Gender-Matched Synonymous Parallelism in the Old Testament," *JBL* 99/3 (1980): 321–341.

34. On the instability of correspondence between grammatical gender and so-called natural gender, see J. M. Anderson, *Morphology, Paradigms, and Periphrases* (Oxford: Oxford University Press, 2011), 269ff; D. E. Baron, *Grammar and Gender* (New Haven: Yale, 1986); and H. Motschenbacher, *Language, Gender, and Sexual Identity: Poststructuralist Perspectives* (*SLS* 29; Amsterdam: John Benjamins, 2010), 63ff. For a feminist argument that grammatical gender may nonetheless have an effect upon modern interpretation, see A. Alvanoudi, *Grammatical Gender in Interaction: Cultural and Cognitive Aspects* (Leiden: Brill, 2014).

35. See Kaiser and Silva, *Introduction to Biblical Hermeneutics*, 52, for a specific caution against extrapolating messages about social gender from grammatical gender in the Hebrew Bible.

36. Most recently published in James H. Charlesworth, ed. *The Old Testament Pseudepigrapha: 2 Volumes* (Peabody: Hendrickson, 2010).

37. See S. Sheinfeld, "The Pseudepigrapha in Current Research," *Religion Compass* (2013): 1–8.

38. See G. S. Oegema and J. H. Charlesworth, eds., *The Pseudepigrapha and Christian Origins: Essays from the Studiorum Novi Testamenti Societas* (New York: T&T Clark, 2008); McDonald, *The Formation of the Christian Biblical Canon*; and J. H. Charlesworth, *The Old Testament Pseudepigrapha and the New Testament* (Cambridge: Cambridge University Press, 1985); as well as Davila, *The Provenance of the Pseudepigrapha*.

39. Any pseudepigrapha cited herein are from Charlesworth's earliest two-volume collection, hereafter *OTP*. J. H. Charlesworth, ed. *Old Testament Pseudepigrapha: 2 Volumes* (Garden City: Doubleday, 1983)

40. There is typical biblical parallelism in the poetic sections of *Ahiqar, Apocalypse of Abraham, Apocalypse of Elijah, Enoch, 3 Enoch, Jubilees, Testament of Moses*, and more, and other books contain vestiges of parallelism from suspected Hebrew originals, such as *Life of Adam and Eve* (See Charlesworth, *OTP 2*, 251). Indeed, the presence of parallelism is often used to help determine whether a pseudepigraphon of uncertain provenance was originally composed in Hebrew, such as in the case of *Questions of Ezra*. See M. E. Stone, "Questions of Ezra," *OTP 1*, 591–600.

41. See Davila, *The Provenance of the Pseudepigrapha*, 190ff.

42. J. J. Collins, "Joseph and Aseneth: Jewish or Christian," *JSP* 14/2 (2005): 97–112.

43. R. S. Kraemer, *When Aseneth Met Joseph: A Late Antique Tale of the Biblical Patriarch and His Egyptian Wife, Reconsidered* (Oxford: Oxford University Press, 1998). Kraemer also still finds it quite possible, despite debates back and forth in recent decades, that "a strong case can be made for Christian composition and redaction," ix.

44. K. Snodgrass, *Stories with Intent: A Comprehensive Guide to the Parables of Jesus* (Grand Rapids: Eerdmans, 2008).

45. In an email to me in 2012, Klyne Snodgrass kindly confirmed that at no point during the research for his book did he come across a gender-based pairing of parables in Hebrew or Greek that might constitute a literary ancestor for the Q pairs.

46. Arnal does this in both "Gendered Couplets in Q" and in his monograph *Jesus and the Village Scribes*.

47. For example, the Mishnah, redacted around 200 C.E. (see Arnal, "Gendered Couplets in Q," 87, n.58).

48. Arnal, "Gendered Couplets in Q," 88–89.

49. Arnal, "Gendered Couplets in Q," 92.

50. Arnal, "Gendered Couplets in Q," 91.

51. Arnal, *Jesus and the Village Scribes*, 168–170.

52. Arnal, "Gendered Couplets in Q," 92.

Chapter 6

Gender Pairs in Contemporaneous and Later Texts

A search for gendered teaching pairs that precede Jesus reveals nothing that can be said to be a direct rhetorical precursor. By contrast, the first and early second centuries seem to be full of examples of various types of gendered pairing in a variety of sources, some of which are connected to early Jesus followers. The presence of gendered pairs in other documents similar in date to Q, along with their afterlife in documents immediately following Q, may indicate that at least some of these documents are connected or share a common source. First- and second-century Jesus-movement literature that makes use of gendered pairing can conceivably be viewed as sharing a common ancestry with Q or at least as sharing a cultural repertoire. Roughly contemporaneous documents can be related to Q as "siblings" whether direct or indirect—texts that have drunk from the same cultural well of inspiration.

It is from an analysis of later early Christian texts that I form arguments that support the notion that Jesus of Nazareth was the innovator of Q's style of gendered pairing. In other words, if there were no gendered pairs before Jesus, but there is gendered pairing in all of the key texts related to Jesus for a century or so after him, this suggests that Jesus' tendency to address both genders in parallel was carried on by the first generation or two of his followers. At the same time, contemporaneous texts outside the Jesus tradition, such *De Vita Contemplativa, Joseph and Aseneth,* and *That Women Too Should Study Philosophy,* work to temper any overenthusiastic claims that Jesus can take sole credit for all gender discourse wherein men and women are depicted as equal in some way.

THE AFTERLIFE OF THE Q GENDER PAIRS

Pairing in Jesus-following Literature

Vestiges of gendered pairs occur in much of the early Christian literature in the decades contemporaneous with and following Q, such as the Gospel of Mark, John's Gospel, the letters of Paul, and, of course, the Gospels of Matthew and Luke from which Q is reconstructed.

The gender-paired sayings in Matthew and Luke are direct literary descendants of Q by definition. But the places in the Gospels of John, Special Luke, Mark, and Paul (1 Cor 7), where other kinds of gender pairing occur, do not seem to share literary dependence. Together, they serve as a cloud of independent[1] witnesses of the tendency toward gender pairing that was first set down in Greek in Q and first spoken by Jesus.

Luke/Acts and Gender Pairs

As mentioned earlier, the most obvious place where gender parallels exist is in the Gospels of Luke and Matthew, from which Q was reconstructed. Matthew has generally been viewed as less interested in the gendered parable pairs of Q than Luke, as Matthew tends to drop one of each pair as though he doesn't see the point of duplication, whereas Luke will retain duplicate parables or even add gender-paired material. For instance, quite aside from the matter of sayings material derived from Q, Luke constructs whole narratives about men matched by whole narratives about women, such as Zechariah and Mary in Luke 1:5–23 or Simeon and Anna in Luke 2—not paired parables, but paired *characters* in Luke's plot.[2] In general, Luke is thought to make fewer alterations to Q than Matthew does.[3] Kloppenborg and Derrenbacker's interpretation of Luke's use of Q's gender pairs over and against Matthew's usage is highly typical: "On the Two Document hypothesis, Luke saw gender pairing in Q [. . .] and developed this. Matthew, by contrast, did nothing to enhance gender pairing and in fact omitted the parable of the drachma."[4]

Although the only text of Q we have is that which has been built backwards from Matthew and Luke, we can already see by the ways in which the pairs are massaged into their gospel settings that the gospels represent redactions of the sayings material. As was noted in earlier chapters, feminist close readings of the treatment of the Q pairs by Luke reveal that while Matthew may be more likely to drop one half of the pairs, he is not the only author who shows disinterest or even discomfort toward them.

Luke may indeed contain numerous "anomalies" in comparison with the other gospels, in terms of having more named women, depicting a greater variety of women, and expanding Q's practice of matching men's stories with women's stories, according to Mary Rose D'Angelo.[5] Yet, she goes on to note, views of Luke/Acts as the women-friendly gospel have not held up to scrutiny in recent scholarship.[6] Turid Seim's analysis of Luke's "double message" around women indicates that although the Gospel of Luke may be more likely than Matthew to retain Q's gendered pairs, it sends mixed signals for women. Seim finds that the gender pairs and other elements (e.g., named female characters) in Luke do indicate that there were plenty of women in the audience and active in the movement, but she notes at the same time that these women elicit tension on the part of the author, as evidenced by the relationships between them and other characters in the gospel, and argues that there is ultimately a crafted curtailing of women's roles in the broader scheme of Luke/Acts.[7] While Matthew may have left out gendered pairing because he did not notice it or was not interested in it, Luke does notice—and actually works to counteract it.

Schaberg and Ringe concur with Seim; they find that Luke's Gospel shows an interest in "controlling women who practice or aspire to practice a prophetic ministry in the church"[8] and they describe Lukan female role models as "prayerful, quiet, grateful women, supportive of male leadership, forgoing the prophetic ministry."[9] Reid's study of women in Luke similarly finds Luke to be "intent on restricting [women] to silent, passive, supporting roles."[10] D'Angelo notes that

> on the one hand, the author of Luke does increase the number of stories about women in the Gospel, and the increase is a deliberate choice on the part of the author. On the other, the roles in which women appear are more restricted by what is acceptable to the convention of the imperial world than are the roles of women in Mark or John.[11]

When Schüssler Fiorenza compares women in Q material to their placement and treatment in Luke, she too argues for a deliberate Lukan program of taming and re-framing any gender-leveling work being wrought in Q. She also wrestles the authorship of gendered parable pairs back from Luke into the hands of Q (read: Jesus), suggesting that these parable pairs are far more likely to have been original to Q and omitted by Matthew.[12]

There is strong agreement among virtually all the recent feminist readings of Luke that take Q into account: Luke has significantly different tendencies than the Q sayings when it comes to the role of women. Yet despite both Matthean and Lukan ambivalence toward the effects and implications of Jesus' gendered parable pairing, both authors apparently still felt obligated to incorporate some of them, even when the rhetorical aims of the original pairs differed from or even conflicted with those of the gospel authors. In short, the treatments of the Q pairs by Matthew and (especially) Luke reveal an interest in changing the rhetorical purpose of the gender pairs.

Table 6.1 Johannine Narrative Gender-pairs

Jesus' mother and the royal official	John 2:1–11 and John 4:46–64
Nicodemus and the Samaritan	John 3:1–12 and John 4:4–42
The blind man and Martha	John 9:1–41 and John 11:1–54
Mary of Bethany and Judas	John 12:1–8
Jesus' mother and the beloved disciple	John 19:25–27
Mary of Magdala and Thomas	John 20:11–18 and John 20:24–29

John's Gospel and Gender Pairs

Scholars have long noted an awareness of binary gender in the Gospel of John. Like Luke does with Simeon and Anna, or Zechariah and Mary,[13] John's author has crafted a narrative balance between female characters and male characters in his gospel.[14] In terms of the unfolding narrative, we find that Nicodemus is paired with the Samaritan Woman, Martha has been paired with Peter, Mary of Bethany is juxtaposed with Judas, and the list goes on. Scholars who have discussed the Johannine narrative gendered pairs agree that there are six sets of characters that deliberately highlight and balance gender in John (see table 6.1).

In terms of genre, these six Johannine pairs are not the pithy, verbally parallel, teaching passages familiar to us from Q; rather, these juxtapose a male example and a female example on a much broader scale within the gospel, at the level of plot, just like the non-parable, narrative gendered pairings of Luke. Nevertheless, they too attest to a pairing of masculine and feminine of which the author/editor was undoubtedly cognizant. Whereas Luke's aim with the narrative pairs seems to depict women in submissive roles more pleasing to his imperial-influenced audience, John's narrative pairs may be working with a Christological aim—to depict a Christ who possesses a balance of masculine and feminine characteristics.[15] Either way, the presence of gendered pairing in the traditionally literarily independent Gospel of John is notable. It may well point to yet another stream of the same tradition of gender pairing that stands *behind* Q, namely the historical Jesus, albeit at the macro level of narrative rather than the micro level of sayings.

Colleen Conway has done extensive work on the pairing of men and women in the plot of the fourth gospel[16] and agrees with previous scholars that there is indeed a "consciousness of gender identity" in the gospel.[17] But Conway pushes against previous scholarship on the six paired women and men in John when she concludes that, although the gospel is indeed conscious of gender and does offer an array of female participants, the message is not one of "a genuine discipleship of equals" about which feminist theologians might rejoice unequivocally; she writes: "in the Gospel of John, women appear free from traditional gender categories in the social realm, but the customary relationship between male and female is reinscribed in the spiritual realm."[18] In other words, although women are given active roles in the narrative, these are limited to the social realm; she demonstrates that Jesus is still depicted as the ultimate male, so readings that find the divine Christ in John to be beyond gender are overly optimistic.[19] Conway concludes that, while there is no question that gender is actively employed in the construction of meaning in the Johannine narrative, that meaning is ambiguous and multifaceted.[20]

Conway's ambivalent reading stands in contrast to that of another scholar who has also discussed gendered parallels in Johannine narrative: Margaret Beirne.[21] Beirne, who also describes this literary element as "gendered pairs," identifies the same six male/female pairings designed by the author of John. Beirne, however, considers these six Johannine pairs to be John's continuation[22] of the narrative gender pairing that she perceives as a Lukan convention. Unlike Conway, Beirne interprets this Johannine attempt to balance both genders in the narrative as a way of modeling a "discipleship of equals," as the title of her work indicates with no uncertainty: *Women and Men in the Fourth Gospel: A Genuine Discipleship of Equals*. Additionally, she proposes that this was a significant part of the Johannine author's project:

> The six nominated "gender pairs" of the fourth gospel are located in literary arrangements suggestive of a balancing of gender and are contextualized with the Johannine Jesus encompassing the major dimensions of the Gospel's theological purpose.[23]

The conclusions of Beirne and Conway differ markedly in terms of their ramifications for women both ancient and modern, but they agree completely in one respect: the fourth gospel contains a crafted pairing of masculine and feminine at the literary level, which seems to have been a conscious choice on the part of the author. This latter point will become significant for my argument regarding the origins of Q's gender pairs, which I discuss in the conclusion to this chapter.

Undisputed Paul and the Gender Pairs

In the authentic writings of Paul, roughly contemporaneous with Q, there are two passages that deserve attention as instances of pairing and/or balancing gender: Galatians 3:28, along with several instructions about marriage in 1 Corinthians 7. In terms of genre, neither of these passages is a set of twin parallel parables with gender as the variable as we find in Q, which is understandable as Paul shows very little interest in or awareness of the sayings material and was not a member of Jesus' movement before the crucifixion. Nor is either case of Pauline pairing a narrative-level gender pairing like the ones seen in Luke or John, which is understandable as Paul's only writings we know of are in epistolary format rather than narrative format. Rather, the Galatians case is more like the "shorter pairs" in Q—a short phrase that mentions two halves in a gender binary and seems to view both sides as (at least in some way) equals. The 1 Corinthians passage is more like the halakhic or legal gender-pairing seen above in *Joseph and Aseneth*, where exactly the same behavioral instructions are given to men and women.

Galatians 3:28: Famously, Galatians 3:28 reads: "There is no longer Jew or Greek, there is no longer slave or free, there is no longer male and female; for all of you are one in Christ Jesus." Of course, this is the verse that launched a thousand books.[24] It has been an interpretive key for the entire New Testament in the hands of all manner of liberators, egalitarians, and feminists.[25] According to Karin B. Neutel, though, the verse has "escaped a thoroughly first-century reading," because "interpretations of this verse tend to be driven by . . . modern notions such as inclusion, equality, or identity."[26]

For our purposes, what is important is not the myriad modern readings of the verse, but the simple fact that "male and female" (ἄρσεν καὶ θῆλυ)[27] are paired in the text, in the same way as the "shorter pairs" in Q. Also similar to Q is that both sides of these sets of terms, while not social equals in the first century (e.g., slaves and free persons), become categories that are leveled in Paul's version of the Jesus movement. When one is "in Christ Jesus," the terms lose their regular distinctions. This renders this text not only similar to the "shorter pairs," but means it is similar in terms of content to those Q parable pairs where each gender may retain its stereotypical roles (male shepherd, female housekeeper), and yet gender is pointedly never a criterion for rejection from or membership in the *basileia* (or, in Paul's case, "in Christ").

1 Corinthians 7: Far more impressive than this wee gender pair in Galatians, however, is the extended series of gendered pairs we find in 1 Corinthians 7. These read:

a) . . . each man should have his own wife, and each woman her own husband. (1 Cor 7:2b)
b) The husband should give to his wife her conjugal rights, and likewise the wife to her husband. (1 Cor 7:3)
c) For the wife does not have authority over her own body, but the husband does, likewise the husband does not have authority over his own body, but the wife does. (1 Cor 7:4)

d) ... the wife should not separate from her husband ... the husband should not divorce his wife. (1 Cor 7:10b-11)
e) ... if any brother has a wife who is an unbeliever, and she consents to live with him, he should not divorce her. And if any woman has a husband who is an unbeliever, and he consents to live with her, she should not divorce him. (1 Cor 12:b–13)
f) For the unbelieving husband is made holy through his wife, and the unbelieving wife is made holy through her husband. (1 Cor 7:14a)
g) Wife, for all you know, you might save your husband. Husband, for all you know, you might save your wife. (1 Cor 7:16)

This is quite a lengthy series of repeated instructions for both men and women, with the same instruction being given to each, implying a type of equality within the community—the inclusion of both men and women as recipients of the letter, and, further, the ability of both believing men and believing women to "make holy" an unbelieving spouse (7:14a). In cases of divorce, celibacy, marriage, and so on, there is no indication in the above passages that women and men have different levels of responsibility, agency, or importance. Both genders are exhorted to adhere to the same guidelines.

Together, these two cases that I have identified from within the genuine Pauline epistles (Galatians and 1 Corinthians) may link gendered pairing in Paul and Q—probably not by means of a literary relationship, but perhaps by means of a shared heritage that goes back earlier than both Q and Paul, to this rhetorical practice of Jesus during his public career, and to the full inclusion of women members that either resulted from—or gave rise to—the rhetoric.

Mark's Gospel and Gender Pairs

In addition to Pauline and Johannine gendered pairing, there is also an instance of a Markan gendered parallel parable pair (Mark 2:21–22 and parallels)—the parables of the Patch and the Wine. This name for the parable set, which has not caught on, was suggested by Alistair Kee in a 1970 article, "so there is no value judgment on the various elements";[28] Kee was deliberately going against all previous nomenclature in a noble effort to break free of a dominant supersessionist reading. Unlike in Paul and John, this pair is in the same genre that we have identified in Q: the full parallel parable pair. The parables of the patched garment and the old wineskin have made their way into both Luke and Matthew, presumably via Mark rather than Q.[29] The twin parables juxtapose a patch of unshrunk cloth in the first part with new wine in the second. The verses in question read:

> No one sews a piece of unshrunk cloth on an old cloak; otherwise, the patch pulls away from it, the new from the old, and a worse tear is made.

And no one puts new wine into old wineskins; otherwise, the wine will burst the skins, and the wine is lost, and so are the skins (Mark 2:21–22).

In the first two parallel lines, a patch that has not been prepared by shrinking will result in the loss of both patch and cloak; in the second parallel lines, wine that is put into old wineskins at too early a stage in its process will result in the loss of both wine and skins.[30]

At first glance, while this is clearly a doubled parable, the twin lessons do not seem to refer to gender at all. Recall, however, that one version of the gender pairs in Q avoids mentioning human gender directly, but rather implies it by using day-to-day tasks associated with either men or women. Sewing is certainly viewed as feminine for the time period in question. "The control of the shuttles and all kinds of wool-work" is said to be relegated completely to women in Plato, *Laws* 805d–806a, and Xenophon says that a knowledge of spinning and "making a cloak" are the absolute basic minimum training with which a good wife should come equipped (*Oikonomikos* 7.5–6). As for the laborers for viticulture, they are most certainly men.[31] So, if sewing can be connected with the female realm and winemaking with the male realm, then Mark 2:21–22 contains a gendered pair. This unique Markan connection to Jesus' gender-pairing was first noted by Denis Fricker.[32] With this gender-implied type of parable pair in mind, the similarity between the Q pairs and this Markan parable set is striking.

Whether or not the author of Mark was aware of it, Mark 2:21–22 indeed seems to constitute a gendered parallel pair. This means that gendered pairing exists within yet another text that is approximately contemporaneous with, yet independent of Q. Together, these begin to build a case that the pairs are an innovation that must go back before Q to Jesus, and, further, were so strongly associated with Jesus that they show up in various ways in almost every sort of text that came out of the Jesus movement in the first century. The appearance of various types of gendered pairing in four independent texts—Paul, Mark, John, and the Luke/Matthew/Q sayings material—strongly suggests that the pairs originated with a stratum of the Jesus movement prior to their two earliest pieces of literary evidence: undisputed Pauline letters and Q, and thus with Jesus himself. This final section examines these textual afterlives of the pairs in light of the criteria for authenticity that are sometimes employed by historical Jesus researchers.

GENDER PAIRING AND THE HISTORICAL JESUS

As I demonstrated earlier, there are no cases before Q in early Jewish and Hellenistic literature where identical story-pairs expressly crafted with human gender balance occur and in relation to a gender-mixed audience. There are, however, numerous cases in the first and early second centuries, including in the major Christian sources immediately following Q. We have seen that in some instances, the post-Q cases of gender pairs in Jesus-movements texts show some discomfort with the gender-pairing tendency of Jesus and work to mute its gender-leveling rhetoric (Luke/Acts, and perhaps John and Matthew). In the case of Mark, it is not certain whether the author connected the one paired saying with gender. And yet, no matter their level of authorial enthusiasm for the gender-pairing, the above passages function as multiple independent attestations to this literary pairing device (Q/Paul/Mark/John). Together, these data work to reinforce the argument that gendered pairing with the intent of reaching a mixed-gender audience as, in some sense, equals, is Jesus' own invention.

Multiple Attestation

The criterion of multiple attestation is one of the various tools that can be used to bolster the likelihood of a tradition's authenticity in historical Jesus research. It is succinctly defined by John P. Meier as follows: "*multiple attestation* focuses on sayings or deeds of Jesus witnessed (i) in more than one independent literary source (e.g., Mark, Q, Paul, or John) and/or (ii) in more than one literary form or genre."[33]

The practice of relying on criteria of authenticity has waned in some circles due to concerns about subjectivity and over-confidence.[34] The criteria have at times been overemphasized as the sole acceptable means of reconstructing anything about the historical Jesus. Some scholars have advocated doing away with the concept of criteria altogether, focusing on the role of orality and memory in developing traditions rather than relying so heavily on texts.[35] Tobias Hägerland asserts that "the longstanding yet mistaken notion in historical Jesus research that the criteria can, in isolation, fulfil the requirement of a method must be abandoned."[36] However, he goes on to note that it seems "both advisable and probable" that the criteria will continue to be used, albeit in combination with other approaches.[37] The fact remains that when something is attested across multiple independent sources, this remains a useful indicator of its prevalence.

The appearances of gender pairs (of various sorts) in Paul, Mark, and John in addition to Q represent four traditionally separate literary traditions: the Q/Matthew/Luke complex, the Gospel of Mark, the Pauline epistles, and the Gospel of John.[38] According to the criterion of multiple attestation, the frequency of these appearances not only in different text groups but also in different genres strongly suggests that the practice of using rhetorical gender balance as a teaching method predates all of these sources (i.e., that, in this case, it originates with Jesus of Nazareth).

Turning our attention to the Johannine use of narrative gender pairing, it is significant that John's Gospel constitutes an early Christian text without, as far as anyone can tell, any direct literary dependence on Q[39] that displays a clear interest in balancing genders at the literary level. Although Conway interprets this balance in a more negative light, and Beirne in a more positive one, both clearly identify a strong tendency in John's narrative to use parallel male and female characters. What is important for the purposes of this section is that another early Christian witness independent from Q is carrying on the tradition of gendered pairing, although at a broader narrative level. John serves as an independent witness to an attention to a qualified gender equality that, while it does not serve as an indicator of what was going on within Q and around the creation of Q, does connect disparate early Jesus movements together by the cord of deliberately gender-balanced language.[40]

We have now found this tendency in several post-Q circles: the Johannine community, the Pauline assemblies, the Gospel of Mark, and perhaps even in *Joseph and Aseneth*, if Kraemer's dating and suggestion of Christian provenance hold.[41] A situation of multiple attestation across different genres and text groups is an indicator that the trend predates the earliest of the traditions; that is, in this case, the gender pairs predate Q, Paul, and Mark. In other words, since: (1) Q, Paul, and Mark are among some of the earliest Christian documents; and (2) they all share an element that was seemingly unheard of before them; and (3) this element is echoed in later but literarily independent early Christian sources (John, *Joseph and Aseneth*?), and kept by Luke and Matthew although they felt compelled to modify it; then (4) it is highly plausible that this shared element, which does not seem to have been identifiable as a trend in early Jewish and Hellenistic literature, can be traced to the historical Jesus. Conclusions like this one, assisted by multiple attestations, are common in Historical Jesus Research.[42]

Embarrassment

Another criterion in Jesus research that makes a great deal of sense is known as the criterion of embarrassment. This is the notion that an author is not likely to invent material that makes his or her own ideology or group look bad in the eyes of the reader; if early Christian authors included Jesus material that was "embarrassing" to them—such as the ignominious manner in which their leader died—then such material is flagged as more likely to be authentic.[43] This criterion is largely responsible for the scholarly consensus around the historicity of events like Jesus' baptism.[44]

The criterion of embarrassment strengthens the connection of the pairs with Jesus as well, given the ways in which Luke/Acts and Matthew have been demonstrated above to frame, avoid, or modify with ambivalence and discomfort the raw form of the gender pairs. We saw that Matthew and Luke do take the parables over, but by dropping one half of a pair or by inserting them into a narrative frame that shifts their focus or meaning, they draw attention away from the gender-leveling function of the rhetorical units at their Q stage. This redaction of the pairs by Luke and Matthew reinforces the likelihood of their authenticity as Jesus sayings, since the ambivalence with which they are sometimes incorporated into the works of Matthew and Luke suggest embarrassment. This may mean that the gender pairs had already been established as authentic and useful in communities prior to Matthew and Luke's Gospels, again strongly indicating their use by Jesus.

THE PAIRS IN NON-JESUS FOLLOWING LITERATURE

In addition to the early Christian textual traditions mentioned above, there are other cases in and around the first century where gender is discussed in ways that are in reminiscent of the Q pairs. These are not the paired male–female parables or paralleled male–female plot lines of Q and the gospels nor are they likely to be literarily related to Q. Yet they show that, while Jesus may have coined a rhetorical device, he did so not anomalously but as a product of his time. The texts of *De Vita Contemplativa*, *Joseph and Aseneth*, and *That Women too Should Study Philosophy* serve to demonstrate that some aspects of Jesus' gender pairs, such as the notion of spiritual gender equality apart from social gender equality, or the notion of women as fully responsible and eligible agents in their own pursuit of virtue and piety, arose in other first-century contexts as well.

De Vita Contemplativa

A discussion of women and men as equals in the first century would be incomplete without reference to the Therapeutae and Therapeutrides, a contemplative community comprising both women and men, known only through Philo of Alexandria's glowing description of them in his *De Vita Contemplativa* (*On the Contemplative Life*). Held up as either gloriously feminist or deeply patriarchal by various scholars in turn, there is no question that the text's depiction of women is complicated, and moreover that the ascetics in question have been highly idealized by Philo—although scholars at least seem to now agree that the group is not fictitious.[45] The Therapeutae are now thought to be historical because the group is geographically located in a rather easily verifiable spot, and because the other ascetic group Philo describes—the Essenes—is also historical.[46] One of the most convincing arguments that the group is not fictitious, though, is the fact that Philo describes women philosophers, whom he would probably, in Taylor's words, "have been more comfortable excluding."[47]

Three aspects of the Therapeutae/Therapeutrides in Philo are pertinent to our discussion of Q's gendered pairs. First, this group of ascetics represents an additional first-century description of women and men as having parity in terms of their intellectual and spiritual capacity and worth; both the men and the women are active agents in their own quests for piety in service to God, and both are held up by Philo as seekers of wisdom. Second, while the text does not particularly employ much parallelism, there are a several instances where Philo takes the time to mention that the women are also active participants. Third, the very text in which this gender parity is recorded and depicted as good nevertheless displays some discomfort with the notion of women as men's equals, just as we see happening in some of the early Christian responses to women's religious value and authority at the outset of the Jewish Jesus movements. I will expand on each of these three points below.

First, the Therapeutrides are accorded intellectual and spiritual autonomy alongside the male Therapeutae in the text. Though most of the book is devoted to describing the merits of the group in general (such as simplicity, devotion to wisdom, and austere eating habits), or to denigrating other groups (especially Greco-Roman banqueters), there are moments when the attention is turned (favorably) to the contemplative women. These moments include a mention of the women's equally invested participation in the joint Sabbath-day ceremonies, when the usually solitary individuals come together (italics mine): "For women too regularly make part of the audience with *the same ardour* and the *same sense of their calling*" (*Contempl.* 3.30). Likewise, when the president is delivering an oration, it is clear that the women, too, are intended recipients of its wisdom; Philo mentions that a partition is designed with an open space so that "the women sitting within ear-shot can easily follow what is said since there is nothing to obstruct the voice of the speaker" (*Contempl.* 3.33).

Second, Philo uses a little gendered pairing when he describes the ancient archetype after which the group's choral harmonizing, performed every seventh Sabbath, is modelled: the crossing of the Red Sea. He writes that immediately upon crossing the sea safely, the Israelites (italics mine) had been "so filled with ecstasy *both men and women* that forming a single choir they sang hymns of thanksgiving to God their Saviour, *the men led by the prophet Moses and the women by the prophetess Miriam*" (*Contempl.* 40.87). Philo continues, describing the music of the "choir of the Therapeutae of either sex" in glowing terms, concluding that the choristers are "worthy of reverence" and that "the end and aim of thoughts, words, and choristers alike is piety" (*Contempl.* 40.88). In these passages, Philo recalls both a male and a female figure from Israel's literary past, as do the parable pairs with the Queen of the South and the Men of Ninevah (Q 11:31–32) and Zarephath and Naaman (Luke 4:25–27). He also accords importance and agency to both men and women singers alike as both are "worthy of reverence" and both have the goal of "piety." Although the passage does not pair gender in the formally paralleled way that can be seen in Q and the gospels, it does participate in the same discourse—that of women and men's equal participation in religious community.

Third, Philo's text shows discomfort with the prominence of women in this community, similar to the discomfort we see around the presence of women as spiritual equals in the Jesus movement after Q. Although the overall thrust of the text is Philo's glowing praise for the group, we can see him trying to narrow the circumstances in which women may participate. This tempering of the women's presence makes sense for an author who elsewhere "associated all that is female with irrationality and corporeality and believed that women were selfish, manipulative creatures."[48] In describing the Therapeutrides' participation in communal events, Philo assures the audience that the women are seated apart from the men (*Contempl.* 3.33, 4.69).

Perhaps more importantly, he mentions that the Therapeutrides are comprised of "mostly aged virgins" (*Contempl.* 8.68). This mention of their virginity is not commensurate with Philo's language for them elsewhere as *gunai* (which does not imply virginity),[49] so the presence of the word "mostly" may indicate Philo's wish to exaggerate this virginal aspect because he is uncomfortable with married women who break out of social norms to choose celibacy.[50] As Boyarin notes, "the society and religious culture depicted by Philo *do* permit parity between men and women and religious, cultural creativity for women as for men,"[51] but this parity comes at an expense: "this autonomy and creativity in the spiritual sphere are predicated on the renunciation of both sexuality and maternity."[52] Whether all (or most) of the women in the historical group were lifelong virgins, for Philo it is only acceptable for the Therapeutrides to devote their lives to the love of wisdom and the pursuit of piety because they are exceptional (virginal, nonsexual) women, rather than because women and men in general should be considered to be social equals. There is another point of comparison with Q here: in both the *basileia* community around Jesus and the community of the Therapeutae, the women's seemingly socio-historical spiritual equality exists in tension with their literary reception; authors pass the tradition along while simultaneously trying to temper its force.

What matters about all of this for our purposes is that this work of Philo provides first-century evidence for another Jewish community that, counter-culturally, eschews the demands of marriage and family in favor of religious pursuits for which gender is not a criterion of inclusion. Whether or not Philo approves of this completely, this text mitigates against the myth of feminist Christian origins that imagines that only the women around Jesus were afforded this type of opportunity. The Therapeutrides, as Philo describes

140   *Chapter 6*

them, seem to provide evidence that other contemporaneous Jewish groups could refuse to conform to typical social gender roles and that other first-century Jewish thinkers could conceive of women with spiritual and intellectual capability and agency.

Musonius Rufus

It would also be remiss to think about first-century discourse around the equality of men and women without reference to the Stoics. As with Philo's Therapeutae, scholarly evaluations of ancient Stoicism have ranged from hailing Stoicism as "at its heart, feminist"[53] to arguing that feminism and Stoicism are "fundamentally and essentially incompatible."[54] In these discussions, a variety of Stoic thinkers recur who claimed that women should be treated the same as men, on topics ranging from women's virtue to women's dress to women's education.[55] One such thinker who falls within our time period is the popular first-century Stoic Musonius Rufus. Among his 21 collected treatises are two arguments in favor of a philosophical education for women.

Musonius Rufus did not leave any writings, but his teaching was recorded by Lucius, his student, and preserved in Stobaeus.[56] His treatise, *That Women Too Should Study Philosophy*,[57] illustrates how the longstanding Stoic notion of women's potential for *moral* equality[58] continued through our time period. In it, he advocates that women should indeed acquire a philosophical education.

This treatise on women and philosophy begins as follows:

> Women as well as men . . . have received from the gods the gift of reason, which we use in our dealings with one another and by which we judge whether a thing is good or bad, right or wrong. Likewise the female has the same senses as the male; namely sight, hearing, smell, and the others. Also both have the same parts of the body, and one has nothing more than the other. Moreover, not men alone, but women too, have a natural inclination toward virtue and the capacity for acquiring it, and it is the nature of women no less than men to be pleased by good and just acts and to reject the opposite of these. If this is true, by what reasoning would it ever be appropriate for men to search out and consider how they may lead good lives, which is exactly the study of philosophy, but inappropriate for women? (Musonius Rufus, *Diatr.* 3.1–2 [Lutz])

So, according to Musonius, both men and women receive divine reason, both engage the world using the same senses, both have similar human bodies, both incline toward acquiring virtue, both are pleased by goodness and justice, and thus it is appropriate for both to study philosophy in order to lead good lives. One might be forgiven for understanding the above as a general argument for women's and men's equality, especially because the arguments for men's and women's equal education are overt, rather than implied, as in the audience behind the parable pairs of Q.

Whereas the gender pairs in Q use male and female examples to teach about Jesus' *basileia* message, implying by their medium that a measure of equality is assumed among their audience, the above passage in Musonius Rufus addresses gender equality directly as its main topic. Musonius is not teaching his philosophical lesson using a hypothetical man who loses a sheep paired with a hypothetical woman who loses a coin, or a raven who doesn't farm paired with a lily who doesn't spin, subtly implying or acknowledging the inclusion of women audience members. Rather, he is remembered here as speaking directly about some ways in which men and women can be considered to be equal.

The second part of Musonius' treatise outlines his reasons *why* women should study philosophy: not to excel as philosophers or hold political sway, but rather to do a better job of their gendered tasks of caring for home, children, and husbands. A woman trained in philosophy will be a "good housekeeper" (3.3), an "untiring defender of children and husband" (3.4), "prepared to nourish her children at her own breast, and to serve her husband with her own hands, and willing to do things which some would consider no better than slaves' work" (3.5), and "a great help to the man who married her" (3.5). Musonius states that such a woman will *not* carry on orating and pontificating when she "ought to be sitting at home spinning" (3.6), but on the contrary, philosophy will help her to be "content with her lot and work with her own hands" (3.7). Engel sums up the whole treatise in one sentence: "If you want your wife to be a better domestic servant, teach her philosophy."[59]

Both the Q pairs and this treatise seem to envision a world where gender does, more or less, differentiate between men and women in dictating their main occupations and daily tasks. Such assumptions in Q are transmitted passively by the gendered examples of men and women's labor that appear in the paired stories, but they are also challenged when the *basileia* is prioritized over family obligations. Gendered occupations in Q are thus descriptive, but not necessarily prescriptive. In Musonius Rufus, however, assigned gender roles are not only overtly praised, but they are put forward as extremely important. Thorsteinsson writes that Musonius is "much in favour of the 'traditional' order when he assigns to (most) women typical tasks relating to the household, and some typical physical outdoor tasks to (most) men"[60] and points out that, after all, Musonius "considered the family and household to be the very foundation of society."[61]

These same social views appear in the other treatise where Musonius addresses gender roles—*Should Daughters Receive the Same Training as Sons*. In it, he asserts that girls should receive the same education as boys, arguing that both men and women possess the same capacity for virtues, such as courage and self-control (Musonius Rufus, *Diatr.* 4.1–3 [Lutz]). Yet, as with the previous treatise, he states that women thus educated will not use their philosophical training for oration and argument, but rather "they will use philosophy for the ends of their life as women" (4.8). By this he, once again, means "women's work" such as spinning (4.5) and takes pains to note that men and women should adhere to their gendered tasks as far as is possible, unless there are exceptional circumstances—for instance, if a man becomes weak and disabled, in which case he might only be fit to help with women's tasks or if extreme need requires even women to help with feats of strength and courage (4.8).

As in the case of Q, we can see that the notion of men and women as socially identical is simply not at stake in the first-century Mediterranean world, but that in certain areas, such as the spiritual, the moral, or the intellectual, women's and men's equality was conceivable. The works of Musonius Rufus confirm, as does Philo's *De Vita Contemplativa*, that overt discussion of the degree to which men and women could be considered equal—at least in certain ways—was a part of the first-century Mediterranean landscape. Musonius Rufus provides another contemporaneous example of a view of women as equal in terms of a capacity for virtue, but not rendered identical in terms of socially gendered roles. As Engel points out, the Stoic belief in the identical nature of men's and women's virtue "did not lead the Stoics to call for a radical change in women's roles or place in society,"[62] just as the gendered pairs of Jesus can demonstrate a belief in women's and men's identical capacity for understanding and promoting the teachings, while also employing and reinforcing typically gendered social roles and tasks.

Joseph and Aseneth

Finally, we return to a text mentioned only briefly in a previous chapter—the novella *Joseph and Aseneth*. Chapter 8: 5–7 is the passage in question. This passage, like Q, contains an instance of a kind of gendered pairing, treats both men and women as individuals who are responsible for their own religious choices, and works to teach an identical lesson to both male and female recipients. If, as some argue, *Joseph and Aseneth* is a Christian text,[63] then it may add to our instances of multiple attestation for gender-pairing in early Christianity. However, as its provenance is difficult to determine, *Joseph and Aseneth* at the very least stands as additional evidence that Jesus of Nazareth was hardly unique in his awareness of gender and his ability to conceive of women and men as equals in a number of ways, even as he coined a new way of addressing them.

Joseph and Aseneth is a Hellenistic historical novella, set in the time of the patriarch Joseph, that explains how the Israelite came to marry his wife

Aseneth, the daughter of an Egyptian priest. In Genesis, we read that "Pharaoh gave Joseph the name Zaphenath-paneah; and he gave him Asenath daughter of Potiphera, priest of On, as his wife" (Genesis 41:45a) and that "before the years of famine came, Joseph had two sons, whom Asenath daughter of Potiphera, priest of On, bore to him" (Genesis 41:50). The biblical story is greatly expanded in *Joseph and Aseneth*, a pseudepigraphon that takes pains to demonstrate that the character of Aseneth, although a foreigner, was a worthy bride, as evidenced by the remarkable divine experiences she underwent prior to their marriage (*Joseph and Aseneth* 10–17).[64] For our purposes, it stands out because of the gender-paired passage found in *Joseph and Aseneth* 8:5–7. Here, Joseph recites an injunction that applies to "a man who worships God," and then adds the same injunction for "a woman who worships God":

> It is not right for a man who worships God, who with his mouth blesses the living God, and eats the blessed bread of life, and drinks the blessed cup of immortality, and is anointed with the blessed unction of incorruption, to kiss a strange woman, who with her mouth blesses dead and dumb idols, and eats of their table the bread of anguish, and drinks of their libations the cup of treachery, and is anointed with the unction of destruction. A man who worships God will kiss his mother and his sister that is of his own tribe and kin, and the wife that shares his couch, who with their mouths bless the living God. So too it is not right for a woman who worships God to kiss a strange man, because this is an abomination in God's eyes. (*Joseph and Aseneth* 8: 5–7)

This remarkable passage is in the context of the character of Joseph being presented with the opportunity to kiss the beautiful but non-Jewish Aseneth. Written in the context of Hellenistic cosmopolitanism,[65] it makes sense for the author to wrestle with the question of marriage with non-Jews and to place in the patriarch's mouth a recitation as to why *male* followers of Joseph's god must not embrace female non-followers; he is man, presented with a decision as to whether to kiss a woman. However, Joseph then repeats and rephrases a (sharply abbreviated) version of the scenario for a *hypothetical female* follower, extrapolating that female followers of Joseph's god (although there are none in the text at this point) also must avoid embracing male non-followers. This is certainly a kind of gendered pairing, similar in some ways to what we find in Q.

An obvious similarity is that the passage uses a measure of parallelism to address both potential male audience members and potential female audience members with the same lesson: do not choose a partner who does not worship our god. Obviously, the literary situation is quite different from that of Q in terms of genre; rather than parable pairs in a collection of a sage's teachings, the passage in *Joseph and Aseneth* is narrative, woven into the plot of a romantic Jewish novel,[66] and this particular part of the novel describes an injunction. Perhaps this gender pair is closer to the allegedly scribal "legal variations on a theme" that Arnal suggests characterize the Q pairs, since the *Joseph and Aseneth* passage proclaims the (il)legality of a certain action by men and reiterates the (il)legality of the same action by women. However, just as with Q, *Joseph and Aseneth* is not a primarily legal text overall, weakening the possibility of scribal wordplay. Rather, *Joseph and Aseneth* is a historicized novella—which in this passage addresses a question of everyday relevance—intermarriage with outsiders and the status of proselytes.[67] This proclamation against marrying foreigners and anxiety around their relationship to the community is a recurring theme in ancient Judaism. One of *Joseph and Aseneth*'s very *raisons d'être* may have been to explain how the Egyptian character of Aseneth came to be a suitable bride for the patriarch Joseph in the book of Genesis (41:45), given the Hebrew Bible's general attitude against intermarriage (e.g., in Genesis 24:3–4, Ezra 10:10, Malachi 2:11).

This gendered pair fits nicely within the aims of the novel, which explains how a patriarch from Israel's past came to marry a foreigner (by depicting the foreigner first having a divine experience—in *Joseph and Aseneth* 14–17—which marks her as an insider by some other criterion than birth). In this case, a potential outcome of the passage in *Joseph and Aseneth* is to make sure that the community's marital norms are also kept by women (or even, in a patriarchal context, *especially* kept by women). This single injunction against kissing an outsider, given to both men and women, implies that both men and women must follow this rule, and thus both men and women are held responsible as active agents in upholding community norms, in some ways calling to mind the expectations of the Q gender pairs for both women and men to participate in the *basileia*.

The Pseudepigrapha is a collection that spans a vast date range and contains books whose dating is undecided. In the case of *Joseph and Aseneth*, it cannot be dated with certainty. In Davila's *The Provenance of the Pseudepigrapha*,[68] he does not come down firmly on a date for the work, whereas Collins specifies its range in current scholarship as spanning 100 B.C.E. and 100 C.E.[69] Kraemer suggests that a Christian provenance is possible.[70] Given that the book can be dated broadly contemporaneously with Q, it serves as an additional indicator that various discourses around men's and women's equal group participation were swirling around the ancient Mediterranean world in the century before and after Jesus of Nazareth.

CONSEQUENCES

Twinned parables that draw from the gender of the audience in order to speak to both men and women do not occur before Jesus of Nazareth, yet they do occur in multiple early sources that are connected to his movement. Q's parable pairing has been modified by some of the later Christian sources in a way that reflects embarrassment or discomfort with their gender-leveling force. Other rhetorical work that refers to men and women in rough parallel, and also seeks to render them equal in certain ways, also exists in first-century texts unrelated or only peripherally related to the Jesus movement.

This chapter's comparisons with contemporaneous texts both inside and outside the Jesus movement connect Jesus more solidly with the innovation of gendered parable pairs as they appear in Q, while also embedding him more solidly *within* his first-century Jewish and Roman context. The consequences are that the "discipleship of equals" model need not be completely discarded along with those lamentable elements of Christian feminist scholarship that malign early Judaism in their clamor to redeem Christian origins from androcentrism and kyriarchy. Jesus of Nazareth indeed inspired an early Jesus movement tradition of women's rhetorical and literary inclusion in gendered pairing, but not within an otherwise barbaric wasteland; the discussion of various ways in which women could be considered equal were happening elsewhere as well.

In other words, the gender pairings in Q, bolstered by gendered pairing in Mark, John, and Paul, indicate that there was innovation within the Galilean Judaism around Jesus toward a (limited) gender equality, that is, a commonly held and experienced discipleship of equals that nonetheless retained socially gendered roles. This circumscribed gender leveling was only made possible by the surrounding context of expanded options for women's group membership already occurring for women since the late Republic and evidenced contemporaneously in sources such as Philo, Musonius Rufus, and *Joseph and Aseneth*. Gender equality did not arise as a feminist Christian phoenix out of the ashes of so-called rigidly patriarchal Judaism. Instead, it was a qualified, apocalyptic equality. It quickly met with resistance, even as it was incorporated into developing Christian traditions, and it was ultimately opposed by the second- and third-century versions of Christianity that came to make their permanent mark on the New Testament canon.

Feminist Christian theologians can make use of the fact that an interest in the equal religious treatment of wo/men appears to have been undeniably important in the original sayings of Jesus. When this importance is examined in juxtaposition with the tension that Q's interest in women causes in the gospels, the common theory that women's agency and power declined steadily and sharply as Christianity developed[71] is once again bolstered. In wielding this knowledge, though, feminist theologians and historians of Christian origins must remember that other first-century traditions outside Jesus movements could also argue, in various ways, for the possibility of women who could function alongside men as full agents in their own pursuit of virtue, salvation, and piety; thus, the narrative of Jesus as lone champion for equality amidst universal misogynistic depravity cannot stand.

When one moves beyond the immediate reception traditions treated here (the Gospels, the genuine Pauline corpus), into Christian texts of the mid-second century and beyond, the systematic rejection of this gender-leveling is obvious. Dewey summarizes this negative development: "Most scholars who address gender roles in early Christianity see a pattern of greater equality between the sexes at the time of Jesus moving to greater and greater conformity with the patriarchal culture by the end of the first century."[72] This programmatic diminishment of the role of women seen by the time of the "pastoral epistles," where women are "saved through childbearing" (1 Tim 2:15) and must be obedient to men (Eph 5:22), and the systematic misogyny of the patristic period, will be covered in the next and final chapter.

My interest is not to cover in detail the steady decline in the role of women in the centuries following Q (except to agree with other scholars that there certainly *was* one.)[73] Yet the contrast between the evidence for gender-leveling in the Jewish movement around Jesus and Q, and the way women's subordination began to solidify within Christianity within a century, certainly highlights the rapid demise of the rhetorical work of gender pairs following the loss of their main innovator. Suffice it to say that any search for a negative foil against which to sharply contrast this gender leveling in the early Jesus movements would do better to focus on its tense reception and eventual near obliteration by later *non-Jewish* Christianity than on the Judaism from which it emerged.

NOTES

1. As is customary, I treat Mark, Q, Paul, and John as independent textual traditions. See Holladay, *A Critical Introduction to the New Testament*, for succinct overviews of the literary independence of Mark, Matthew/Luke/Q (133), and John (198–199). For a remarkable old relic arguing for Mark's use of Q, see B. H. Streeter's "St. Mark's Knowledge and Use of Q," *Studies in the Synoptic Problem* (ed. W. Sanday; Oxford: Clarendon, 1911), 165–183. Not everyone is convinced that John is a strictly independent source; see, e.g. B. Shellard, "The Relationship of Luke and John: A Fresh Look at an Old Problem," in *JTS* (*n.s.*) 46/1 (1995): 71–98.

2. For a complete list of these narrative-level pairs (which also contains the Q-derived pairs), see M. R. D'Angelo, "Women in Luke-Acts: A Redactional View," *JBL* 109 (1990): 444–445.

3. See Crook, "The Synoptic Parables," 23–48.

4. R. A. Derrenbacker, Jr. and J. S. Kloppenborg, "Self-Contradiction in the IQP? A Reply to Michael Goulder," *JBL* 120/1 (Spring 2001): 72.

5. D'Angelo, "Women in Luke-Acts," 441–461.

6. D'Angelo, "Women in Luke-Acts," 441–442.
7. Seim, *The Double Message* (i.e., that the Gospel of Luke contains mixed messages for women).
8. Schaberg and Ringe, "Gospel of Luke," 493.
9. Schaberg and Ringe, "Gospel of Luke," 493.
10. Reid, *Choosing the Better Part?*, 53.
11. D'Angelo, "Women in Luke-Acts," 442.
12. See, *inter alia*, Schüssler Fiorenza, *In Memory of Her*, esp. 145–146.
13. D'Angelo, "Women in Luke-Acts," 444–445.
14. For a brief bibliography of those who have worked on this from the 1970s to the present, see Conway, "Gender Matters," 78, n.3.
15. A. D. Myers, "Gender, Rhetoric and Recognition Characterizing Jesus and (Re)defining Masculinity in the Gospel of John," *JSNT* 38/2 (2015): 191–218.
16. See her reworked dissertation, *Men and Women in the Fourth Gospel: Gender and Johannine Characterization* (Atlanta: Scholars, 1999) and "Gender Matters," 79–103.
17. Conway, "Gender Matters," 80.
18. Conway, "Gender Matters," 102.
19. Conway, "Gender Matters," 101.
20. Conway, "Gender Matters," 103.
21. Beirne, *Women and Men in the Fourth Gospel*.
22. Because of the research for this book, I am now rethinking the dating of Luke/Acts and the independence of John. When one is not oblivious to gender, alternative hypotheses emerge.
23. Beirne, *Women and Men in the Fourth Gospel*, 41.
24. Maly reckons that Gal 3:28 is "doubtless the most frequently quoted text in any discussion of the role of women in the Church," in "Women and the Gospel of Luke," 104.
25. To name but a few that illustrate the diversity: B. Kahl, "No Longer Male: Masculinity Struggles behind Galatians 3:28," *JSNT* 79 (2000): 37–49; J. Kugler, "Galatians 3:26-28 und die Vielen Geslechter der Glaubenden: Impuls fur eine Christliche Geschlechtsrollepastoral jenseits von Sex und Gender," in *Geschlecht quer gedacht: Widerstandspotenziale und Gestaltungsmoglichkeiten in Kirchlicher Praxis* (ed. M. E. Aigner and J. Pock; Munster: Werkstatt Theologie, 2009), 53–70; F. Machingura and P. Nyakuhwa, "Sexism: A Hermetical Interrogation of Galatians 3:28 and Women in the Church of Christ in Zimbabwe," *Journal of Pan African Studies* 8/2 (2015): 92–113; J. Punt, "Power and Liminality, Sex and Gender, and Gal 3:28: A Postcolonial, Queer Reading of an Influential text," *Neotest* 44/1 (2010): 140–166; G. Röhser, "Mann und Frau in Christus: Eine Verhältnisbestimmung von Gal 3,28 und 1 Kor 11,2-16," *SNTU* 22 (1997): 57–78. For an overview of the interpretations of the verse between 1990 and 2014, see D. Francois Tolmie, "Tendencies in the Interpretation of Galatians 3:28 since 1990," *AT* 19 (2014): 105–129.
26. K. B. Neutel, *A Cosmopolitan Ideal: Paul's Declaration "Neither Jew Nor Greek, Neither Slave Nor Free, Nor Male and Female" in the Context of First Century Thought* (London: Bloomsbury T&T Clark, 2015), 2.

27. See Neutel's important discussion of the word "and" in "male and female" (as opposed to "nor" in the other two pairs in the verse): Neutel, *A Cosmopolitan Ideal, Part 4* ("Nor Male and Female: Marriage at the End of the World"), where it is argued that the pairing as it stands could refer to there being no post-eschaton *marriage*.

28. A. Kee, "The Old Coat and the New Wine: A Parable of Repentance," in *NovT* 12/1 (January 1970): 18.

29. It is also found in Matthew 9:14–17 and Luke 5:33–39, and appears in saying 47 of the *Gospel of Thomas*. It is not included in the critical edition of Q.

30. Kee, "The Old Coat and the New Wine," 20–21.

31. Although several elite Roman feminine names have been found reported as managers and owners of viticultural enterprises (S. Dixon, *Reading Roman Women* [London: Duckworth, 2001], 97), it is almost certain that the "grittiest work of the vintage" was done by (male) contract labor. D. L. Thurmond, *A Handbook of Food Processing in Classical Rome: For Her Bounty No Winter* (Leiden: Brill, 2006), 111. Viticulture is so important in the ancient Mediterranean that it is said to make up a third of the "Mediterranean Triad" of wheat, olive oil, and wine. See C. Renfrew, *The Emergence of Civilisation: The Cyclades and the Aegean in The Third Millennium BC* (Oxford: Oxbow, 1972), 280.

32. Fricker, *Quand Jésus Parle au Masculin-Féminin*, Chapter 7.

33. Meier, *A Marginal Jew, Volume 4*, 15.

34. See Rafael Rodríguez, "Authenticating Criteria: The Use and Misuse of a Critical Method," *JSHJ* 7 (2009): 152–167.

35. See, for example, Horsley and Draper, *Whoever Hears You Hears Me*. See also Dale C. Allison, *Constructing Jesus: Memory, Imagination, and History* (London: SPCK, 2010) and R. Rodríguez, *Structuring Early Christian Memory* (London: T&T Clark, 2010).

36. Tobias Hägerland, "The Future of Criteria in Historical Jesus Research," *JSHJ* 13 (2015): 63.

37. Hägerland, "The Future of Criteria," 65.

38. Although, Wills, in his *The Quest of the Historical Gospel*, argues using genre criticism that John and Mark, although independent from one another, had access to an earlier shared gospel tradition.

39. For recent arguments for the literary independence of John from the Synoptic Gospels, see R. E. Brown, *The Death of the Messiah* (2 vols.: New York: Doubleday, 1994); Meier, *A Marginal Jew*, volumes 1 through 4, *passim*; and D. M. Smith, *John among the Gospels* (2nd ed.; Columbia: University of South Carolina Press, 2001), esp. 195–241. For an earlier, classic argument, see P. Gardner-Smith, *St. John and the Synoptic Gospels* (Cambridge: Cambridge University Press, 1938). For a survey of the unconvinced, see Shellard, "The Relationship of Luke and John."

40. For an example of the recently renewed appreciation for the Gospel of John as a source for historical Jesus research and not only a source for early Christianity, see R. Horsley and T. Thatcher, *John, Jesus, and the Renewal of Israel* (Grand Rapids: Eerdmans, 2013). The establishment of a "John, Jesus, and History" group of the Society of Biblical Literature has resulted in the following two volumes so far: P. N. Anderson, F. Just, and T. Thatcher, eds., *John, Jesus, and History, Volume 1: Critical*

Appraisals of Critical Views (Atlanta: SBL, 2007) and *John, Jesus, and History, Volume 2: Aspects of Historicity in the Fourth Gospel* (Atlanta: SBL, 2009).

41. Kraemer, *When Aseneth Met Joseph*.

42. See S. Porter, *The Criteria for Authenticity in Historical Jesus Research: Previous Discussion and New Proposals* (JSNTSup 191; Sheffield: Sheffield Academic, 2000) for a thorough discussion of the current state of criteria for historical Jesus research as well as a history of past issues in the development of the criteria.

43. The criterion of embarrassment was added to the arsenal of Historical Jesus researchers in the 1950s. For a discussion of this criterion, see Porter, *The Criteria for Authenticity for Historical Jesus Research*.

44. Hägerland, "The Future of Criteria," 65.

45. See, for example, Troels Engberg-Pedersen, "Philo's De Vita Contemplativa as a Philosopher's Dream," *JSJ* 30 (1999): 40–64.

46. Joan E. Taylor, *Jewish Women Philosophers of First Century Alexandria: Philo's "Therapeutae" Reconsidered* (Oxford: Oxford University Press, 2003), 10.

47. Taylor, *Jewish Women Philosophers*, 11. See also H. Szesnat, "Mostly Aged Virgins: Philo and the Presence of the Therapeutrides at Lake Mareotis," *Neotestamentica* 32/1 (1998): 191–201.

48. S. Golberg, "The Two Choruses Become One: The Absence/Presence of Women in Philo's *On the Contemplative Life*," *JSJ* 39 (2008): 459–470.

49. Szesnat, "Mostly Aged Virgins," 191–201.

50. Joan E. Taylor, "The Women 'Priests' of Philo's *De Vita Contemplativa*: Reconstructing the Therapeutae," in *On the Cutting Edge: The Study of Women in Biblical Worlds* (ed. J. Schaberg, A. Bach, E. Fuchs; NY: Continuum, 2004), 109–110.

51. D. Boyarin, *A Radical Jew: Paul and the Politics of Identity* (Berkeley: University of California Press, 1994), 189.

52. Boyarin, *A Radical Jew*, 189.

53. As in L. Hill, "The First Wave of Feminism: Were the Stoics Feminist?" *History of Political Thought* 22/1 (2001): 40. See also W. Klassen, "Musonius Rufus, Jesus, and Paul: Three First-Century Feminists," *From Jesus to Paul: Studies in Honour of Francis Wright Beare* (Waterloo: Wilfrid Laurier University Press, 1984), 185–206 or E. Asmis, "The Stoics on Women," *Feminism and Ancient Philosophy* (London: Routledge, 1996), 68–94.

54. D. M. Engel, "Women's Role in the Home and the State: Stoic Theory Reconsidered," *Harvard Studies in Classical Philology* 101 (2003): 268.

55. Engel collects the recurring passages that have been used to claim Stoics for feminism, from the Old Stoa through Late Stoicism, in "Women's Role," 268.

56. P. W. Van Der Horst, "Musonius Rufus and the New Testament: A Contribution to the Corpus Hellenisticum," *Novum Testamentum* 16/4 (1974): 306–315.

57. All citations from Musonius Rufus are from C. E. Lutz, "Musonius Rufus: 'The Roman Socrates,'" *YCS* 10 (1947): 3–147.

58. Engel, "Women's Role," 269. For a detailed study of the equality of men's and women's capacity for virtue across a number of Stoic thinkers, see L. Tuomela, "Virtues of Man, Woman - or Human Being?: An Intellectual Historical Study on the

Views of the Later Stoics Seneca the Younger, Musonius Rufus, Epictetus, Hierocles and Marcus Aurelius on the Sameness of the Virtues of Man and Woman," (PhD diss., University of Helsinki, 2014).

59. Engel, "Women's Role," 283.

60. R. M. Thorsteinsson, *Roman Christianity and Roman Stoicism: A Comparative Study of Ancient Morality* (Oxford: Oxford University Press, 2010), 50.

61. Thorsteinsson, *Roman Christianity and Roman Stoicism*, 50.

62. Engel, "Women's Role," 272–273.

63. For an excellent capturing and reframing of this polarized discussion, see J. Hicks-Keeton, "Aseneth Between Judaism and Christianity: Reframing the Debate," *JSJ* 49:2 (2018): 189–222.

64. References to the text are from C. Burchard, "Joseph and Aseneth," in *Old Testament Pseudepigrapha, Volume 2* (ed. J. Charlesworth; Garden City: Doubleday, 1985), 177–248.

65. Its range of dates will be discussed below.

66. Regarding the genre of *Joseph and Aseneth*, Lawrence Wills includes the work in his recent collection of ancient Jewish novels: L. M. Wills, *The Jewish Novel in the Ancient World* (Ithaca: Cornell University Press, 1995, repr. 2015), 158–184; see also L. M. Wills, "Jewish Novellas in a Greek and Roman Age: Fiction and Identity," *JSJ* 42 (2011): 141–165.

67. See H. C. Kee, "The Socio-Cultural Setting of Joseph and Aseneth," *NTS* 29 (1983): 394–413 and "The Socio-Religious Setting and Aims of *Joseph and Asenath*" (*SBLSP* 1976; Missoula: Scholars, 1976), 183–192.

68. See Davila, *The Provenance of the Pseudepigrapha*, 190ff.

69. J. J. Collins, "Joseph and Aseneth: Jewish or Christian," *JSP* 14/2 (2005): 97–112.

70. R. S. Kraemer, *When Aseneth Met Joseph: A Late Antique Tale of the Biblical Patriarch and His Egyptian Wife, Reconsidered* (Oxford: Oxford University Press, 1998). Kraemer also still finds it quite possible, despite debates back and forth in recent decades, that "a strong case can be made for Christian composition and redaction," ix.

71. For a catalogue of strong evidence for early Christian women in leadership (and the suppression thereof), see U. E. Eisen, *Amtsträgerinnen im frühen Christentum. Epigraphische und literarische Studien* (Göttingen: Vandenhoeck & Ruprecht, 1996).

72. Dewey, "Women in the Synoptic Gospels," 59.

73. For a clear demonstration of a deliberate decline in women's value in the early Church, see K. J. Torjesen, *When Women Were Priests: Women's Leadership in the Early Church and the Scandal of Their Subordination* (New York: HarperOne, 1995). For an interesting look at the decline's relationship to men's higher literacy levels, see J. Dewey, "From Storytelling to Written Text: The Loss of Early Christian Women's Voices," *BTB* 26 (1996): 71–78.

Chapter 7

Conclusions and Next Directions

Those who work on Q are beginning to understand that it is more than a solution to the Synoptic problem; it should play a more important role in our quest to understand rural first-century Judaism and Christian origins.[1] My research shows that there is one particular element in Q—its innovative technique of pairing gendered parallel parables—that should play a much greater role in our investigations into where women and gender fit into those origins. We have been doing a better job of making use of Q for the former task for a century. Now it is time to focus more intensely on the latter task.

Turid Seim asserts in her seminal work on the gender pairs in Luke that, "in order to combat the massive process that has rendered women invisible, it is an essential task to make them visible again in text and history."[2] So often, however, we lack the necessary information to uncover the lives and perspectives of ancient women; ancient data that could make women visible have been preserved only through thickly male-centered perspectives or have simply not been preserved at all. With Q, however, the evidence has been right before our eyes for a hundred years; it has been *our inattention to feminist questions* that have obscured what these data can tell us about early Jewish women in first-century Galilee and beyond. William Arnal has noted that there are *two* systemic means by which women have been "systematically effaced from the historical record"; the first is by "androcentric source materials," but the second is by "androcentric historical readings of those sources."[3] There is nothing that we as historians can do to change the fact that our source materials are male-centered. What is lost is lost forever. That said, there *is* a great deal we can do about our own readings of the material that is available to us. Male-centered readings and male readers have certainly failed to make use of Q to its fullest extent in terms of understanding gender in the early Jesus movement.

Sometimes, shining the light of woman-centered approaches onto ancient androcentric data only serves to reinforce the paucity of information about ancient women and to make even more obvious and elucidate in greater detail the well-known patriarchal and kyriocentric systems of oppression and inequality. In the case of Q, however, it is clear that women-centered approaches can instead uncover areas where it has only been *current* oversights and assumptions, rather than the evidence itself, that have served to obscure wo/men's past.[4] Androcentric scholarly interests have blinded us to the presence of deliberately gender-balanced rhetoric in Jesus' teachings. A lack of diversity both in scholars themselves and in scholarly interpretive strategies have in this case resulted in a lack of attention, for the better part of a century, to Q's remarkably important, and readily apparent, information about the place of first-century women in the earliest strata of the Jesus movement.

My choice to highlight gender as an interpretive lens for Q is not guided only by my own feminist curiosity about antiquity. In this case, the ancient data have driven the research: binary gender is an unmistakable focus of Q. While it is best practice to be vigilant about bringing questions about gender to antique evidence in an anachronistic way, as some early feminist readings may have done in overhasty enthusiasm, the sayings material unquestionably, in both its form and its content, begs us to explore what it says about gender. Q's Jesus clearly works to create and/or mirror an intellectual and spiritual parity between men and women.

A series of verbally parallel parable pairs where the single variable is a gendered male/female binary flags to the reader that gender is not only present in the text, but is somehow one of its foci. Furthermore, the repetition of this and similar devices throughout Q, Matthew, Luke, Paul, Mark to a lesser degree, and John to a large degree, bears witness to an interest in gender—or at least a rhetorical momentum—on the part of several independent artifacts from the earliest stratum of the Jesus movement. There is thus solid footing from which to assert that Jesus of Nazareth took an interest in gender, alongside other Roman and Jewish thinkers.

It is only when the sayings of Jesus are studied with the question of women at the forefront that their own deliberate and repeated attention to gender is revealed, and their meaning clarified. When the gendered pairs are compared with their broader literary context, the level to which they are an innovation in antiquity is revealed to be both commensurate with their context and rhetorically unique. My task here has neither been to pass judgment upon whether or not this specific attention to gender in Q counts as emancipatory nor to extrapolate widely and wishfully from it, but rather to describe it[5] in detail and in context, working toward discerning the role of women in and around Q, and even toward understanding the teachings of the historical Jesus

Conclusions and Next Directions 153

toward women. For this reason, this project remains significant whether one goes so far as to stratify Q in the footsteps of Kloppenborg or doubts Q's very existence in the footsteps of Goodacre. As Schottroff writes of her work on women in the Q pairs:

> the results should be equally useful for those who presume a distinction between Q1 and Q2 and for those who doubt the very existence of Q. They all may read the following discussion as a description of some central elements of the Jesus movement or of the message of Jesus."[6]

Even if one is not convinced by the two-source hypothesis, the gendered pairs form part of what Jesus scholars deem to be authentic material that dates back to his Galilean career. With or without Q, the parallel parable pairs are sayings that text-critics, redaction-critics, and historical Jesus scholars connect with Jesus. Their importance as deliberately gender-aware and, in their way, gender-leveling evidence, remains.

The present project is the first book-length work in English to treat the parallel parable pairs of Q with a view to the ways in which these pairs not only uncover some realities of women in the earliest Jesus movements but also something of Jesus of Nazareth's attitude toward them. I concur with Denis Fricker when he concludes that a pairing of female figures with male figures is a process undertaken by Jesus himself[7] and that the pairs "seem to have been an original and remarkable mode of expression in the discourse of the historical Jesus."[8] However, my findings diverge from Fricker's where he finds the pairs "firmly rooted in Semitic poetry" and "their argumentation . . . in Hellenistic rhetoric."[9] I assert instead that the pairs enjoy a certain rhetorical uniqueness.

My research sides with Arnal, Levine, and Schottroff in its findings that the sayings source Q is otherwise androcentric. It also affirms, along with Batten, Corley, and Levine that there was, in the late Republic, a relaxing of restrictions for some women, and that such a development most certainly did not originate with Christianity, over and against Judaism and Hellenism. However, *contra* Arnal and Levine, and in agreement with Schottroff and Schüssler Fiorenza, I read Q against the androcentric grain and argue that the gender pairs are very solid evidence that women and men were (qualified) equals in the oldest stratum of the Jesus movements in a limited but nevertheless important way.

My distinct contributions to the discussion are twofold:

First, I have described *in which ways* the pairs reveal men and women to be equal in the earliest period of the Jesus movement and in which ways they reinforce gender inequalities. Namely, the gender pairs view men and women as identical in terms of their spiritual/religious inclusion and eschatological agency, while retaining socially gendered roles that are more or less *status quo*, similar to the equality described by Musonius Rufus. Even these socially gendered roles, though, are disrupted to some degree in Q when we take into account those reconstructions of the Q people that hint that itinerant prophecy was a possible occupation for both male and female community members and when we take into account the encouragement of a breakdown of patriarchal familial boundaries when these boundaries clash with the group's *basileia* message. This parsing of when and in what ways women and men are equal in Q—and when and in what ways they are not—is a way through the controversy found in the initial scholarship on women and the pairs. Rather than a question of *whether or not* Q challenges the patriarchy/kyriarchy of the day, it is a question of determining *in which ways* Q presents challenges to patriarchy and in which ways it does not.

Second, I have corroborated Fricker's findings that the pairs are a theological innovation of Jesus. I hope I have done so without resorting to anti-Jewish readings that pit the Jesus movement against earlier and adjacent forms of early Judaism in a false dichotomy. Rather, I have worked with Batten and Corley to incorporate current research on the broader status of women at the rise of the Roman Empire, placing the women of the Jesus movement in context with women in other movements, acknowledging overall continuities as well as highlighting the rhetorical creativity of the pairs.

What the parable pairs of Q, in comparative literary context, can tell us about women in the earliest communities around Jesus shows that we are far from finished, making adequate use of the data available to us. If Q is, in James Robinson's provocative words, "The Gospel of Jesus,"[10] then it is Jesus' gospel, rather than the canonical Gospels, in which we find showcased one of the most remarkable treatments of women as spiritually and intellectually equal to men in all of early Christianity. At the same time, careful analysis of the text also reveals that the "Gospel of Jesus" cannot, for a historian, be used as straight evidence for something we can call "egalitarianism" or "feminism" by modern definitions. Whether it can serve in this way for a theologian is, of course, another matter.

WHAT HAPPENED?

The unique type of intellectual/spiritual/religious equality conferred upon the women in Jesus of Nazareth's movement as evidenced in the gendered pairs did not survive long in the decades after his crucifixion.[11] Countertrends that actively sought to dictate what women should and should not do in the Jesus movement began as early as the Deutero-Pauline epistles[12] and the Gospel of Luke.[13] In diametric contrast with the rhetorical work of the gender pairs, there was a strong push to force women back into socially acceptable roles by the time of the Pastoral Epistles in the second century,[14] and these countertrends had developed in directions that denigrated womanhood quite drastically by the time of the so-called Church Fathers. The "Fathers" blame not only Eve but all women for sin, caution men to avoid them as temptresses, and generally view Christianity as a movement for and about men.[15] While the patristic period cannot be painted with a too-generalized brush,[16] it must be said that women on the whole are criticized by patristic authors as useless except for procreative purposes[17] (which are nonetheless viewed as disgusting).[18] Patristic authors encouraged women to somehow shed their womanhood in order to participate in any sort of holiness[19] and even blamed women as a group for the existence of sin, and thus for Jesus' death.[20] This loss of something seemingly special to the earliest followers of Jesus, and others in the first century, raises the question: What happened?

Augustan Reforms

Alicia Batten frames the issue in her article on the gender pairs:

> As is commonly known, Christianity later became a patriarchal religion despite these exciting beginnings. Hence, continuing to study its development in light of larger forces will perhaps better enable us to understand why Christianity appears so quickly to have forgotten some of its own origins.[21]

Among the "larger forces" Batten flags as important for inclusion in future study if we wish to understand what happened to destroy "these exciting beginnings," is the Augustan marital and moral reform program.[22] I agree; the success of the Augustan reforms would be a fruitful context in which to investigate why the limited freedoms enjoyed by the women in and around Q do not seem to have continued. The move in early Christianity toward more typical gender relations does correspond roughly to the increase in non-Jewish membership; a Gentile demographic eventually came to dominate the Jesus movement, in its transformation into the Church. Perhaps non-Jewish urban community members were more firmly entrenched in upper-class Roman gender norms than were the rural Jewish artisans and peasants at the movement's origins, and this influenced the decline of the leveling of social categories in Christian communities.[23] Perhaps it is possible that the shifts within the Jesus movement from gender equality to gender hierarchy were not coincidental, but rather were linked to the shift from majority Jewish to majority non-Jewish membership, and thus more exposed to the lasting influence of the highly successful moral reforms of Augustus, whose programmatic policies and portrayals of the proper place of women were embraced and enlarged throughout the Roman Empire long after his death.[24] Although it is not within the scope of this project—nor perhaps within the scope of the possible—to explain the demise of the gendered innovations that are revealed in the Q gender pairs, future scholarship would do well to take Augustan moral and marital reforms, and their success among the populations that eventually overtook the Jewish Jesus movement, as a possible starting point.

Apocalypticism

Another lens through which it will be good to explore the brevity of women's greater equality in first-century Judaism is certainly apocalypticism. John the Baptist, Jesus, and Paul shared a minority Jewish view that the End of Days was immanent—or indeed was already beginning.[25] When "the axe already lies at the root of the tree" (Q 3:9)—that is, when everything is about to be destroyed, made new, and permanently set to rights through divine cataclysm—typical social categories such as class, wealth, marital status, gender, and occupation can lose importance in light of the urgent need to prepare. Schüssler Fiorenza discusses the "difficult practical problems in everyday life" that stem from the breakdown of "patriarchal status divisions."[26] Those second-century Christian writings which scramble to get women behaving like good Roman citizens again—quietly devoted to marriage and childbearing and eschewing leadership roles—smack of groups who are realizing that the End of Days may not be quite so close[27] and who must continue life in community without drawing negative attention or being too disruptive of the social order.[28] The study of women in Q is poised to contribute to the conversation that investigates the early Christian loss of women's leadership in light of the shift away from Jewish apocalypticism.

Women Scholars and Scholarship about
Women Advance Textual Criticism

Additionally, this project brings into focus the need for text-critical attention to be paid to the gender pairs when the next critical edition of Q is being prepared. Recent feminist research on the Lukan use of the pairs (at least those who take Q into account as a text) must give pause to the tendency to classify parable pairs as original to Luke out of an older, erroneous perception that Luke is more inclusive of women. Given the present study, at least some of the "Lukan" parable pairs now seem far more likely to have originated in Q too, despite their absence from Matthew.

Furthermore, it is worth investigating why the gender pairs appear in more than one of Kloppenborg's proposed strata.[29] If Q can be divided into two main formational periods, and gender pairs occur in *both* of them, then this makes them—and their repercussions for women—all the more central to those early Jesus communities. Conversely, perhaps the presence of the pairs across both strata actually mitigates the likelihood of stratification.

These two questions, of why the gender pairs were weakened as Christianity gradually coalesced away from Judaism, and of what the gender pairs can teach us text-critically about Q, should continue to keep Q and its gendered pairs at the fore as an important source of data for the development of the varieties of early Judaism and the development of Christian origins.

Finally, for those feminist Christian readers who are frustrated with misogyny and inequality in their religious institutions and their world, I hope this book has vindicated and inspired them by showing that, at the birth of Jesus' movement, women were a priority. Jesus deliberately, systematically, and creatively included us.

NOTES

1. Kloppenborg states that Q has come to "make a real difference in how Christian origins are imagined." *Q: The Earliest Gospel*, vii.
2. Seim, *The Double Message*, 8.
3. Arnal, "Gendered Couplets in Q," 75.
4. The example *par excellence* of the extent to which androcentric readings and readers can completely misinterpret plain and plentiful data is Brooten's work on female leaders in ancient synagogues (Brooten, *Women Leaders in the Ancient Synagogue*). I have written on these "politics of citation" and the deliberate erasure and diminishment of women scholars as well as of information on ancient women in S. Parks, "'The Brooten Phenomenon': Moving Women from the Margins in Second-Temple and New Testament Scholarship," *The Bible & Critical Theory* 14/2 (2018): 1–20 and in S. Parks "Historical-Critical Ministry? The Biblical Studies Classroom as Restorative Secular Space," *New Blackfriars* 100/1086 (2019): 229–244. Arnal uses Brooten to illustrate how androcentric interpretation can stand in blatant contradiction to ancient data: "A case in point is Bernadette Brooten's persuasive argument that the ancient Jewish synagogue (although far from promoting the equality of men and women) was not devoid of important female members and participants. Most traditional scholarship, however, has argued the general exclusion of women from the synagogue and, indeed, from any important role in Hellenistic and Roman Judaism. [. . .] The evidence for women taking on significant roles in early Judaism has either been ignored or dismissed by (mostly male) scholars." Arnal, "Gendered Couplets in Q," 75, n.1.
5. In the words of T. Ilan: "The terms 'improvement' and 'deterioration' are not relevant to the question of women's status and condition [. . .] the role of the historian is to *describe* changes and developments without making value judgements." *Jewish Women in Greco-Roman Palestine: An Inquiry into Image and Status* (Tubingen: Mohr Siebeck, 1995), 6. Further, according to Brooten, "how could one evaluate the

complex historical phenomena of Jewish women's lives with the categories 'positive,' 'ambivalent,' and 'negative'? Even as categories for describing attitudes, this is not adequate." "Early Christian Women and their Cultural Context," 75–76.

6. Schottroff, "The Sayings Source Q," 511.

7. Fricker, *Quand Jésus Parle au Masculin-Féminin*, 377.

8. Fricker, *Quand Jésus Parle au Masculin-Féminin*, 380. My translation.

9. Fricker, *Quand Jésus Parle au Masculin-Féminin*, 79. My translation.

10. See J. Robinson, *The Gospel of Jesus: In Search of the Original Good News* (New York: HarperCollins, 2005).

11. See H. Kung's *Women in Christianity* (London: Continuum, 2001), one of the many monographs in which it is argued that, while active roles—including leadership roles—for women seemed to pose no problem for Jesus and the earliest Christians, they were viewed as increasingly problematic as Christianity developed. See also Torjesen, *When Women Were Priests*, and Eisen, *Amtsträgerinnen im frühen Christentum*.

12. H. C. Kee, who notes a shift away from gender-leveling ethics in the historical Jesus toward a potentially ambivalent role for women in the authentic letters of Paul, to a definitively confining and submissive role for women by the time of the Deutero-Paulines and pastoral epistles in "The Changing Role of Women in the Early Christian World," *Theology Today* 49/2 (1992): 225–238.

13. As is argued with concision and clarity in Schaberg and Ringe, "Gospel of Luke."

14. Kee, "The Changing Role of Women in the Early Christian World," 231–232.

15. See B. Clack, ed., *Misogyny in the Western Philosophical Tradition: A Reader* (New York: Routledge, 1999), 49–94.

16. For her work on the patristic period that pushes past the well-known misogyny to attempt to uncover evidence for more complex women's roles, see E. Clark's volumes, *Jerome, Chrysostom, and Friends: Essays and Translations* (New York: Mellen, 1979) and *Ascetic Piety and Women's Faith: Essays on Late Ancient Christianity* (Lewiston: Mellen, 1986).

17. "I don't see what sort of help woman was created to provide man with, if one excludes the purpose of procreation. If woman was not given to man for help in bearing children, for what help could she be? To till the earth together? If help were needed for that, man would have been a better help for man. The same goes for comfort in solitude. How much more pleasure is it for life and conversation when two friends live together than when a man and a woman cohabitate?" Augustine, *De genesi ad litteram*, 9, 5–9.

18. "I consider that nothing so casts down the manly mind from its heights as the fondling of women, and those bodily contacts which belong to the married state." Augustine, *Soliloq.* 1.10. "The whole of her bodily beauty is nothing less than phlegm, blood, bile, rheum, and the fluid of digested food. [. . .] If you consider what is stored up behind those lovely eyes, the angle of the nose, the mouth and cheeks you will agree that the well-proportioned body is merely a whitened sepulchre, total inner filth." Chrysostom, *Exhortation to the Fallen Theodore*, 14.

19. "As long as a woman is for birth and children she is different from man as body is from soul. But when she wishes to serve Christ more than the world, then she will cease to be a woman, and will be called man." Jerome, *Commentary on Ephesians*, 3.5.

20. For example, "The curse God pronounced on your sex still weighs on the world. [. . .] You are the devil's gateway. [. . .] You are the first that deserted the divine laws. All too easily you destroyed the image of God, Adam. Because you deserved death, it was the son of God who had to die." Tertullian, *On the Apparel of Women* 1.1.

21. Batten, "More Queries for Q," 49.

22. "Augustus' laws on marriage are a significant indication that women were becoming too free." Batten, "More Queries for Q," 49. See also Hallett, "Women in Augustan Rome," 372–384.

23. On the role of elite women in early Christian rhetoric and reality, see S. Matthews, *First Converts: Rich Pagan Women and the Rhetoric of Mission in Early Judaism and Christianity* (Stanford: Stanford University Press, 2002).

24. M. Beard, J. North, and S. Price cover the Augustan reforms and their aftermath in *Religions of Rome, Volume 1: A History* (New York: Cambridge University Press, 1998), 186–210, and J. M. G. Barclay deals with Jewish interactions with and responses to the reforms in *Negotiating Diaspora: Jewish Strategies in the Roman Empire* (London: T&T Clark, 2004). See also, on the widespread and long-lasting influence of Augustus via "social media," P. Zanker, *The Power of Images in the Age of Augustus* (transl. A. Shapiro; Ann Arbor: University of Michigan Press, 1988).

25. See P. Fredriksen, *Paul: The Pagans' Apostle* (New Haven: Yale University Press, 2017), esp. 30.

26. See E. Schüssler-Fiorenza, "Rhetorical Situation and Historical Reconstruction in 1 Corinthians," in *Christianity at Corinth: The Quest for the Pauline Church* (ed. E. Adams and D. G. Horrell; Louisville: Westminster John Knox, 2004), 157–158.

27. This is succinctly articulated by B. Ehrman, "From Paul's Female Colleagues to the Pastor's Intimidated Women: The Oppression of Women in Early Christianity," in *The New Testament: A Historical Introduction to the Early Christian Writings* (6th ed.; Oxford: Oxford University Press, 2016), 460.

28. See Margaret Y. MacDonald, *The Pauline Churches: A Socio-Historical Study of Institutionalization in the Pauline and Deutero-Pauline Writings* (Cambridge: Cambridge University Press, 1988) and Carolyn Osiek, Margaret Y MacDonald, and Janet H. Tulloch, A *Woman's Place: House Churches in Earliest Christianity* (Minneapolis: Fortress, 2006).

29. See Kloppenborg, *The Formation of Q*.

Appendix
The Q Gender Pairs in English

Listed in this appendix, in English translation, are all of the gendered pairs discussed in this book as authentic sayings material. Those that appear in the critical edition of Q are my own translation, when noted, and those that do not appear in the critical edition are taken from the Revised Standard Version of Luke. They appear below in the order in which they occur in Luke's gospel. For anyone wishing to view the pairs in the context of Q, there are numerous affordable and compact English translations of Q available, such as the one edited by James Robinson for Fortress Press in 2002.[1]

THE FULL GENDER PAIRS

Many Widows including Zarephath/Many Lepers including Naaman

> But in truth, I tell you, there were many widows in Israel in the days of Elijah, when the heaven was shut up three years and six months, when there came a great famine over all the land; and Elijah was sent to none of them but only to Zarephath, in the land of Sidon, to a woman who was a widow.
> And there were many lepers in Israel in the time of the prophet Elisha; and none of them was cleansed, but only Naaman the Syrian. (Luke 4:25–27 RSV)

Persistent Friend/Persistent Widow

> And he said to them, "Which of you who has a friend will go to him at midnight and say to him, 'Friend, lend me three loaves; for a friend of mine has arrived on a journey, and I have nothing to set before him'; and he will answer from within, 'Do not bother me; the door is now shut, and my children are with me in bed; I cannot get up and give you anything'? I tell you, though he will not get

up and give him anything because he is his friend, yet because of his importunity he will rise and give him whatever he needs."

He said, "In a certain city there was a judge who neither feared God nor regarded man; and there was a widow in that city who kept coming to him and saying, 'Vindicate me against my adversary.' For a while he refused; but afterward he said to himself, 'Though I neither fear God nor regard man, yet because this widow bothers me, I will vindicate her, or she will wear me out by her continual coming.'" (Luke 11:5–8, 18:2–5 RSV)

Bread/Fish

What person of you, whose son[2] asks him for bread, will give him a stone? Or again when he asks for a fish, will give him a snake? (Q 11:11–12)

Queen of the South/Ninevite Men

The Queen of the South will be raised at the judgment with this generation and condemn it, for she came from the ends of the earth to listen to the wisdom of Solomon, and look, something more than Solomon is here!

Ninevite men [ἄνδρες] will arise at the judgment with this generation and condemn it, for they repented at the announcement of Jonah, and look, something more than Jonah is here! (Q 11:31–32)

Ravens/Lilies

Consider the ravens: They neither sow nor reap nor gather into barns, and yet God feeds them. Are you not better than the birds?

Consider[3] the lilies, they neither card[4] nor toil nor spin; yet I tell you: Not even Solomon in all his glory was arrayed like one of these. (Q 12:24, 27)

Mustard seed, yeast

What is the *basileia* of God like, and with what am I to compare it? It is like a seed of mustard, which a man[5] took and threw into his garden. And it grew and developed into a tree, and the birds of the sky nested in its branches.

And again: With what am I to compare the *basileia* of God? It is like yeast, which a woman took and hid in three measures of flour until it was fully fermented. (Q 13:18–21)

Lost Sheep/Lost Coin

Which man[6] is there among you who has a hundred sheep, on losing one of them, will not leave the ninety-nine in the mountains and go hunt for the lost one? And if it should happen that he finds it, I say to you that he rejoices over it more than over the ninety-nine that did not go astray.

Or what woman who has ten coins, if she were to lose one coin, would not light a lamp and sweep the house and hunt until she finds? And on finding she calls the friends and neighbors, saying: Rejoice with me, for I found the coin which I had lost. (Q 15:4–5a, 7–9)

Two Men/Two Women

I tell you, there will be two men [δύο] in the field; one [εἷς] is taken and one [εἷς] is left.
Two women [δύο] will be grinding at the mill; one [μία] is taken and one [μία] is left. (Q 17:34–35)

THE SHORTER GENDER PAIRS

Tax Collectors and Prostitutes

For John came to you, and the tax collectors [τελῶναι] and [prostitutes?][7] responded positively, but the religious authorities rejected him. Q 7:29–30?

Division in the Household

For I have come to divide son against father, and daughter against her mother, and daughter-in-law against her mother-in-law. (Q 12:53)

Parents and Children

The one who does not hate father and mother cannot be my disciple; and the one who does not hate son and daughter cannot be my disciple. (Q: 14:26)

NOTES

1. Robinson, *The Sayings of Jesus*.
2. I have taken the translation of this whole saying directly from the Q critical edition, except for changing "child" to "son" here. The Greek is υἱός.
3. I have chosen to begin both sayings with "consider" in English, in the interest of greater parallelism, as I believe this is the translation that makes the most sense. However, the critical edition does not seem to have had the gender pairs in mind at all when considering English renderings, as it translates the first instance as "consider" and the second instance as "observe." Both reconstructions in the critical edition are conjectural; in the first parable, "consider" is reconstructed from [κατανοήσ]ατε and in the second parable, "observe" is reconstructed from κατα[[(μάθε)]]τε. Since the portions within square brackets signify conjecture, and portions within double square brackets signify extreme conjecture, there is no reason not to reconstruct both

parables as beginning with κατανοήσατε—"consider," and thus enjoy parallel beginnings for these parallel lessons.

4. I have here modified the text from the Q translation in the critical edition, which reads "Observe the lilies, how they grow: They do not work nor do they spin" (which is how the verse also appears in the gospels). As the text-critical note in the critical edition notes, there was already a scribal error here at the level of Q: "The original reading οὐ ξαίνει ("do not card") is, already in Q, corrupted by a scribal error into αὐξάνει." Robinson, Hoffmann, and Kloppenborg, eds., *The Critical Edition of Q*, 344. I have thus translated the verse as it likely originally circulated, since the original version of the saying is in a more parallel form. The scholarship that went into this decision is highly informed by a palimpsest of this text in Codex Sinaiticus, discovered under ultraviolet light, which confirms that the original version of the pair contains superior literary parallelism. In the underlying text—a rendering that is also preserved in saying 36 of the *Gospel of Thomas*—the lilies and the ravens are each connected to a trio of negative verbs: ravens neither sow nor reap nor gather into barns, and lilies neither *card* nor toil nor spin (as seen above, the difference in Greek between "they grow," αὐξάνει, and "they do not card," οὐ ξαίνει, is very slight); this was uncovered by T. C. Skeat in 1938, who also confirmed its reinforcement in *Thomas*. See H. J. M. Milne and T. C. Skeat, *Scribes and Correctors of the Codex Sinaiticus* (London: Trustees of the British Museum, 1938). James Robinson pointed out the importance of this discovery as a proof that Q was a written Greek text. See J. Robinson, "The Nag Hammadi Gospels and the Fourfold Gospel" in *The Earliest Gospels* (London: T&T Clark, 2004), 84–85, as well as his earlier "A Written Greek Sayings Cluster Older than Q," 61–77 and his "The Pre-Q Text of the (Ravens and) Lilies: Q 12:22–31 and P. Oxy 655 (*Gos. Thom.* 36)," in *Text und Geschichte* (Marburg: Elwert, 1999), 143–180.

5. The critical edition has "person" here, as is its consistent translation custom for the Greek ἄνθρωπος. However, as argued above, I suggest that in this context of gender pairings, the word is not inclusive but is clearly functioning in opposition to the γυνή in its parallel saying.

6. As mentioned above, this translation is from the critical edition of Q, with the exception of my translation "man." Q translates τίς ἄνθρωπος as "which person" in keeping with the typical inclusive translation choices throughout the critical edition, but in cases where τίς ἄνθρωπος stands in literary opposition to τίς γυνή in a parallel verse, it stands to reason that "man" better captures what is happening rhetorically.

7. The word in square brackets is my reconstruction, as the critical edition of Q leaves a lacuna in the place of "prostitutes." If the original saying were "prostitutes" (as in Matthew) then it forms a little gendered pair. The text-critical notes leave the question open as to whether the Lukan or the Matthean version appeared in Q. Robinson, Hoffmann, and Kloppenborg, eds., *The Critical Edition of Q*, 138.

Bibliography

Achtemeier, Elizabeth. "The Impossible Possibility: Evaluating the Feminist Approach to Bible and Theology." *Interpretation* 42 (1988): 45–57.
Adler, William. "The Pseudepigrapha in the Early Church." In *The Canon Debate*, edited by L. M. McDonald and J. A. Sanders, 211–228. Peabody: Hendrickson, 2002.
Allen, Willoughby Charles. "The Book of Sayings Used by the Editor of the First Gospel." In *Studies in the Synoptic Problem*, edited by William Sanday, 234–286. Oxford: Clarendon, 1911.
Allison, Dale C. *Constructing Jesus: Memory, Imagination, and History*. London: SPCK, 2010.
Allison, Dale C. *The Intertextual Jesus: Scripture in Q*. Harrisburg: Trinity Press International: 2000.
Alvanoudi, Angeliki. *Grammatical Gender in Interaction: Cultural and Cognitive Aspects*. Leiden: Brill, 2014.
Anderson, John M. *Morphology, Paradigms, and Periphrases*. Oxford: Oxford University Press, 2011.
Anderson, Paul N., Felix Just, and Tom Thatcher, eds. *John, Jesus, and History Volume 1: Critical Appraisals of Critical Views*. Atlanta: SBL, 2007.
———, eds. *John, Jesus, and History, Volume 2: Aspects of Historicity in the Fourth Gospel*. Atlanta: SBL, 2009.
Arnal, William E. "Gendered Couplets in Q and Legal Formulations: From Rhetoric to Social History." *Journal of Biblical Literature* 116/1 (1997): 75–94.
———. *Jesus and the Village Scribes: Galilean Conflicts and the Setting of Q*. Minneapolis: Fortress, 2001.
———. "The Synoptic Problem and the Historical Jesus." In *New Studies in the Synoptic Problem*, edited by P. Foster, A. Gregory, J. S. Kloppenborg, and J. Verheyden, 371–432. Leuven: Peeters, 2011.
Asmis, Elizabeth. "The Stoics on Women." In *Feminism and Ancient Philosophy*, edited by Julie K. Ward, 68–94. London: Routledge, 1996.

Baker, Cynthia M. *Jew*. New Brunswick: Rutgers, 2016.

———. *Rebuilding the House of Israel: Architectures of Gender in Jewish Antiquity*. Stanford: Stanford University Press, 2002.

Barclay, John M. G. *Negotiating Diaspora: Jewish Strategies in the Roman Empire*. London: T&T Clark, 2004.

Baron, Dennis E. *Grammar and Gender*. New Haven: Yale, 1986.

Barrera, Julio Trebolle. *The Jewish Bible and the Christian Bible: An Introduction to the History of the Bible*. Translated from the Spanish by Wilfred G. E. Watson. Leiden: Brill, 1998.

Barr, James. "Which Language did Jesus Speak: Some Remarks of a Semitist." *Bulletin of the John Rylands Library* 53 (1970): 9–29.

Batten, Alicia. "More Queries for Q: Women and Christian Origins." *Biblical Theology Bulletin* 24/2 (1994): 44–51.

Bauckham, Richard. *Gospel Women: Studies of the Named Women in the Gospels*. Grand Rapids: Eerdmans, 2002.

Beard, Mary, John North, and Simon Price. *Religions of Rome, Volume 1: A History*. York: Cambridge University Press, 1998.

Beavis, Mary Ann. "Christian Origins, Egalitarianism, and Utopia." *Journal of Feminist Studies in Religion* 23/2 (Fall 2007): 27–49.

———. "Parable and Fable." *Catholic Biblical Quarterly* 52 (1990): 473–498.

Beirne, Margaret M. *Women and Men in the Fourth Gospel: A Genuine Discipleship of Equals*. London: Sheffield Academic, 2003.

Berlin, Adele. "Grammatical Aspects of Biblical Parallelism." *Hebrew Union College Annual* 50 (1979): 17–43.

Besançon Spencer, Aida. "Jesus' Treatment of Women in the Gospels." In *Discovering Biblical Equality: Complementarity without Hierarchy*, edited by R. W. Pierce and R. Merrill Groothius, 126–141. Leicester: Apollos, 2005.

Bielman, Anne. "Female Patronage in the Greek Hellenistic and Roman Republican Periods." In *A Companion to Women in the Ancient World*, edited by S. L. James and S. Dillon, 238–248. Chichester: Wiley Blackwell, 2012.

Binz, Stephen J. *Women and the Gospels: Friends and Disciples of Jesus*. Grand Rapids: Baker, 2011.

Blumenthal, Christian. *Basileia bei Lukas: Studien zur erzälehrischen Entfaltung der lukanischen Basileiakonzeption*. Freiburg: Herder, 2016.

Boring, Eugene. *Introduction to the New Testament*. Louisville: Westminster John Knox, 2012.

Boyarin, Daniel. *Dying for God: Martyrdom and the Making of Christianity and Judaism*. Stanford: Stanford University Press, 1999.

———. *A Radical Jew: Paul and the Politics of Identity*. Berkeley: University of California Press, 1994.

Brenner, Athalya. "Introduction." In *Feminist Companion to the Hebrew Bible in the New Testament*, edited by Athalya Brenner, 15–30. Sheffield: Sheffield Academic, 1996.

Brocke, Edna. "Do the Origins Already Contain the Malady?" In *A Feminist Companion to the Hebrew Bible in the New Testament*, edited by A. Brenner, 349–354. Sheffield: Sheffield Academic, 1996.

Brooten, Bernadette. "Early Christian Women and their Cultural Context: Issues of Method in Historical Reconstruction." In *Feminist Perspectives on Biblical Scholarship*, edited by A. Yarbro Collins, 65–91. Chico: Scholars, 1985.

———. *Women Leaders in the Ancient Synagogue: Inscriptional Evidence and Background Issues*. Chico: Scholars, 1982.

Brown, Francis, S. R. Driver, and Charles A. Briggs. *A Hebrew and English Lexicon of the Old Testament*. Oxford: Oxford University Press, 1907.

Brown, Raymond E. *The Death of the Messiah*. 2 volumes. New York: Doubleday, 1994.

Burchard, Christoph. "Joseph and Aseneth." In *Old Testament Pseudepigrapha, Volume 2*, edited by J. Charlesworth, 177–248. Garden City: Doubleday, 1985.

Burkett, Delbert. *Rethinking the Gospel Sources II: The Unity and Plurality of Q*. Atlanta: Society of Biblical Literature, 2009.

Burridge, Richard A. *Four Gospels, One Jesus?* 2nd edition. Grand Rapids: Eerdmans, 2005.

Butler, Judith. *Undoing Gender*. London: Routledge, 2014.

Camp, Claudia. *Wisdom and the Feminine in the Book of Proverbs*. Decatur: Almond, 1985.

Carastathis, Anna. "The Concept of Intersectionality in Feminist Theory." *Philosophy Compass* 9/5 (2014): 304–314.

Catchpole, David R. *The Quest for Q*. Edinburgh: T&T Clark, 1993.

Chancey, Mark A. *The Myth of a Gentile Galilee*. Cambridge: Cambridge University Press, 2002.

Charlesworth, James H. *The Old Testament Pseudepigrapha and the New Testament*. Cambridge: Cambridge University Press, 1985.

———, ed. *Old Testament Pseudepigrapha: 2 Volumes*. Garden City: Doubleday, 1983–1985. Recently republished by Peabody: Hendrickson, 2010.

Chesnutt, Randall. "Revelatory Experiences Attributed to Biblical Women." In *Women Like This: New Perspectives on Jewish Women in the Greco-Roman World*, edited by Amy-Jill Levine, 107–126. Atlanta: Scholars, 1991.

Clack, Beverley, ed. *Misogyny in the Western Philosophical Tradition: A Reader*. New York: Routledge, 1999.

Clark, Elizabeth. *Ascetic Piety and Women's Faith: Essays on Late Ancient Christianity*. Lewiston: Mellen, 1986.

———. *Jerome, Chrysostom, and Friends: Essays and Translations*. New York: Mellen, 1979.

Collins, John J. *The Bible After Babel: Historical Criticism in a Postmodern Age*. Grand Rapids: Eerdmans, 2005.

———. "Joseph and Aseneth: Jewish or Christian." *Journal for the Study of the Pseudepigrapha* 14/2 (2005): 97–112.

———, ed. *Oxford Handbook of Apocalyptic Literature*. Oxford: Oxford University Press, 2014.

Conway, Colleen. "Gender Matters in John." In *A Feminist Companion to John: Volume II*, edited by Amy-Jill Levine, 79–103. Cleveland: Pilgrim, 2003.

———. *Men and Women in the Fourth Gospel: Gender and Johannine Characterization*. Atlanta: Scholars, 1999.

Corley, Kathleen E. *Private Women, Public Meals: Social Conflict in the Synoptic Tradition.* Peabody: Hendrickson, 1993.

———. "Jesus, Egalitarian Meals, and Q." Paper presented at the annual meeting of the SBL. San Francisco, November 1992.

———. *Women and the Historical Jesus: Feminist Myths of Christian Origins.* Santa Rosa: Polebridge, 2002.

Cotter, Wendy. "Prestige, Protection and Promise: A Proposal for the Apologetics of Q." In *The Gospel Behind the Gospels: Current Studies on Q*, edited by Ronald A. Piper, 117–138. Leiden: Brill, 2014.

Crenshaw, Kimberlé. "Demarginalizing the Intersection of Race and Sex: A Black Feminist Critique of Anti-Discrimination Doctrine, Feminist Theory, and Anti-Racist Politics." *University of Chicago Legal Forum* 140 (1989): 139–167.

Cromhout, Markus. *Jesus and Identity: Reconstructing Judean Ethnicity in Q.* Eugene: Cascade, 2007.

Crook, Zeba. "The Synoptic Parables of the Mustard Seed and the Leaven: A Test-Case for the Two-Document, Two-Gospel, and Farrer-Goulder Hypotheses." *Journal for the Study of the New Testament* 22/78 (2000): 23–48.

Crossan, John Dominic. *The Essential Jesus: Original Sayings and Earliest Images.* San Francisco: Harper, 1998.

———. *The Historical Jesus: The Life of a Mediterranean Jewish Peasant.* Edinburgh: T&T Clark, 1991.

———. "Itinerants and Householders in the Earliest Kingdom Movement." In *Reimagining Christian Origins*, edited by E. Castelli and H. Taussig, 113–129. Valley Forge: Trinity Press International, 1996.

Dale, Moyra. "Dismantling Socio-Sacred Hierarchy: Gender and Gentiles in Luke-Acts." *Priscilla Papers* 31/2 (2017): 19–23.

Dancy, John C. *The Divine Drama: The Old Testament as Literature.* Cambridge: Lutterworth, 2001.

D'Angelo, Mary Rose. "Women in Luke-Acts: A Redactional View." *Journal of Biblical Literature* 109 (1990): 441–461.

Davila, James. *The Provenance of the Pseudepigrapha: Jewish, Christian, or Other. Supplements to the Journal for the Study of Judaism in the Persian, Hellenistic, and Roman Periods* 105. Leiden: Brill, 2005.

Davis, Andrew R. "The Literary Effect of Gender Discord in the Book of Ruth." *Journal of Biblical Literature* 132/3 (2013): 495–513.

De Beauvoir, Simone. *The Second Sex.* New York: Vintage, 1973.

De Conick, April D. *Recovering the Original Gospel of Thomas: A History of the Gospel and Its Growth.* London: T&T Clark, 2006.

Dell, Katharine. "Proverbs." In *The New Oxford Annotated Bible, New Revised Standard Version with Apocrypha*, edited by Michael D. Coogan, Marc Z. Brettler, Carol A. Newsom, and Pheme Perkins, 895–896. Fully revised fourth edition. Oxford: Oxford University Press, 2010.

Derrenbacker, Robert A. Jr. and John S. Kloppenborg. "Self-Contradiction in the IQP? A Reply to Michael Goulder." *Journal of Biblical Literature* 120/1 (Spring 2001): 57–76.

Dewey, Joanna. "From Storytelling to Written Text: The Loss of Early Christian Women's Voices." *Biblical Theology Bulletin* 26 (1996): 71–78.

———. "Women in the Synoptic Gospels: Seen But Not Heard?" *Biblical Theology Bulletin* 27/2 (1997): 53–60.

Dillon, Richard J. "Ravens, Lilies, and the Kingdom of God (Matthew 6:25-33/ Luke 12:22-31)." *Catholic Biblical Quarterly* 53 (1991): 605–627.

Dixon, Suzanne. *Reading Roman Women.* London: Duckworth, 2001.

Dobbs-Allsopp, Frederick William. "Poetry, Hebrew." In *The New Interpreter's Dictionary of the Bible* 4, edited by K. Doob Sakenfeld, 550–558. Nashville: Abingdon, 2009.

Dowling, Elizabeth V. *Taking Away the Pound: Women, Theology, and the Parable of the Pounds in the Gospel of Luke.* London: T&T Clark, 2007.

Duby, Georges, and Michelle Perrot, series editors. *A History of Women in the West.* Cambridge: Harvard University Press, 1994–1996.

Duling, Dennis C. "'Egalitarian' Ideology, Leadership, and Factional Conflict within the Matthean Group." *Biblical Theology Bulletin* 27 (1997): 124–137.

———. "Millennialism." In *The Social Sciences and New Testament Interpretation*, edited by R. Rohrbaugh, 183–205. Peabody: Hendrickson, 1996.

Dunn, James D. G. *Jesus Remembered: Christianity in the Making, Volume 1.* Grand Rapids: Eerdmans, 2003.

Dvorsky, George, and James Hughes. "Postgenderism: Beyond the Gender Binary." *Institute for Ethics and Emerging Technologies White Papers* (March 2008): 1–18.

Easton, Burton Scott. *The Gospel According to St. Luke.* Edinburgh: T&T Clark, 1926.

Edwards, James R. *The Hebrew Gospel and the Development of Synoptic Tradition.* Grand Rapids: Eerdmans, 2009.

Ehrman, Bart. "From Paul's Female Colleagues to the Pastor's Intimidated Women: The Oppression of Women in Early Christianity." Pages 460–473 in *The New Testament: A Historical Introduction to the Early Christian Writings.* 6th edition. Oxford: Oxford University Press, 2016.

Eisen, Ute E. *Amtsträgerinnen im frühen Christentum. Epigraphische und literarische Studien.* Göttingen: Vandenhoeck & Ruprecht, 1996.

Elliott, John H. "Jesus was not an Egalitarian: A Critique of an Anachronistic and Idealist Theory." *Biblical Theology Bulletin* 32 (2002): 75–91.

Engberg-Pedersen, Troels. "Philo's *De Vita Contemplativa* as a Philosopher's Dream." *Journal for the Study of Judaism* 30 (1999): 40–64.

Engel, David M. "Women's Role in the Home and the State: Stoic Theory Reconsidered." *Harvard Studies in Classical Philology* 101 (2003): 267–288.

Evans, Craig A. *Matthew.* New York: Cambridge University Press, 2012.

Fassberg, Steven E. "Which Semitic Language Did Jesus and Other Contemporary Jews Speak?" *Catholic Biblical Quarterly* 74/2 (2012): 263–280.

Fowler, H. T. "Paul, Q, and the Jerusalem Church." *Journal of Biblical Literature* 43 (1924): 9–14.

Flender, Helmut. *Heil und Geschichte in der Theologie des Lukas.* Munich: Kaiser, 1965.

Fredriksen, Paula. *Paul: The Pagans' Apostle*. New Haven: Yale University Press, 2017.

———. *Sin: The Early History of an Idea*. Princeton: Princeton University Press, 2012.

Frenschkowski, M. "Galiläa oder Jerusalem? Die Topographischen und Politischen Hintergründe der Logienquelle." In *The Sayings Source Q and the Historical Jesus*, edited by Andreas Lindemann, 535–560. Leuven: Leuven University Press, 2001.

Freyne, Sean. *Jesus, A Jewish Galilean: A New Reading of the Jesus Story*. London: T&T Clark, 2004.

Fricker, Denis. "La femme, la famille, et la communauté dans la source des *logia*." *Revue des Sciences Religieuses* 79/1 (2005): 97–116.

———. *Quand Jésus Parle au Masculin-Féminin: Étude Contextuelle et Exégétique d'une Forme Littéraire Originale*. Paris: Gabalda, 2004.

Fricker, Denis, and Nathalie Siffer. *Q ou la source des paroles de Jésus*. Paris: Cerf, 2010.

Funk, Robert W., Roy W. Hoover, and the Jesus Seminar. *The Five Gospels: What Did Jesus Really Say? The Search for the Authentic Words of Jesus*. New York: HarperOne, 1997.

Gabel, John B., and Charles B. Wheeler. *The Bible As Literature: An Introduction*. New York: Oxford University Press, 1986.

Gamliel, Tova. "Textual Categories and Gender Images in a Women's Wailing Performance." *Social Analysis* 51/3 (2007): 23–54.

Gardner-Smith. P. *St. John and the Synoptic Gospels*. Cambridge: Cambridge University Press, 1938.

Garnsey, Peter. *Food and Society in Classical Antiquity*. Cambridge: Cambridge University Press, 1999.

Gench, Frances Taylor. *Back to the Well: Women's Encounters with Jesus in the Gospels*. Louisville: Westminster John Knox, 2004.

Goff, Matthew. "Wisdom and Apocalypticism." In *The Oxford Handbook of Apocalyptic Literature*, edited by J. J. Collins, 52–68. Oxford: Oxford University Press, 2014.

Golberg, Shari. "The Two Choruses Become One: The Absence/Presence of Women in Philo's *On The Contemplative Life*." *Journal for the Study of Judaism* 39 (2008): 459–470.

Good, Deirdre. "Beyond the Canon." In *Women's Bible Commentary Twentieth Anniversary Edition: Revised and Updated*, edited by C. A. Newsom, S. H. Ringe, and J. E. Lapsley, 633–639. Louisville: Westminster John Knox, 2012.

Goodacre, Mark. *The Case Against Q*. Harrisburg: Trinity Press International, 2002.

———. "Criticising the Criterion of Multiple Attestation: The Historical Jesus and the Question of Sources." In *Jesus, Criteria, and the Demise of Authenticity*, edited by C. Keith and A. Le Donne, 152–172. New York: T&T Clark, 2012.

Gravett, Sandra L. "Literature, Old Testament As." In *Eerdmans Dictionary of the Bible*, edited by D. N. Freedman, 812–814. Grand Rapids: Eerdmans, 2000.

Guijarro, Santiago. "Domestic Space, Family Relationships, and the Social Location of the Q People." *Journal for the Study of the New Testament* 27/1 (2004): 69–81.

———. "La Coexistence de différents sens du terme *euaggelion* aux origines du christianisme." *Revue théologique de Louvain* 45 (2014): 481–501.

Guy, Laurie. "The Interplay of the Present and Future in the Kingdom of God (Luke 19:11-44)." *Tyndale Bulletin* 48/1 (1997): 119–137.
Hägerland, Tobias. "The Future of Criteria in Historical Jesus Research." *Journal for the Study of the Historical Jesus* 13 (2015): 43–65.
Hallett, Judith P. "Women in Augustan Rome." In *A Companion to Women in the Ancient World*, edited by S. L. James and S. Dillon, 372–384. Chichester: Wiley Blackwell, 2012.
Hanson, Kenneth C. "All in the Family: Kinship in Agrarian Roman Palestine." In *The Social World of the New Testament*, edited by J. H. Neyrey and E. C. Stewart, 25–46. Peabody: Hendrickson, 2008.

———. "The Galilean Fishing Economy and the Jesus Tradition." *Biblical Theology Bulletin* 27 (1997): 99–111.

———. "Kinship." Pages 62–79 in *The Social Sciences and New Testament Interpretation*. Edited by R. Rohrbaugh. Peabody: Hendrickson, 1996.
Harrington, Daniel J. "The Old Testament Apocrypha in the Early Church and Today." In *The Canon Debate*, edited by L. M. McDonald and J. A. Sanders, 196–210. Peabody: Hendrickson, 2002.
Hartin, P. J. "The Wisdom and Apocalyptic Layers of the Sayings Gospel Q: What Is Their Significance?" *HTS Teologiese Studies / Theological Studies* 50/3 (1994): 556–582.

———. "The Woes against the Pharisees: (Matthew 23:1-39): The Reception and Development of Q 11, 39-52 within the Matthean Community." In *From Quest to Q: Festschrift James Robinson*, edited by J. M. Asgeirsson, K. de Troyer, and M. W. Meyer, 265–284. Leuven: Leuven University Press, 2000.
Hengel, Martin. *Judentum und Hellenismus: Studien zu ihrer Begegnung unter Berücksichtigung Palästinas bis zur Mitte des 2 Jh.s v.Chr*. Tübingen: J. C. B. Mohr, 1973.

———. *The Septuagint as Christian Scripture*. London: T&T Clark, 2002.
Herzog II, W. R. *Parables as Subversive Speech: Jesus as Pedagogue of the Oppressed*. Louisville: Westminster John Knox, 1989.
Hicks-Keeton, Jill. "Aseneth Between Judaism and Christianity: Reframing the Debate." *Journal for the Study of Judaism* 49/2 (2018): 189–222.
Hill, Lisa. "The First Wave of Feminism: Were the Stoics Feminist?" *History of Political Thought* 22/1 (2001): 13–40.
Hoffmann, R. Joseph, ed. *Julian's Against the Galileans*. Translated by R. Joseph Hoffmann. Amherst: Prometheus Books, 2004.
Holladay, Carl R. *A Critical Introduction to the New Testament*. Nashville: Abingdon, 2005.
Horsley, Richard. "The Gospel of Imperial Salvation: Introduction." In *Paul and Empire*, edited by R. Horsley, 10–24. Harrisburg: Trinity Press International, 1997.
Horsley, Richard, and Tom Thatcher. *John, Jesus, and the Renewal of Israel*. Grand Rapids: Eerdmans, 2013.
Horsley, Richard with Jonathan A. Draper. *Whoever Hears You Hears Me: Prophets, Performance, and Tradition in Q*. Harrisburg: Trinity Press International, 1999.
Houlden, Leslie. "Introduction to the New Testament." In the *Oxford Bible Commentary*, edited by J. Barton and J. Muddiman, 830–843. New York: Oxford University Press, 2001.

Howes, Llewellyn. "Whomever You Find, Invite": The Parable of the Great Supper (Q 14:16–21, 23) and the Redaction of Q." *Neotestamentica* 49/2 (2015): 321–350.

Ilan, Tal. *Jewish Women in Greco-Roman Palestine: An Inquiry into Image and Status*. Tubingen: Mohr Siebeck, 1995.

Ingolfsland, Dennis. "Kloppenborg's Stratification of Q and Its Significance for Historical Jesus Studies." *Journal of the Evangelical Theological Society* 46/2 (2003): 217–232.

James, Sharon L., and Sheila Dillon, eds. *A Companion to Women in the Ancient World*. Chichester: Wiley Blackwell, 2012.

Jervis, L. Ann. "Suffering for the Reign of God: The Persecution of Disciples in Q." *Novum Testamentum* 44/4 (2002): 313–332.

Johnson, Lee A., and Robert C. Tannehill. "Lilies Do Not Spin: A Challenge to Female Social Norms." *New Testament Studies* 56/4 (2010): 475–490.

Johnson-Debaufre, Melanie. *Jesus Among Her Children: Q, Eschatology, and the Construction of Christian Origins*. Cambridge: Harvard University Press, 2005.

Jones, Brice. *Matthean and Lukan Special Material: A Brief Introduction with Texts in Greek and English*. Eugene: Wipf and Stock, 2011.

Joseph, Simon J. "'For Heaven and Earth to Pass Away?': Reexamining Q 16:16–18, Eschatology, and the Law." *Zeitschrift für die Neutestamentliche Wissenschaft* 105/2 (2014): 169–188.

———. *Jesus, Q, and the Dead Sea Scrolls: A Judaic Approach to Q*. Tübingen: Mohr Siebeck, 2012.

Julicher, Adolf. *Die Gleichnisreden Jesu*. Freiburg: J. C. B. Mohr (Paul Siebeck), 1888.

Kahl, Brigitte. "No Longer Male: Masculinity Struggles behind Galatians 3:28." *Journal for the Study of the New Testament* 79 (2000): 37–49.

Kähler, Martin. *The So-Called Historical Jesus and the Historic-Biblical Christ*. Translated by Carl E. Braaten. Philadelphia: Fortress, 1964.

Kaiser, Walter C. Jr., and Moises Silva. *Introduction to Biblical Hermeneutics: The Search for Meaning*. Grand Rapids: Zondervan, 1994.

Kee, Alistair. "The Old Coat and the New Wine: A Parable of Repentance." *Novum Testamentum* 12/1 (January 1970): 13–21.

Kee, Howard Clark. "The Changing Role of Women in the Early Christian World." *Theology Today* 49/2 (1992): 225–238.

———. "The Socio-Cultural Setting of Joseph and Aseneth." *New Testament Studies* 29 (1983): 394–413.

———. "The Socio-Religious Setting and Aims of *Joseph and Asenath*." In *Society of Biblical Literature Seminar Papers* 1976, edited by George MacRae, 183–192. Missoula: Scholars, 1976.

Keith, Alison. "Women in Augustan Literature." In *A Companion to Women in the Ancient World*, edited by S. L. James and S. Dillon, 385–399. Chichester: Wiley Blackwell, 2012.

Keith, Chris, and Anthony Le Donne, eds. *Jesus, Criteria, and the Demise of Authenticity*. New York: T&T Clark, 2012.

Kirk, Alan. *The Composition of the Sayings Source: Genre, Synchrony, and Wisdom Redaction in Q*. Leiden: Brill, 1998.

Klassen, William. "Musonius Rufus, Jesus, and Paul: Three First-Century Feminists." In *From Jesus to Paul: Studies in Honour of Francis Wright Beare*, edited by Peter Richardson and John C. Hurd, 185–206. Waterloo: Wilfrid Laurier University Press, 1984.

Klopas, Jane. "Jesus and Women: Luke's Gospel." *Theology Today* 43/2 (1986): 192–202.

Kloppenborg, John S. "Discursive Practices in the Sayings Gospel Q and the Quest of the Historical Jesus." In *The Sayings Source Q and the Historical Jesus*, edited by Andreas Lindemann, 149–190. Leuven: Leuven University Press, 2001.

———. *Excavating Q: The History and Setting of the Sayings Gospel*. Minneapolis: Fortress, 2000.

———. *The Formation of Q: Trajectories in Ancient Wisdom Collections*. Minneapolis: Fortress, 2007.

———. "Introduction." In *The Shape of Q: Signal Essays on the Sayings Gospel*, edited by J. S. Kloppenborg, 1–22. Minneapolis: Fortress, 1994.

———. "The Lost Gospel of Q: The Earliest Record of Jesus' Galilean Followers." Annual Peter Craigie Memorial Lecture. University of Calgary, 2001.

———. "On Dispensing with Q: Goodacre on the Relation of Luke to Matthew." *New Testament Studies* 49 (2003): 210–236.

———. "Q, Bethsaida, Khorazin, and Capernaum." In *Q in Context II: Social Setting and Archaeological Background of the Sayings*, edited by M. Tiwald, 61–90. Göttingen: Vandenhoeck & Ruprecht, 2015.

———. *Q: The Earliest Gospel: An Introduction to the Original Stories and Sayings of Jesus*. Louisville: Westminster John Knox, 2008.

———. *Q Parallels: Synopsis, Concordance, and Critical Notes*. Sonoma: Polebridge, 1988.

———. "The Sayings Gospel Q: Recent Opinion on the People Behind the Document." *Currents in Research: Biblical Studies* 1 (1993): 9–34.

Kloppenborg, John S., and Leif E. Vaage. "The Sayings Gospel Q and Method in the Study of Christian Origins." In *Early Christianity, Q and Jesus*, edited by John S. Kloppenborg and Leif E. Vaage, 1–14. Atlanta: Scholars, 1991.

Kloppenborg, John S., ed. *Conflict and Invention: Literary, Rhetorical, and Social Studies on the Sayings Gospel Q*. Valley Forge: Trinity Press International, 1995.

Koester, Helmut. *History and Literature of Early Christianity, Volume 2*. 2nd edition. Berlin: de Gruyter, 2000.

Kopas, Jane. "Jesus and Women: Luke's Gospel." *Theology Today* 43/2 (1986): 192–202.

Koperski, Veronica. "Is 'Luke' a Feminist or Not? Female-Male Parallels in Luke-Acts." In *Luke and his Readers: Festschrift A. Denaux*, edited by R. Bieringer, G. Van Belle, and J. Verheyden, 25–48. Leuven: Peeters, 2005.

Kraemer, Ross Shepard, and Mary Rose D'Angelo, eds. *Women and Christian Origins*. Oxford: Oxford University Press, 1999.

Kraemer, Ross Shepard. *When Aseneth Met Joseph: A Late Antique Tale of the Biblical Patriarch and His Egyptian Wife, Reconsidered*. Oxford: Oxford University Press, 1998.

Kraybill, Donald. *The Upside-Down Kingdom*. 4th revised edition. Harrisonburg: Herald, 2011.

Kugler, J. "Galatians 3:26-28 und die Vielen Geselechter der Glaubenden: Impuls fur eine Christliche Geschlechtsrollepastoral jenseits von Sex und Gender." In *Geschlecht quer gedacht: Widerstandspotenziale und Gestaltungsmoglichkeiten in Kirchlicher Praxis*, edited by M. E. Aigner and J. Pock, 53–70. Munster: Werkstatt Theologie, 2009.

Kung, Hans. *Women in Christianity*. London: Continuum, 2001.

Leiman, Sid Z. *The Canonization of Hebrew Scripture*. Hamden: Archon, 1976.

LeMon, Joel M., and Brent A. Strawn. "Parallelism." In *Dictionary of the Old Testament: Wisdom, Poetry, and Writings*, edited by T. Longman III and P. Enns, 502–515. Downer's Grove: InterVarsity, 2008.

Levine, Amy-Jill. "Introduction." In *A Feminist Companion to John: Volume 1*, edited by Amy-Jill Levine, 1–14. London: Sheffield Academic, 2003.

———. "Matthew, Mark, and Luke: Good News or Bad?" In *Jesus, Judaism, and Christian Anti-Judaism*, edited by P. Fredriksen and A. Reinhartz, 77–98. Louisville: Westminster John Knox, 2002.

———. "Second-Temple Judaism, Jesus, and Women: Yeast of Eden." In *A Feminist Companion to the Hebrew Bible in the New Testament*, edited by A. Brenner, 302–331. Sheffield: Sheffield Academic, 1996.

———. *Short Stories by Jesus: The Enigmatic Parables of a Controversial Rabbi*. New York: HarperCollins, 2014.

———. "The Word Becomes Flesh: Jesus, Gender, and Sexuality." In *The Historical Jesus in Recent Research*, edited by J. D. G. Dunn and S. McKnight, 509–523. Winona Lake: Eisenbrauns, 2005.

———. "This Widow Keeps Bothering Me." In *Finding a Woman's Place: Essays in Honor of Carolyn Osiek*, edited by D. L. Balch and J. T. Lamoreaux, 124–150. Eugene: Pickwick, 2011.

———. "Who's Catering the Q Affair? Feminist Observations on Q Paraenesis." *Semeia* 50 (1990): 145–161.

———. "Women in the Q Communit(ies) and Traditions." In *Women and Christian Origins*, edited by R. S. Kraemer and M. R. D'Angelo, 150–170. New York: Oxford University Press, 1999.

———, ed. *A Feminist Companion to Luke*. London: Sheffield Academic, 2002.

———, ed. *A Feminist Companion to Matthew*. Sheffield: Sheffield Academic, 2001.

———, ed. *Women Like This: New Perspectives on Jewish Women in the Greco-Roman World*. Atlanta: Scholars, 1991.

Lieber, Laura S. "Jewish Women: Texts and Contexts." In *A Companion to Women in the Ancient World*, edited by S. L. James and S. Dillon, 329–342. Chichester: Wiley Blackwell, 2012.

Lieu, Judith. "'Impregnable Ramparts and Walls of Iron': Boundary and Identity in Early 'Judaism' and 'Christianity'." *New Testament Studies* 48 (2002): 297–313.

Loader, William, ed. *The Pseudepigrapha on Sexuality: Attitudes toward Sexuality in Apocalypses, Testaments, Legends, Wisdom, and Related Literature*. Grand Rapids: Eerdmans, 2011.

Loades, Ann. "Feminist Interpretation." In *The Cambridge Companion to Biblical Interpretation*, edited by J. Barton, 81–94. Cambridge: Cambridge University Press, 1998.

Lowth, Robert. *De sacra poesi Hebraeorum praelectiones academicae (Lectures on the Sacred Poetry of the Hebrews)*. Oxford: Clarendon, 1753.

Lowth, Robert. *Isaiah: A New Translation, with a Preliminary Dissertation and Notes, Critical, Philological, and Explanatory*. Boston: Pierce, 1834.

Lutz, Cora E. "Musonius Rufus: 'The Roman Socrates.'" *Yale Classical Studies* 10 (1947): 3–147.

MacDonald, Margaret Y. *The Pauline Churches: A Socio-Historical Study of Institutionalization in the Pauline and Deutero-Pauline Writings*. Cambridge: Cambridge University Press, 1988.

Machingura, Francis and Paradzai Nyakuhwa. "Sexism: A Hermetical Interrogation of Galatians 3:28 and Women in the Church of Christ in Zimbabwe." *Journal of Pan African Studies* 8/2 (2015): 92–113.

Mack, Burton. "The Kingdom that Didn't Come: A Social History of the Q Tradents." Pages 608–635 in *SBL Seminar Papers* 27. Missoula: Scholars, 1988.

———. *The Lost Gospel: The Book of Q and Christian Origins*. San Francisco: HarperSanFrancisco, 1993.

———. *Who Wrote the New Testament: The Making of the Christian Myth*. New York: HarperCollins, 1995.

Malick, David E. "The Significance of Three Narrative Parallels of Men and Women in Luke 1, John 3-4, and Acts 9." *Priscilla Papers* 28/3 (2014): 15–25.

Malina, Bruce J. "Understanding New Testament Persons." In *The Social Sciences and New Testament Interpretation*, edited by R. Rohrbaugh, 41–61. Peabody: Hendrickson, 1996.

Maly, Eugene H. "Women and the Gospel of Luke." *Biblical Theology Bulletin* 10/3 (1980): 99–104.

Martin, Dale B. *Sex and The Single Savior: Gender and Sexuality in Biblical Interpretation*. Louisville: Westminster John Knox, 2006.

Marzano, Annalisa. *Harvesting the Sea: The Exploitation of Marine Resources in the Roman Mediterranean*. Oxford: Oxford University Press, 2013.

Mason, Steve. "Jews, Judaeans, Judaizing, Judaism: Problems of Categorization in Ancient History." *Journal for the Study of Judaism* 38 (2007): 457–512.

Matthews, Shelly. *First Converts: Rich Pagan Women and the Rhetoric of Mission in Early Judaism and Christianity*. Stanford: Stanford University Press, 2002.

Mattila, Sharon Lea. "Jesus and the Middle Peasants?: Problematizing a Social-Scientific Concept." *Catholic Biblical Quarterly* 72 (2010): 291–313.

McDonald, Lee Martin. *The Formation of the Christian Biblical Canon: Revised and Expanded Edition*. Peabody: Hendrickson, 1995.

McDonald, Lee Martin, and James A. Sanders, eds. *The Canon Debate*. Peabody: Hendrickson, 2002.

McKinlay, Judith E. "Reading Biblical Women Matters." In *The Oxford Handbook of Biblical Narrative*, edited by Danna Nolan Fewell, 398–410. New York: Oxford University Press, 2016.

Meier, John P. *A Marginal Jew.* 5 vols. New Haven: Yale University Press, 1991–2015.

Merz, Annette. "How a Woman Who Fought Back and Demanded her Rights became an Importunate Widow: The Transformations of a Parable of Jesus." In *Jesus from Judaism to Christianity: Continuum Approaches to the Historical Jesus*, edited by Tom Holmen, 49–86. London: T&T Clark, 2007.

Michaud, Jean-Paul. "Quelle(s) communauté(s) derriere la Source Q?" In *The Sayings Source Q and the Historical Jesus*, edited by Andreas Lindemann, 577–606. Leuven: Leuven University Press, 2001.

Millard, Alan. "Literacy in the Time of Jesus." *Biblical Archaeology Review* 29 (2003): 36–45.

———. *Reading and Writing in the Time of Jesus.* Sheffield: Sheffield Academic, 2000.

Milne, Herbert John Mansfield, and Theodore Cressy Skeat. *Scribes and Correctors of the Codex Sinaiticus.* London: Trustees of the British Museum, 1938.

Mitchell, Linda E. "Codes of Law and Laws: Ancient Greek and Roman Law." In *The Oxford Encyclopedia of Women in World History*, edited by B. G. Smith, 422–426. Oxford: Oxford University Press, 2008.

Moreland, Milton C. "Q and the Economics of Early Roman Galilee." In *The Sayings Source Q and the Historical Jesus*, edited by Andreas Lindemann, 561–575. Leuven: Leuven University Press, 2001.

Moss, Candida. "Current Trends in the Study of Early Christian Martyrdom." *Bulletin for the Study of Religion* 41/3 (2012): 22–29.

Motschenbacher, Heiko. *Language, Gender, and Sexual Identity: Poststructuralist Perspectives.* Studies in Language and Society 29. Amsterdam: John Benjamins, 2010.

Moxnes, Halvor. *The Economy of the Kingdom: Social Conflict and Economic Relations in Luke's Gospel.* Philadelphia: Fortress, 1988.

———. "Honor and Shame." In *The Social Sciences and New Testament Interpretation*, edited by R. Rohrbaugh, 19–40. Peabody: Hendrickson, 1996.

Moyise, Steve. *Jesus and Scripture: Studying the New Testament Use of the Old Testament.* Grand Rapids: Baker Academic, 2011.

Mroczek, Eva. *The Literary Imagination in Jewish Antiquity.* Oxford: Oxford University Press, 2016.

Murphy, Cullen. *The Word According to Eve.* Boston: Houghton Mifflin, 1998.

Myers, Alicia D. "Gender, Rhetoric and Recognition Characterizing Jesus and (Re) defining Masculinity in the Gospel of John." *Journal for the Study of the New Testament* 38/2 (2015): 191–218.

Najman, Hindy. "The Inheritance of Prophecy in Apocalypse." In *The Oxford Handbook of Apocalyptic Literature*, edited by J. J. Collins, 36–51. Oxford: Oxford University Press, 2014.

Neirynck, Frans. "The Reconstruction of Q and IQP / CritEd Parallels." In *The Sayings Source Q and the Historical Jesus*, edited by Andreas Lindemann, 53–148. Leuven, Leuven University Press, 2001.

Neutel, Karin B. *A Cosmopolitan Ideal: Paul's Declaration "Neither Jew Nor Greek, Neither Slave Nor Free, Nor Male and Female" in the Context of First Century Thought.* London: Bloomsbury T&T Clark, 2015.

Neyrey, Jerome. "What's Wrong with this Picture: John 4, Cultural Stereotypes of Women, and Public and Private Space." In *A Feminist Companion to John: Volume 1*, edited by Amy-Jill Levine, 98–125. London: Sheffield Academic, 2003.

Oakman, Douglas E. "The Ancient Economy." In *The Social Sciences and New Testament Interpretation*, edited by R. Rohrbaugh, 126–143. Peabody: Hendrickson, 1996.

———. "Jesus and Agrarian Palestine: The Factor of Debt." Pages In *The Social World of the New Testament: Insights and Models*, edited by Jerome H. Neyrey and Eric Clark Stewart, 63–84. Peabody: Hendrickson, 2008.

———. *Jesus and the Economic Questions of His Day*. Lewiston: Mellen, 1986.

———. "Was Jesus a Peasant? Implications for Reading the Jesus Tradition." In *The Social World of the New Testament: Insights and Models*, edited by Jerome H. Neyrey and Eric Clark Stewart, 123–140. Peabody: Hendrickson, 2008.

O'Brien, Julia M., ed. *The Oxford Encyclopedia of the Bible and Gender, Volume 1 ASI-MUJ*. New York: Oxford University Press, 2014.

Oegema, Gerbern S. *Apocalyptic Interpretation of the Bible*. New York: T&T Clark, 2012.

———. "Non-Canonical Writings and Biblical Theology." In *The Changing Face of Judaism, Christianity, and Other Greco-Roman Religions in Antiquity*, edited by I. Henderson and G. Oegema with S. Parks, 491–512. Gutersloh: Gutersloher Verlagshaus, 2006.

Oegema, Gerbern S., and James H. Charlesworth, eds. *The Pseudepigrapha and Christian Origins: Essays from the Studiorum Novi Testamenti Societas*. New York: T&T Clark, 2008.

Ogden Bellis, Alice. *Helpmates, Harlots, and Heroes: Women's Stories in the Hebrew Bible*. Louisville: Westminster John Knox, 2007.

Osiek, Carolyn, and David L. Balch. *Families in the New Testament World: Households and House Churches*. Louisville: Westminster John Knox, 1997.

Osiek, Carolyn, Margaret Y MacDonald, and Janet H. Tulloch. A *Woman's Place: House Churches in Earliest Christianity*. Minneapolis: Fortress, 2006.

Parker, David C. *An Introduction to the New Testament Manuscripts and Their Texts*. Cambridge: Cambridge University Press, 2008.

Parks, Sara. "'The Brooten Phenomenon': Moving Women from the Margins in Second-Temple and New Testament Scholarship." *The Bible & Critical Theory* 14/2 (2018): 1–20.

———. "Historical-Critical Ministry? The Biblical Studies Classroom as Restorative Secular Space." *New Blackfriars* 100/1086 (2019): 229–244.

Parvey, Constance F. "The Theology and Leadership of Women in the New Testament." In *Religion and Sexism*, edited by R. Radford Ruether, 139–146. NY: Simon and Schuster, 1974.

Patterson, Stephen J. *The Gospel of Thomas and Jesus*. Sonoma: Polebridge, 1993.

———. "An Unanswered Question: Apocalyptic Expectation and Jesus' Basileia Proclamation." *Journal for the Study of the Historical Jesus* 8/1 (2010): 67–79.

Perrin, Norman. *Rediscovering the Teaching of Jesus*. London: SCM, 1967.

Petersen, David L., and Kent Harold Richards. *Interpreting Hebrew Poetry*. Minneapolis: Fortress, 1992.

Peters, Janelle. "Gendered Activity and Jesus's Saying Not to Worry." *Neotestamentica* 50/1 (2016): 35–52.
Philo. *Volume 4: Every Good Man Is Free. On the Contemplative Life. On the Eternity of the World. Against Flaccus. Apology for the Jews. On Providence.* Translated by F. H. Colson. LCL. 1941.
Pilch, John J. "Are there Jews and Christians in the Bible?" *Harvard Theological Studies* 53/1 (1997): 119–125.
Piper, Ronald A. "In Quest of Q: The Direction of Q Studies." In *The Gospel Behind the Gospels: Current Studies on Q*, edited by R. A. Piper, 1–18. Leiden: Brill, 1995.
———. "Jesus and the Conflict of Powers in Q: Two Q Miracle Stories." In *The Sayings Source Q and the Historical Jesus*, edited by Andreas Lindemann, 317–350. Leuven: Leuven University Press, 2001.
———. "Wealth, Poverty, and Subsistence in Q." In *From Quest to Q: Festschrift James Robinson*, edited by J. M. Asgeirsson, K. de Troyer, and M. W. Meyer, 219–264. Leuven: Leuven University Press, 2000.
———. *Wisdom in the Q-Tradition: The Aphoristic Teaching of Jesus*. Cambridge: Cambridge University Press, 1989.
Plaskow, Judith. "Anti-Judaism in Christian Feminist Interpretation." In *Searching the Scriptures: A Feminist Introduction*, edited by E. Schüssler Fiorenza, 7–29. New York: Crossroad, 1993.
———. "Christian Feminism and Anti-Judaism." *Cross Currents* 33 (1978): 306–309.
———. "Feminist Anti-Judaism and the Christian God." *Journal of Feminist Studies in Religion* 7/2 (1991): 99–108.
Polaski, Sandra. *A Feminist Introduction to Paul*. Danvers: Chalice, 2005.
Porter, Stanley E. *The Criteria for Authenticity in Historical Jesus Research: Previous Discussion and New Proposals. Journal for the Study of the New Testament: Supplement Series* 191. Sheffield: Sheffield Academic, 2000.
Portier-Young, Anathea. "Jewish Apocalyptic Literature as Resistance Literature." In *The Oxford Handbook of Apocalyptic Literature*, edited by J. J. Collins, 145–162. Oxford: Oxford University Press, 2014.
Powell, Mark Allen, ed. *Harper Collins Bible Dictionary: Revised and Updated*. New York: HarperCollins, 2011.
Punt, J. "Power and Liminality, Sex and Gender, and Gal 3:28: A Postcolonial, Queer Reading of an Influential Text." *Neotestamentica* 44/1 (2010): 140–166.
Racine, Jean-François, and Madeleine Beaumont. "Three Approaches to the Position of Women in the Q Document: Hal Taussig, Luise Schottroff, and Amy-Jill Levine." In *Women also journeyed with Him: Feminist Perspectives on the Bible*, edited by G. Caron, 99–116. Collegeville: Liturgical Press, 2000.
Raditsa, Leo Ferrero. "Augustus' Legislation Concerning Marriage, Procreation, Love Affairs and Adultery." In *Aufstieg und Niedergang der römischen Welt: Geschichte und Kultur Roms im Spiegel der neueren Forschung* 2/13, edited by Hildegard Temporini, 278–339. Berlin: de Gruyter, 1980.
Redfield, Robert. *Peasant Society and Culture*. Chicago: University of Chicago Press, 1956.
Reed, Jonathan. *Archaeology and the Galilean Jesus: A Re-examination of the Evidence*. Harrisburg: Trinity Press International, 2000.

Reid, Barbara E. *Choosing the Better Part? Women in the Gospel of Luke*. Collegeville: Liturgical Press, 1996.

Reinhartz, Adele. "A Fork in the Road or a Multi-Lane Highway? New Perspectives on 'The Parting of the Ways' Between Judaism and Christianity." In *The Changing Face of Judaism, Christianity and Other Greco-Roman Religions in Antiquity*, edited by G. Oegema and Ian Henderson with Sara Parks Ricker, 278–293. Gütersloh: Gütersloher Verlagshaus, 2005.

———. "The Vanishing Jews of Antiquity." *Marginalia Review of Books*, 24. June 2014. No pages. Accessed July 15, 2015. http://marginalia.lareviewofbooks.org/vanishing-jews-antiquity-adele-reinhartz.

Renfrew, Colin. *The Emergence of Civilisation: The Cyclades and the Aegean in The Third Millennium BC*. Oxford: Oxbow, 1972.

Resseguie, James L. "Literature, New Testament As." In *Eerdmans Dictionary of the Bible*, edited by D. N. Freedman, 815–817. Grand Rapids: Eerdmans, 2000.

Robbins, Vernon K. "The Social Location of the Implied Author of Luke-Acts." In *The Social World of Luke-Acts*, edited by J. H. Neyrey, 305–332. Peabody: Hendrickson, 1991.

Robinson, James. "The Critical Edition of Q and the Study of Jesus." In *The Sayings Source Q and the Historical Jesus*, edited by Andreas Lindemann, 27–52. Leuven: Leuven University Press, 2001.

———. *The Gospel of Jesus: In Search of the Original Good News*. New York: HarperCollins, 2005.

———. "The Nag Hammadi Gospels and the Fourfold Gospel." In *The Earliest Gospels: The Origins and Transmission of the Earliest Christian Gospels–The Contribution of the Chester Beatty Gospel Codex P^{45}*, edited by Charles Horton, 69–87. London: T&T Clark, 2004.

———. "The Pre-Q Text of the (Ravens and) Lilies: Q 12:22–31 and P. Oxy 655 (*Gos. Thom.* 36)." Pages 143–180 in *Text und Geschichte*. Marburg: Elwert, 1999.

———. *The Sayings Gospel Q in Greek and English with Parallels from the Gospels of Mark and Thomas*. Leuven: Peeters, 2001.

———. *The Sayings of Jesus: The Sayings Gospel Q in English*. Minneapolis: Fortress, 2002.

———. "A Written Greek Sayings Cluster Older than Q: A Vestige." *Harvard Theological Review* 92 (1999): 61–77.

Robinson, James, Paul Hoffmann, and John Kloppenborg, eds. *The Critical Edition of Q: Synopsis including the Gospels of Matthew and Luke, Mark and Thomas, with English, German, and French translations of Q and Thomas*. Minneapolis: Fortress, 2000.

Rodríguez, Rafael. "Authenticating Criteria: The Use and Misuse of a Critical Method." *Journal for the Study of the Historical Jesus* 7 (2009): 152–167.

———. *Structuring Early Christian Memory*. London: T&T Clark, 2010.

Rohrbaugh, Richard L. "Introduction." In *The Social Sciences and New Testament Interpretation*, edited by R. Rohrbaugh, 1–15. Peabody: Hendrickson, 1996.

———. "The Preindustrial City." In *The Social Sciences and New Testament Interpretation*, edited by R. Rohrbaugh, 107–125. Peabody: Hendrickson, 1996.

Röhser, G. "Mann und Frau in Christus: Eine Verhältnisbestimmung von Gal 3,28 und 1 Kor 11,2-16." *Studien zum Neuen Testament und seiner Umwelt* 22 (1997): 57–78.

Rollens, Sarah E. *Framing Social Criticism in the Jesus Movement.* Tübingen: Mohr Siebeck, 2014.

———. "The Kingdom of God is Among You: Prospects for a Q Community." In *Christian Origins and the Establishment of the Early Jesus Movement,* edited by Stanley E. Porter and Andrew W. Pitts, 224–241. Leiden: Brill, 2018.

Roth, Dieter T. *The Parables in Q.* London: T&T Clark, 2018.

Sanders, Ed Parish. *The Historical Figure of Jesus.* London: Penguin, 1993.

Schaberg, Jane. "Luke." In *Women's Bible Commentary: Twentieth-Anniversary Edition Revised and Updated,* edited by Carol A. Newsom, Sharon H. Ringe, and Jacqueline E. Lapsley, 363–380. Louisville: Westminster John Knox, 1998.

Schaberg, Jane, and Sharon Ringe. "Gospel of Luke." In *Women's Bible Commentary: Twentieth-Anniversary Edition Revised and Updated,* edited by Carol A. Newsom, Sharon H. Ringe, and Jacqueline E. Lapsley, 493–511. Louisville: Westminster John Knox, 2012.

Schmid, Josef. *Matthäus und Lukas: Eine Untersuchung des Verhältnisses ihrer Evangelien.* Freiburg: Herder & Herder, 1930.

Schottroff, Luise. "Feminist Observations on the Eschatology of the Sayings Source." Paper presented at the 1992 annual meeting of the SBL. San Francisco, November 1992.

———. "Itinerant Prophetesses: A Feminist Analysis of the Sayings Source Q." In *Current Studies on Q,* edited by R. A. Piper, 347–360. Leiden: Brill, 1995.

———. *Lydia's Impatient Sisters: A Feminist Social History of Early Christianity.* London: SCM, 1995.

———. "The Sayings Source Q." In *Searching the Scriptures 2: A Feminist Commentary,* edited by Elizabeth Schüssler Fiorenza, 510–534. New York: Crossroad, 1994.

Schulz, Siegfried. *Q: Die Spruchquelle der Evangelisten.* Zurich: Theologischer Verlag, 1964.

Schurmann, Heinz. *Traditionsgeschichtliche Untersuchungen zu den synoptischen Evangelien.* Dusseldorf: Patmos-Verlag, 1968.

Schüssler Fiorenza, Elisabeth. *Bread Not Stone.* Boston: Beacon, 1995.

———. *But She Said: Feminist Practices of Biblical Interpretation.* Boston: Beacon, 1992.

———. "Critical Feminist Studies in Religion." *Critical Research on Religion* 1/43 (2013): 43–50.

———. *Discipleship of Equals: A Critical Feminist Ekklesialogy of Liberation.* New York: Crossroad, 1993.

———. "Feminist/Women Priests – An Oxymoron?" *New Women/New Church* (Fall 1995): 10–18.

———. *In Memory of Her.* New York: Crossroad, 1983.

———. *Jesus and the Politics of Interpretation.* New York: Continuum, 2000.

———. *Jesus, Miriam's Child, Sophia's Prophet: Critical Issues in Feminist Christology.* New York: Continuum, 1995.

———. "Jesus of Nazareth in Historical Research." In *Thinking of Christ: Proclamation, Explanation, Meaning,* edited by T. Wiley, 29–48. New York: Continuum, 2003.

———. "The Praxis of Coequal Discipleship." Pages In *Paul and Empire: Religion and Power in Roman Imperial Society,* edited by R. A. Horsley, 224–241. Harrisburg: Trinity, 1997.

———. "Remembering the Past in Creating the Future: Historical-Critical Scholarship and Feminist Biblical Interpretation." In *Feminist Perspectives on Biblical Scholarship,* edited by A. Yarbro Collins, 43–64. Chico: Scholars, 1985.

———. *Rhetoric and Ethic: The Politics of Biblical Studies.* Minneapolis: Fortress, 1999.

———. "Rhetorical Situation and Historical Reconstruction in 1 Corinthians." In *Christianity at Corinth: The Quest for the Pauline Church,* edited by Edward Adams and David G. Horrell, 145–160. Louisville: Westminster John Knox, 2004.

———. *Sharing Her Word: Feminist Biblical Interpretation in Context.* Boston: Beacon, 1998.

———. *Wisdom Ways: Introducing Feminist Biblical Interpretation.* Maryknoll: Orbis, 2001.

———, ed. *Feminist Biblical Studies in the 20th Century.* Atlanta: Society of Biblical Literature, 2014.

Seim, Turid. *The Double Message: Patterns of Gender in Luke & Acts.* New York: T&T Clark, 2004.

Sevrin, J.-M. "Thomas, Q et le Jesus de l'histoire." In *The Sayings Source Q and the Historical Jesus,* edited by Andreas Lindemann, 461–478. Leuven: Leuven University Press, 2001.

Sheinfeld, Shayna. "The Pseudepigrapha in Current Research." *Religion Compass* 7/5 (2013): 1–8.

Shellard, Barbara. "The Relationship of Luke and John: A Fresh Look at an Old Problem." *The Journal of Theological Studies, New Series* 46/1 (1995): 71–98.

Sheppard, Gerald T. "Poor." In *Mercer Dictionary of the Bible,* edited by W. E. Mills, 700–701. Macon: Mercer University Press, 1990.

Siegele-Wenschkewitz, Leonore. "In the Dangerous Currents of Old Prejudices: How Predominant Thoughts have Disastrous Effects and What could be Done to Counter Them." In *A Feminist Companion to the Hebrew Bible in the New Testament,* edited by A. Brenner, 342–348. Sheffield: Sheffield Academic, 1996.

Simkins, Ronald A. "The Widow and Orphan in the Political Economy of Ancient Israel." *Journal of Religion & Society Supplement* 10 (2014): 20–33.

Sloan, David B. "The τίς ἐξ ὑμῶν Similitudes and the Extent of Q." *Journal for the Study of the New Testament* 38/3 (2016): 339–355.

———. "What If the Gospel according to the Hebrews Was Q?" Paper presented at the Annual Meeting of the SBL. Boston, MA, 18 Nov 2017.

Smith, Dwight Moody. *John among the Gospels.* 2nd edition. Columbia: University of South Carolina Press, 2001.

Snodgrass, Klyne. *Stories with Intent: A Comprehensive Guide to the Parables of Jesus*. Grand Rapids: Eerdmans, 2008.

Soulen, Richard N., and R. Kendall Soulen. "Historical Critical Method." Pages 88–89 In *Handbook of Biblical Criticism, Fourth Edition*. Louisville: Westminster John Knox, 2011.

Spencer, Franklin Scott. *Salty Wives, Spirited Mothers, and Savvy Widows: Capable Women of Purpose and Persistence in Luke's Gospel*. Grand Rapids: Eerdmans, 2012.

Stone, Michael E. "Questions of Ezra." In *Old Testament Pseudepigrapha, Volume 1*, edited by J. H. Charlesworth, 591–600. Garden City: Doubleday, 1983.

Streeter, Burnett Hillman. "St. Mark's Knowledge and Use of Q." In *Studies in the Synoptic Problem*, edited by W. Sanday, 165–183. Oxford: Clarendon, 1911.

Szesnat, Holger. "Mostly Aged Virgins: Philo and the Presence of the Therapeutrides at Lake Mareotis." *Neotestamentica* 32/1 (1998): 191–201.

Takaoglu, Turan. "Archaeological Evidence for Grain Mills in the Greek and Roman Troad." In *Vom Euphrat bis zum Bosporus: Kleinasien in der Antike*, edited by Engelbert Winter, 673–679. Bonn: Dr. Rudolph Habelt, 2008.

Taylor, Joan E. *Jewish Women Philosophers of First Century Alexandria: Philo's "Therapeutae" Reconsidered*. Oxford: Oxford University Press, 2003.

Taylor, Joan E. "The Women 'Priests' of Philo's *De Vita Contemplativa*: Reconstructing the Therapeutae." In *On the Cutting Edge: The Study of Women in Biblical Worlds*, edited by Jane Schaberg, Alice Bach, and Esther Fuchs, 102–122. New York: Continuum, 2004.

Theissen, Gerd. *Le christianisme de Jésus: ses origines sociales en Palestine*. Paris: Relais Desclée 6, 1978.

———. *Social Reality and the Early Christians*. Minneapolis: Fortress, 1992.

Theissen, Gerd, and Annette Merz. *The Historical Jesus: A Comprehensive Guide*. Minneapolis: Fortress, 1998.

Thorsteinsson, Runar M. *Roman Christianity and Roman Stoicism: A Comparative Study of Ancient Morality*. Oxford: Oxford University Press, 2010.

Thurmond, David L. *A Handbook of Food Processing in Classical Rome: For Her Bounty no Winter*. Leiden: Brill, 2006.

Thurston, Bonnie Bowman. *Women in the New Testament: Questions and Commentary*. New York: Crossroad, 1998.

Tolmie, D. Francois. "Tendencies in the Interpretation of Galatians 3:28 since 1990." *Acta Theologica* 19 (2014): 105–129.

Torjesen, Karen Jo. *When Women Were Priests: Women's Leadership in the Early Church and the Scandal of their Subordination*. New York: HarperOne, 1995.

Tuckett, C. "Q and the 'Church': The Role of the Christian Community within Judaism according to Q." In *A Vision for the Church: Studies in Early Christian Ecclesiology in Honour of J. P. M. Sweet*, edited by Markus Bockmuehl and Michael B. Thompson, 65–77. Edinburgh: T&T Clark, 1997.

Tuckett, C. M. *Q and the History of Early Christianity: Studies on Q*. Edinburgh: T&T Clark, 1996.

Tuomela, Liisa. "Virtues of Man, Woman - or Human Being?: An Intellectual Historical Study on the Views of the Later Stoics Seneca the Younger, Musonius Rufus,

Epictetus, Hierocles and Marcus Aurelius on the Sameness of the Virtues of Man and Woman." PhD dissertation. University of Helsinki, 2014.

Vaage, Lief. *Galilean Upstarts: Jesus' First Followers According to Q*. Valley Forge: Trinity Press International, 1994.

Van Der Horst, P. W. "Musonius Rufus and the New Testament: A Contribution to the Corpus Hellenisticum." *Novum Testamentum* 16/4 (1974): 306–315.

Vassiliadis, Petros. "Original Order of Q: Some Residual Cases." In *Logia: Les Paroles de Jésus—the Sayings of Jesus*, edited by J. Delobel, 379–387. Leuven: Leuven University Press, 1982.

Vermes, Geza. *Jesus the Jew: A Historian's Reading of the Gospels*. Minneapolis: Fortress, 1981.

Von Harnack, Adolf. *The Sayings of Jesus: The Second Source of St. Matthew and St. Luke*. London: Williams & Norgate, 1908.

Watson, Wilfred G. E. "Gender-Matched Synonymous Parallelism in the Old Testament." *Journal of Biblical Literature* 99/3 (1980): 321–341.

White, L. Michael. *Scripting Jesus: The Gospels in Re-Write*. New York: HarperOne, 2010.

White, Sidnie Ann. "Women: Second Temple Period." In *The Oxford Guide to People and Places of the Bible*, edited by Bruce M. Metzger and Michael D. Coogan, 330–334. Oxford: Oxford University Press, 2001.

Wills, Lawrence. *The Jewish Novel in the Ancient World*. Ithaca: Cornell University Press, 1995. Reprinted 2015.

———. "Jewish Novellas in a Greek and Roman Age: Fiction and Identity." *Journal for the Study of Judaism* 42 (2011): 141–165.

———. *The Quest of the Historical Gospel: Mark, John, and the Origins of the Gospel Genre*. London: Routledge, 1997.

Winkler, John J. *The Constraints of Desire: The Anthropology of Sex and Gender in Ancient Greece*. New York: Routledge, 1990.

Yaghjian, Lucretia B. "Ancient Reading." In *The Social Sciences and New Testament Interpretation*, edited by R. Rohrbaugh, 206–230. Peabody: Hendrickson, 1996.

Yarbro Collins, Adela, ed. *Feminist Perspectives on Biblical Scholarship*. Chico: Scholars, 1985.

Yoder, John Howard. *The Politics of Jesus*. 2nd edition. Grand Rapids: Eerdmans, 1994.

Zanker, Paul. *The Power of Images in the Age of Augustus*. Translated by Alan Shapiro. Ann Arbor: University of Michigan Press, 1988.

Index of Ancient Sources

Page references for figures are italicized.

Q 3:2-3, 56
Q 3:8, 38
Q 3:9, 35, 156
Q 3:21-22, 35
Q 4:1-13, 35, 38, 56
Q 6:20-22, 39
Q 6:31, 35
Q 6:43-44, 32
Q 7:1-10, 33, 38
Q 7:22, 38
Q 7:28, 34
Q 7:29-30, *82*, 94–95, 163
Q 7:31-32, 96
Q 7:32, *82*
Q 7:34, 95
Q 9:58, 120
Q 10:2, 32, 56
Q 10:3, 32
Q 10:5-12, 37
Q 10:8-9, 34
Q 10:12-14, 38
Q 10:13-15, 32
Q 10:15, 120
Q 10:16, 37
Q 11:5-8, 87
Q 11:11-12, 84, 116, 162
Q 11:14, 33

Q 11:16, 56
Q 11:29-30, 38
Q 11:31-32, 38, 80, *82*, 85, 89, 138, 162
Q 11:39-52, 39
Q 11:42, 38
Q 11:51, 38
Q 11:52, 34, 38
Q 12:11, 38
Q 12:23, 2
Q 12:24, 1, 32, 80, *82*, 162
Q 12:27, 80, *82*, 162
Q 12:29-31, 34, 38
Q 12:51-53, 14, 96, 101
Q 12:53, 12, *82*, 163
Q 13:18-21, 34, *82*, 90, 162
Q 13:30, 39
Q 13:34-35, 38
Q 14:11, 39
Q 14:26, 2, *82*, 98, 163
Q 15:4-5a, 2, 79–80, *82*, 91–92, 95, 121, 162–63
Q 15:7, 2
Q 15:7-9, 79–80, *82*, 91–92, 95, 121, 162–63
Q 15:8-10, 2
Q 16:16, 34
Q 16:17, 38

Q 17:6, 32
Q 17:20-21, 34
Q 17:26-27, 38
Q 17:34-35, *82*, 93, 163
Q 22:30, 38

Genesis 24:3-4, 144
Genesis 41:45a, 143–44
Genesis 41:50, 143
Judges 9:8-15, 115
2 Samuel 12:1-7, 115
1 Kings 10:1-13, 89
2 Chronicles 9:1-12, 89
Ezra 10:10, 144
Psalm 85:11, 117
Proverbs 1:20, 116
Proverbs 12:1, 116
Amos 5:24, 116
Micah 7:5-6, 97
Jonah 3:5, 89
Malachi 2:11, 144

Matthew 7:9-10, 84
Matthew 11:19, 95
Matthew 21:23, 95
Matthew 21:32, 94–95

Mark 1:1, 55
Mark 2:21-22, 133–34
Mark 4, 56
Mark 4:30-32, 90
Mark 6:14-29, 35

Luke 1:5-23, 128
Luke 2, 128
Luke 4:25-27, *82*, 84–85, 87, 138, 161
Luke 7:30, 94–95
Luke 7:34, 95
Luke 7:39, 95
Luke 11:5-8, 81, *82*, 86, 161–62
Luke 11:11-12, 84, 88
Luke 14:26, 98
Luke 18:1-8, 81
Luke 18:2-5, *82*, 86–87, 161–62
Luke 18:6-8, 87–88

John 2:1-11, *130*
John 3:1-12, *130*
John 4:4-42, *130*
John 4:46-64, *130*
John 9:1-41, *130*
John 11:1-54, *130*
John 12:1-8, *130*
John 19:25-27, *130*
John 20:11-18, *130*
John 20:24-29, *130*

1 Corinthians 7, 128, 131
Galatians 3:28, 131
Ephesians 5:22, 146
1 Timothy 2:15, 146
Gospel of Thomas, 55–56
Sirach 14:20, 116
Sirach 14:26, 116
Sirach 21:22, 116
Sirach 21:26, 116

De Vita Contemplativa, 17
Contemp. 3.30, 138
Contemp. 3.33, 138–39
Contemp. 4.69, 139
Contemp. 8.68, 139
Contemp. 40.87, 138
Contemp. 40.88, 138
Diatr. 3.1-2, 140
Diatr. 3.3, 141
Diatr. 3.4, 141
Diatr. 3.5, 141
Diatr. 3.6, 141
Diatr. 3.7, 141
Diatr. 4.1-3, 141–42
Diatr. 4.5, 142
Diatr. 4.8, 142
Joseph and Aseneth 8:5-7, 142–43
Joseph and Aseneth 10–17, 143–44
Laws, 134
Oikonomikos, 134
Progymnasmata, 119
That Women Too Should Study Philosophy, 127

Index of Modern Authors

Arnal, William, 12–13, 37, 55, 64, 66, 81, 83, 92–93, 99, 111, 113, 120–22, 144, 151, 153

Barrera, J. T., 56
Batten, Alicia, 11, 13, 55, 60–62, 64, 66–67, 77, 98, 102, 111, 113, 153–55
Beavis, Mary Ann, 65–66
Beirne, Margaret, 3, 131, 136
Berlin, Adele, 117
Boyarin, Daniel, 139
Brooten, Bernadette, 59
Butler, Judith, 10

Camp, Claudia, 9
Chancey, Mark, 38
Chesnutt, Randall, 9
Collins, John J., 144
Conway, Colleen, 130–31, 136
Corley, Kathleen, 11, 13, 55, 59, 62, 64–67, 77, 95, 98, 102, 111, 113, 153–54
Crook, Zeba, 90
Crossan, John Dominic, 100

Dale, Moyra, 51
D'Angelo, Mary Rose, 128–29
Davila, James, 119, 144
de Beauvoir, Simone, 10

Derrenbacker, Robert, 128
Dewey, Joanna, 54, 146
Dillon, Richard, 54
Duling, Dennis, 38, 40
Dunn, James D. G., 32

Elliott, John, 65–66, 100
Engel, David, 141–42

Fredriksen, Paula, 51
Fricker, Denis, 2, 51, 55, 57, 59, 77, 81, 96, 111, 113, 115, 117, 134, 153–54

Goodacre, Mark, 153
Gravett, Sandra, 116

Hägerland, Tobias, 135
Herzog II, W. R., 87
Horsley, Richard, 30
Houlden, Leslie, 56

Johnson, Lee A., 83
Jones, Brice, 85

Kähler, Martin, 33
Kee, Alistair, 133
Kloppenborg, John, 29, 31, 33, 35, 38
Koester, Helmut, 33
Kraemer, Ross Shepard, 144

Levine, Amy-Jill, 12–13, 39, 55, 57, 63–64, 66, 88–89, 91, 99, 102, 153

Mack, Burton, 3, 30, 35, 57
Malick, David, 51
Martin, Dale, 6
Meier, John P., 135
Merz, Annette, 2, 54, 87–88, 98

Neutel, Karin B., 132

Piper, Ronald, 33, 36
Plaskow, Judith, 63
Portier-Young, Anathea, 52, 55

Racine, Jean-Francois, 11, 55, 59–60, 77
Reed, Jonathan, 32
Reid, Barbara, 129
Ringe, Sharon, 54, 99, 129
Robinson, James, 2, 29, 56, 154, 161

Rohrbaugh, Richard, 57
Roth, Dieter, 81

Sanders, E. P., 33–34, 39
Schaberg, Jane, 54, 99, 129
Schottroff, Luise, 55, 58–60, 63, 66, 77, 83, 91, 97–99, 153
Schüssler Fiorenza, Elisabeth, 4, 6–7, 10, 36, 66, 87–89, 91, 98, 100, 129, 153, 156
Seim, Turid, 52–53, 129, 151
Siffer, Nathalie, 2
Sloan, David, 86–87
Snodgrass, Klyne, 119

Tannehill, Robert C., 83
Theissen, Gerd, 2, 36, 58, 63
Thorsteinsson, Runar, 141

Watson, Wilfred, 117

Subject Index

androcentrism, 4, 12, 17, 58–60, 63–66, 88–89, 99–100, 102, 121–22, 145, 151–53
anti-Judaism, 4, 13, 15, 63, 65–66, 112. *See also* supersessionism
apocalypticism, 14, 31, 33–36, 41, 90, 93, 98–99, 145, 156
Apocrypha, 33, 114–15, 117, 123n13
Augustus, 59, 61, 113, 155;
    Augustan marriage reforms, 61, 113, 123n7, 155–56

basileia, 2, 5, 12, 14, 16, 18, 31, 33–37, 40, 58, 64–65, 83–85, 88–91, 94, 97–101, 111–12, 123, 132, 139, 141, 144, 154, 162

"discipleship of equals", 13, 16, 25n61, 63, 66, 100, 112, 130–31, 145

feminist interpretation, 3–4, 7–8, 12–13, 15, 27, 58–59, 63, 65–67, 91, 102, 112, 128–30, 145, 151–52, 156

Galilee, 1, 12, 29, 31–33, 38–39, 52, 67, 121, 151;
    Galilean provenance for Q, 29–31
gender:
    in antiquity, 10;
    as binary, 10–11, 152;
    equality, 2–5, 11, 13–17, 19n12, 37, 54, 58–67, 83, 93, 98–101, 112–13, 133, 136–37, 139–42, 145–46, 154–56;
    gendered roles/norms, 4–5, 9, 11–12, 14–17, 60, 67, 83–84, 91, 93, 98–100, 140–42, 145–46, 154–55;
    inclusivity, 11, 16, 60–61, 65, 91, 99, 112

Hebrew Bible, 38, 85, 88, 90, 111, 114–15, 117, 119, 122, 123n13, 144
Hellenistic literature, 2–3, 5, 13, 17, 67, 111, 113–14, 119, 122, 134, 136, 142
historical criticism, 5–7
historical Jesus, 3, 8–9, 17, 28, 39, 51, 55, 59, 62, 100–101, 112, 122–23, 130, 134–36, 152;
    criterion of embarrassment, 136–37;
    criterion of multiple attestation, 3, 135–36, 142;
    Historical Jesus Research, 1, 3, 17, 62, 112, 134–36

John, Gospel of, 1, 3, 16, 53, 128–36, 145, 152

John the Baptist, 34, 39, 56, 94–96, 156, 163
Joseph and Aseneth, 17, 112, 119, 122, 127, 132, 136–37, 142–45
Judaism, 4, 9, 13, 30, 36, 38, 55–56, 61, 63–66, 102, 111–12, 144–46, 151, 153–54, 156–57;
　Galilean, 15, 39–40, 113, 145;
　Second-Temple, 13, 37–38, 40

Luke, Gospel of, 1–3, 14, 28–30, 40, 51–57, 84–90, 92, 94–95, 99, 128–30, 132–37, 151–52, 154, 156, 161;
　Luke/Acts, 16, 51, 53–54, 56, 86, 128–29, 136;
　Luke's "double message", 53, 129

Mark, Gospel of, 3, 14, 16, 28–30, 33, 55–57, 81, 86, 90, 128–29, 133–36, 145, 152;
　Markan priority, 28–29.
　See also Synoptic Problem
Matthew, Gospel of, 1–2, 14, 28–30, 53–57, 84–87, 89–90, 92, 94–95, 128–29, 133–37, 152, 156
Musonius Rufus, 14, 17, 140–42, 145, 154

parables, 1–2, 12, 32, 34, 52–57, 59, 77–96, 100–101, 111, 115–22, 128, 130–34, 136–38, 141, 143–45, 156;
　definition of, 18n3;
　gender parable pairs, 4–5, 10, 16, 27, 31, 34, 40, 51–53, 56, 86, 96, 102, 111–14, 118, 120, 128–29, 145, 151–54
parallel gender pairs, 2–3, 10–11, 18n7, 79, 95, 102, 113–14, 118, 120, 133–34, 151–53;
　full pairs, 15, 78, 80–82, 93;
　gender doublets, 2, 18n7, 118;
　shorter pairs, 15, 78, 80–81, 84, 94, 96, 112, 132, 163;
　taxonomy of, 77, 80–81
parallelism, 81, 83–84, 89–90, 93, 97–98, 111, 115–22, 138, 143;
　antithetical, 116;
　synonymous, 115–17, 119, 122
Pastoral Epistles, 65, 146, 155
Paul, letters of, 3, 15–16, 29–30, 33, 38, 52, 56, 59, 128, 131–36, 145, 152, 156
Philo of Alexandria, 4, 14, 111–12, 137–40, 142, 145
Pseudepigrapha, 4, 114, 117–19, 144

Q:
　background in scholarship, 28–30;
　critical edition of, 29, 53, 81, 85–87, 89, 92, 94–95, 98, 156, 161;
　Jewishness of, 38, 52;
　provenance, 31–32;
　"Q People", 14, 27, 30–31, 39–40, 63, 154;
　strata of development, 8, 31, 35–36, 46n51, 63, 156–57

sapiential tradition, 14, 31, 35–36, 41.
　See also wisdom sayings
Stoicism, 4, 17, 140, 142
supersessionism, 4, 15, 38, 58, 64, 66–67, 102, 111, 133.
　See also anti-Judaism
Synoptic Problem, 29, 90, 151;
　two-source hypothesis, 28–30, 90, 153.
　See also Mark, Gospel of, Markan priority

Therapeutrides/Therapeutae, 14, 137–40

wisdom sayings, 35, 40.
　See also sapiential tradition

About the Author

Sara Parks was born in New Brunswick, Canada, and received her MA in New Testament and Christian Origins and her PhD in Early Judaism from McGill University in Montreal. She is Assistant Professor in New Testament Studies at the University of Nottingham. Dr. Parks specializes in women in the Hellenistic and Early Roman periods and has recently published articles on the gendered politics of citation in Second Temple scholarship and on the Biblical Studies classroom as restorative secular space. She is working on an undergraduate textbook on women and gender in the ancient Mediterranean world.

www.ingramcontent.com/pod-product-compliance
Lightning Source LLC
Chambersburg PA
CBHW021850300426
44115CB00005B/89